Not Without a Storm

towards a communist manifesto for the age of globalisation

CLIFF SLAUGHTER

A fearful eye thou hast: where is that blood
That I have seen inhabit in those cheeks?
So foul a sky clears not without a storm:
Pour down thy weather ...

Shakespeare
King John, IV, 2.

INDEX BOOKS
London

Published 2006 by Index Books (Indexreach Ltd)
3 The Quadrant, Richmond, Surrey TW9 1BF
www.indexbooks.co.uk
sales@indexbooks.co.uk

Other books by Cliff Slaughter:

A New Party for Socialism
Marx and Marxism, an introduction
Marxism, Ideology and Literature
Marxism and the Class Struggle
Coal is our Life (with N. Dennis and L.F. Henriques)

A C.I.P. catalogue record for this book is available from the British Library

ISBN-10: 1-871518-26-1
ISBN-13: 978-1-871518-26-9

This one is for Vivien, without whom
it wouldn't have happened

ACKNOWLEDGEMENTS

The information contained in this book is not the result of any original research on my part. It consists in large part of examples which shout out at us from the daily and weekly press together with extracts from the writings of people infinitely more qualified than I am in their own fields (dangers to the environment, 'underdevelopment', etc.). My own concern is to pose the responsibility of working towards what Marx called 'practical consciousness' of the world in which these problems arise and must be resolved. They are problems that threaten the very survival of our species and even of the planet itself.

It has been something of a struggle to produce *Not Without a Storm* – against the mainstream of Marxist commentary which, as I indicate below, does not seem to me to confront with sufficiently radical rethinking or rigour the crisis humanity faces. My greatest debt, consistently acknowledged in the text, is to István Mészáros. Besides him many other comrades and friends have made the book possible. Some of them – Janos Borovi, Steve Drury, John Lea, Claude Meillassoux, Bob Myers – are among those whose work I have plundered in the chapters that follow. But I have had invaluable encouragement and help from all the comrades in the Movement for Socialism in Britain, including Terry Brotherstone (particularly in the editing of this volume) and, in other ways, Clare Cowen, Bridget Leach, Liz Leicester and Dave Temple; and from co-thinkers in other countries, including some of those whose work centres on *Carré Rouge* – a journal which, as I explain in the Introduction, has been a particular inspiration.Thanks to Andy Robertson for typesetting and Brian Eley for the cover design.

Perhaps readers will find the book very repetitive. In part this will be because of the way in which it has been put together. But, in general, I do not apologise. My acknowledgements should conclude with one to my late father, Fred Slaughter. Already celebrated by the age of twenty as a Methodist preacher in the mining villages of County Durham, he later became a militant atheist and communist soapbox agitator and propagandist. He passed on to me his secret. 'First tell 'em what you're going to tell 'em. Then tell 'em. Then tell 'em what you've told 'em.'

Cliff Slaughter
Leeds, September 2005

CONTENTS

INTRODUCTION

Jerusalem or Pandaemonium?

> Pandaemonium is the Palace of All the Devils. Its building began c.1660. It will never be finished – it has to be transformed into Jerusalem. The building of Pandaemonium is the real history of Britain over the last three hundred years. That history has never been written …
>
> Humphrey Jennings, c. 1942.[1]

> The people are the power to come. Oppressed, unprotected, abandoned; left to the ebb and flow of the tides of the market, now taken on to work, now cast off to starve, committed to the shifting laws of demand and supply, slaves of Capital – the whited name of old accursed Mammon – … [T]hey are, I say, the power … likely to come to set up yet another Power not existing in England now …
>
> George Meredith, 1874-75.[2]

> And did the Countenance Divine
> Shine forth upon our clouded hills?
> And was Jerusalem builded there
> Among these dark satanic mills?
>
> William Blake, 1804-09.[3]

My starting point in this book is a twofold conviction. First, the existing social order driven by the imperatives of globalised capital is an ever-growing threat to humanity's very survival. Second, the objective conditions for a social revolution to overcome it exist – and must be mastered.

For the last half-century the expression of such a conviction on these weighty matters has 'gone out of fashion'. This trend became especially prevalent following the collapse of Stalinism (conventionally, but perversely, called 'communism') in 1989-91, and the widely acclaimed – but equally perversely described – 'death of Marxism'. Mrs Thatcher's 'there is no alternative' is now widely circulated as good ideological coin. In writing this book I have made the assumption that those who genuinely believe this will not be reading it. In this category are all the 'politicians' I know anything about in the older capitalist countries of Western Europe and North America.

Far more people are too busy trying to make a living to give much thought to the question. This is probably a much larger category than was the case a generation or so ago. Many who once believed in the prospect of some reformed 'alternative' to the present order offered by self-styled socialist and communists, have had to face the reality that these 'leaders' have abandoned all promises of any general progressive change. Liberal commentators conventionally refer to such people as 'apathetic', but they are only responding to the reality of the recognition that the politics in which they were once encouraged to believe now offers them nothing. I hope that there will be those who, directly or indirectly, may at some point find something in this book that will encourage them to re-engage in political discussion.

But what I say in this book is directed, first and foremost, and very deliberately, at three major categories of reader. First, I want to address those who look to protest against – and resist the consequences of – the rule of globalised capital, but who, if they are to succeed, need – so I shall argue – a more comprehensive and properly historical understanding of our present reality. Protest has its place, and has often been the precursor of effective actual resistance or even of revolutionary movements, but everyone knows that protest by itself cannot effectively confront globalised capital.

Second are trade unionists, thrown into necessarily defensive struggles against the ravages of globalised capital. They are finding it increasingly difficult to win even limited victories, and are growing ever more conscious that their existing unions – which in the UK still mostly refuse to break with New Labour and all try to substitute 'partnership' for struggle – are inadequate for even their most basic needs. Politically, many have long ago rejected the formula – which once seemed to deliver the Welfare State – that there should be a division of labour between 'the industrial and the political arms' of the movement. They seek a unified working-class way forward. But on the base of what theoretical conceptions and what politics? And how can the lessons in practical internationalism, explored in the 1984-85 miners' strike and, more particularly, by the Liverpool dockers in the 1990s, be developed in a manner that serves the refoundation of working-class, socialist internationalism?

The third category comprises those sincerely committed to political formations that claim to have a Marxist theory, organisation and programme, but which cling to conceptions which may have had relevance, however limited, some decades ago, but which are now an obstacle to achieving the kind of understanding, organisation and programme necessary. There is often a failure to understand that a whole period of the capital system's development (that of its ascendancy), and of the class struggle, has definitely ended. I count myself as having belonged, until a few years ago, to those who failed in this respect. I make it quite explicit in what follows that, for me, it was the work of István Mészáros – in particular his *Beyond Capital* – which made possible the necessary development in understanding. Most important of all is Mészáros's demonstration that with 'globalisation' the capital system has encountered its historical limits, its structural crisis.

Perhaps I should address this last point in a more brutal manner. All of us who for a good part of the twentieth century tried to work as Marxists in the working-class movement must begin by facing up to one big, sobering fact. It is this: despite all that work, the world's working people remain, in the new millennium, at the mercy of a capital system that has survived all their struggles, and which confronts them with greater threats than ever before. Millions have died in wars and man-made famines, and many more face the same fate today and in the near future. If there are socialists who think they must simply persist in the activities, forms of organisation and policies they have always known, then they will make no contribution to the cause they embrace. If they persist in holding to the conceptions of the epoch they held in the last century, they are doomed to be seen as political dinosaurs.

If we are to truly take responsibility for our part in failing to effectively challenge the march of destructive capital, we have to work in all humility to understand why we failed. Addressing that question is the central motive of the following pages. But this is not at all to say that the communist project is now outdated, or that our political lives were wasted, that Marxism has been proved wrong. Quite the contrary! What must be understood is that it is only now, with the globalisation of capital, that the objective conditions for socialist revolution are maturing. The struggles of the past – even including the many defeats and betrayals – are the source of inspiration and the spur to a new understanding. But that new understanding cannot come from this history alone. There has to be a refoundation of the working-class movement, which includes a refoundation of Marxism. This book is no more than an attempt to come to terms with István Mészáros's work as the beginning of that refoundation.

There are those who will call me a 'revisionist', a term with which I am very familiar. Well, I am indeed seeking to revise what should be revised. To put the matter clearly. I write now with the same aims, and with the same basic theoretical and political convictions that I had more than half a century ago when I became a communist. But I am now convinced that, in confronting global capital, a refounded, working-class internationalism is urgently necessary, and that it requires a development of our theoretical understanding and its unity with socialist practice. It goes without saying that underlying this is the deeply held conviction, insisted on by Mészáros, that Marx was right in discovering the working class as the structural antagonist of capital, its revolutionary opposite. I learned long ago that Stendhal was right to say, in his *Life of Henri Brulard,* that the only class with the energy to make effective change is the class which 'has to struggle with real needs'.[4] Walter

Benjamin showed a profound understanding of this:

> Not man or men but the struggling, oppressed class itself is the depository of historical knowledge. In Marx it appears as the last enslaved class, as the avenger that completes the task of liberation in the name of generations of the downtrodden.[5]

To those sociologists and others who warn that such reference to Marx will put readers off, I reply that Marx's work is the only viable starting-point, and that, at the same time, it also provides the only basis on which to say something usefully new. Furthermore, while I never believed the academic cautions, there is, in any case, recent evidence that, to many non-academic minds, the ideological offensive to declare Marx irredeemably passé has failed. Francis Wheen's intelligent 1999 biography, *Karl Marx*, has been a best seller. There was little other significance in a BBC public poll in mid-2005 to vote for the world's greatest philosopher. But the fact that it was won by Marx – with twice as many votes as for the second-placed David Hume – suggests that, in the anglophone world at least, he is far from having been dismissed from general consciousness.

Not Without a Storm is subtitled 'work in progress', and so it is. In a sense it is an interim report, unconventional in form. This is in part because the book is to some degree a collective work, in part because I feel strongly that something like this needs to be published urgently, as an invitation to others to participate in the discussion it seeks to promote.

To revisit all this in a more personal way. Twice in my political life I have been directly involved in crises that were life-changing for people seriously committed to the cause that, already in the mid-nineteenth century, had been identified as essential to the future of humanity – the cause of communism. The first was in 1956-7. In the aftermath of Nikita Khrushchev's 'secret speech' partially revealing the crimes of Stalin, and of the Red Army's brutal suppression of the anti-Stalinist Hungarian revolution, the world Communist movement was afforded the opportunity to face the reality of the political and moral corruption with which it had been infected. For me, in my late twenties already a long-standing (though relatively insignificant) Yorkshire member of the Communist Party of Great Britain, this had to mean re-examining what those I had been taught to excoriate for standing against that corruption had to say.

As a result of that re-examination, I joined the Trotskyist movement. From 1957 until 1985 I was a member – for much of the time a leading member – of the political organisation in which T G (or Gerry) Healy was the dominant figure. It was 'The Group' when I joined it; in 1959 it became the Socialist Labour League (publishing *The Newsletter,* edited at first by Peter Fryer,[6] and then, from 1969, the daily *Workers Press*); and from 1973 the Workers Revolutionary Party (replacing *Workers Press* with the *News Line* in 1976). An account of how a small number of comrades made their political way from the CPGB to Healy's group, and of the work they were able to do in the late 1950s, has been published by Terry Brotherstone in a mid-1990s volume dedicated to Tom Kemp.[7]

What became of the Healy movement remains, to say the least, a vexed question, but this is not the place to deal with it. The implosion of the WRP in 1985 – an event that briefly hit the headlines of the mainstream media – was, however, the second major 'crisis of communism' in my personal political life. Healy was expelled from his own party when he refused to answer irrefutable charges of – *inter alia* – sexual exploitation of young comrades. A number of Party members had made periodic efforts – as I now see, entirely inadequate efforts – to moderate Healy's increasingly unfounded 'revolutionary' political prognoses and crazed philosophical pronouncements. But we now found ourselves forced to confront the depths of the anti-communist, moral corruption he had brought on the movement.

The painfully necessary opportunity to do this came as the result of the conjunction of two sets of events. The first was the most important class struggle in Britain since the General Strike of 1926 – the 1984-5 miners' strike.[8] This revealed how theoretically unprepared the WRP was to deal with the reality of the crisis the working class now faced. The second was the decision of a small, courageous group of WRP members, working at the Party centre in London, to expose Healy. They did so in a carefully prepared way that would maximise the possibility of gaining the support of Party members against his controlling authority in the organisation, an authority that had been bolstered since the early 1970s by his recruitment to his clique of 'leaders' of celebrities. Prominent amongst these were the actors Vanessa and Corin Redgrave, who seemed mesmerised by Healy's plebeian energy and old-school political oratory.

What happened to the WRP will not be the main concern of the majority of those reading *Not Without a Storm*, which is about the present and the future, not about the past for its own sake. To those readers for whom – because of the enormous, and in some cases personally and politically destructive, impact of the WRP experience on their own lives[9] – explaining the events of 1984-5 remains a (if not the) central question, I would say this. Such an explanation, I am sure, can only be significantly advanced on the basis of the kind of work that this book attempts. By that I mean work that seeks to understand where we are now (the nature of the period we have entered), and how we got here (the nature of the period we have come through). We cannot understand the significance of our past, including our mistakes, if we do not know – if we do not wrestle over how to deepen our knowledge of – the present circumstances and the future possibilities of our class, the working class.

Not Without a Storm does not look like a book in the conventional sense – a work, that is, with chapters of relatively uniform structure and layout. It is not as much of a collective enterprise as I once hoped it would be. The political fragmentation that has followed on from the so-called 'collapse of communism' (it should be 'collapse of Stalinism') in 1989-91 has affected all of us, not only those who maintained their Stalinist faith, or intellectual subservience to the apparent immovability of 'actually existing socialism', until the last. Nevertheless some of the chapters that follow are substantially compilations of the work of others. With some of these writers I have been in direct, regular communication. This has either been through the Movement for Socialism, which some of us formed in the mid-1990s when it became clear that rescuing the Workers Revolutionary Party (and what we had called the Workers International to Reconstruct the Fourth International) was no way forward. Or else it has been through my contact with comrades such as those in Workers' Left Unity (Iran) and those who – also forced fundamentally to rethink – produce the journal *Carré Rouge,* founded by François Chesnais and Charles Jérémie, in Paris. I have also benefited from work published in the Glasgow-based journal *Critique,* which since 1973 (and unlike most other left-wing publications) made a sustained and serious analysis of the Soviet system, and in which a version of chapter 4 of the present book first appeared.[10]

My original intention was to publish this book two or three years ago, maintaining a greater continuity in the progress of the collective work in which I have been involved than has proved possible.[11] Its appearance now, however incomplete it may seem, is to encourage discussion between those with political histories similar to mine and the categories of reader I defined above. The times are pressing, the tasks large. The theoretical direction I think our forward movement might take is – very provisionally – indicated in chapters 4 and 8.

This book is about communism – the social-metabolic order and culture which must be attained if humanity is to survive the mortal dangers consequent on the continued rule of capital. It will be, as Marx wrote, 'an association, in which the free development of each is the condition for the free development of all'. The overcoming of capital's rule, the socialist revolution, does not mean the replacement of one form of exploitation by another, as was the case with all earlier revolutions. Instead, it marks the end of all class society.

In the social order ruled by capital, the mass of humanity is deprived of any independent means of production and compelled to sell itself to the owners of capital. That capital is nothing other than the result of past labour, stored-up labour. Thus dead labour rules over the living. Capital's rule constitutes an external force or 'second nature' constraining living humanity. The history of humanity is, on the one side, that of progress through manual and mental labour towards an understanding of nature, enjoyment of its gifts, and freedom from its hostility and dangers. The capitalist mode of production of the last few hundred years led to an unprecedented advance in this respect. But the 'second nature' of mankind's alienation under the rule of capital cuts off living labour from nature, and bars the way to the potential freedom which human labour has made possible. Only the overcoming of the social metabolic order of the capital system will create a truly human exchange with the rest of nature, because it must put an end, not only to that system, but also to exploitation and class society as such.

In the third volume of *Capital*, Marx wrote:

> From the standpoint of a higher socio-economic formation, the private property of particular individuals in the earth will appear just as absurd as the private property of one man in other men. Even an entire society, a nation, or all simultaneously existing societies taken together, are not owners of the earth, they are simply its possessors, its beneficiaries, and have to bequeath it in an improved state to succeeding generations, as *boni patres familias* (good heads of the household).[12]

And Mészáros summarises the issue as follows:

> ... how to reconstitute, at a level fully consonant with the historically achieved productive development of society, the necessary unity of the working subjects with the attainable objective conditions of their meaningful life-activity.[13]

Clearly, this historical imperative goes beyond the revolutionary conquest of state power by the working class. And here we face ever more complex and difficult problems. Marx showed that communism was no utopia but a condition prepared and necessitated by capitalism's own inexorable drive for accumulation, which brings highly developed productive forces and the world market. Without these productive forces and 'universal intercourse' there could be no communism. In our own 21st century, however, it would be fatal not to take into account the fact that the continued imprisonment of these productive forces by capital has already resulted in their becoming destructive on a massive scale. The self-reproduction of capital, its unending and overriding quest for accumulation, has become, in Mészáros's words, a 'destructive self-reproduction'.

Communists have already had to learn (especially after the Soviet experience) the bitter lesson that the overthrow of capitalist state power plus nationalisation of the means of production is not enough to bring socialism. And this is not a matter only of the impossibility of 'socialism in a single country'. Beyond state power and changed property relations, there is the long struggle to overcome capital's hierarchical domination and control so that 'living labour' truly controls production.

But there is now a new consideration: the destructive consequences on the global scale of the perpetuation of capital's rule must surely be confronted even before the conquest of power. That is to say: the working-class and socialist movement must take responsibility now for defending and protecting the natural and human conditions and resources of the future positive social metabolic order. Indeed, in today's conditions of globalised capital, with its uncontrolled plunder of natural resources and impoverishment of countless millions in Asia, Africa and Latin America, such defence and protection is an absolute precondition of the necessary unification of all the human forces exploited by and opposed to capital.

Not Without a Storm begins with a brief look at what is called 'globalisation' and its results (contrasting it with Marx's idea of 'universal intercourse' as one of the conditions for the transition to socialism). It then tries to show the situation of the working class, in order to ask the following question. In a world that has undergone so much change since Marx's day, what can be the concrete meaning of his call for the 'proletarians of all lands' to unite: 'You have nothing to lose but your chains, you have a world to win'?

The epigraphs at the head of this introduction are all quotations from men who were not Marxists. And they were all from one country – England. Jennings, a pioneering filmmaker who died not long after the second world war, rejected the idea that the marriage of science and technology that made the Industrial Revolution defined the inevitable course of social progress. He sought to release the imagination of men and women in a way that would allow them to control science and technology for human need. Meredith was a prolific latter-nineteenth-century poet and novelist whose widely read fictions were, in the Victorian manner, designed to instruct while they entertained. In *Beauchamp's Career* an unconventional ex-naval hero fails to win election as a radical politician, but eventually dies rescuing a working-class lad from drowning – leaving witnesses contemplating the value of the exchange of life involved. Readers are challenged by the tragic metaphor to consider whether the being of the apparently weak young worker may hold the key to the fulfilment of the ideal for England's future that Beauchamp could not bring about through the ballot box. The great early nineteenth-century poet and artist William Blake, and his much-sung *Jerusalem*, need no introduction.

Many who sing *Jerusalem*, however, do not perhaps realise that it comes from a long poem written in the first decade of the nineteenth century, *Milton*. In it, England's great seventeenth-century revolutionary poet, the Puritan John Milton, is called back from heaven to aid Blake in the cause of fighting the dehumanising effects of the machine economy; and of envisioning a true paradise in 'England's green and pleasant land'. And it was Milton who – in *Paradise Lost*, in 1667 – gave the name 'pandaemonium', the place of all the demons, to hell. The hell Jennings confronted in his creative and scholarly work was nothing less than the social metabolism that evolved following the defeat – with the Restoration of the monarchy in 1660 – of the English Revolution of the 1640s. This political process made possible, in the late-eighteenth and nineteenth centuries, the capital system's 'first industrial revolution'. By the last quarter of the nineteenth century it was becoming clear – as Meredith's metaphorical climax hints – that this was a hell that could not complete itself, could not, from within, become a human formation. And for Jennings, three-quarters of a century on, the idea that the Welfare State legislation of the 1940s had accomplished such a completion was clearly an illusion. Transformation – accomplished by collective human creativity – was required.

The main point of all this in the present context – that is, as prologue to what follows – is that the focus on England, apparently parochial, is not that at all. In the late 1860s, Marx based much of his first volume of *Capital* on the empirical base others had created for the study of the 'condition of England' or, rather, Britain. Was this relevant to workers elsewhere, he asked, replying to the question he had put in the mouths of German workers particularly: '*De te fabula narratur*' – 'This will be your story'. It is a measure of the changes of the last few decades that it was still possible a generation or so ago to discuss such matters in a framework predicated on the diversity of national experience in different parts of the world. As we proceed into the 21st century, the experience of the workers of all countries is already essentially interconnected, though the lives of many in the 'advanced' countries have never seemed more desirably different from most in Africa and elsewhere. The collective grasping of that globalised interconnection (and contradiction) in consciousness, and the actualisation of that collective consciousness into a 'truly human society' – under conditions in which the barbaric alternative is all too thinkable – is the great task we have inherited. But this is a forecast that cannot be delivered easily or without prediction of pain. The necessary changes will not come 'without a storm'. It is a storm for which uncompromising theoretical and practical preparation is essential as we face the choice between building Jerusalem and hellish destruction. Human, and even planetary, survival is at stake.

It is in the nature of this book that its work is ongoing, and that, at each point of apparent completion, it seems already superseded. It is impossible, in making a final revision of this introduction (in September 2005) not to reflect on the impact of Hurricane Katrina in Louisiana and Mississippi and on the aftermath of the destruction in New Orleans. Reading about it, seeing the images, in one sense, makes much of *Not Without a Storm* seem redundant. Forget George W Bush's tears over a 'natural disaster'. The wanton destruction of the environment in the interests of big business has nowhere been more tragically systematic than along the 1,500 miles of the coastline of the Gulf of Mexico in the American South. Scientists had given clear warnings of the threat to New Orleans, a city built in a bowl and protected – as the local press had long campaigned about – by inadequate levees.

The rapid polarisation of wealth in the richest and most powerful nation in the world has been suddenly and brutally exposed. 'New Orleans was Third World long before the hurricane,' wrote Cornel West in the *Observer*.[14] The average income in parts of the city is less than $8,000 a year. The truth about the impact of the ruthless drive over the past few years to shut down social and welfare services at last has to be written about and published. The racist oppression and exploitation of poor black people is now brutally highlighted. The ruling class in the nineteenth century was forced to free its slaves. Now its descendants inflict this humanitarian atrocity, this vicious crime, on a people whose grandparents and great-grandparents created, even in their inhuman conditions, the wonders of New Orleans music. Nor, in the aftermath of Katrina, was the rescue of human beings the priority, but rather the restoration of capital's 'law and order' – the law and order of the perpetrators of the disaster. The criminal culture of the ruling class inevitably produced the murder, rape and looting that broke out. Meanwhile hundreds of fraudulent relief and charity organisations were set up on the internet. Here, in horrific concentration, and before our eyes, is the pandaemonium the capital system must produce.

Yes, indeed: 'So foul a sky clears not without a storm'.

---

[1] A note by Humphrey Jennings, quoted by Charles Madge in Mary-Lou Jennings and Charles Madge (eds.), *Pandaemonium: 1660-1886, the coming of the machine as seen by contemporary observers* by Humphrey Jennings (London, 1995, first published in 1985 from texts and notes assembled by the author, 1937-50), p. 5. The date 1942 is a guess – Madge refers to an 'early note' for a proposed introduction: 1942 was the year in which the foundation document of the Welfare State, the Beveridge Report, appeared. Jennings (b. 1906) was killed researching a prospective film location in Greece in 1950.

[2] George Meredith, *Beauchamp's Career* (3 vols., London, 1876, first published in the *Fortnightly Review*, August 1874-December 1875), chap. XXIX. Meredith's character thought too that the power of the workers was also in danger of 'seduction … by another Power not mighty in England now' – a reactionary power.

[3] William Blake, *Milton* (various editions; written,1804-09), Introduction.

[4] Stendhal was the literary name of Marie-Henri Beyle (1783-1842), who participated in the Napoleonic Wars and was a pioneer of the nineteenth-century French novel. The quote is from his autobiographical novel, *The Life of Henri Brulard* (London, 1995, written 1835-36, first published 1890).

[5] Walter Benjamin, 'Theses on the Philosophy of History', in his *Illuminations*, edited and with an introduction by Hannah Arendt (London, 1999; first published, 1970), p. 251.

[6] Peter Fryer was the *Daily Worker* correspondent whose eyes were opened by his experience reporting – and having his reports suppressed – on the Hungarian revolution. See Peter Fryer, *Hungarian Tragedy* (London, 1956 and later editions, especially the expanded one published in 1997). Fryer's courageous, and never adequately acknowledged, role in the mid-1950s crisis of communism was crucial in my experience. From time to time when he served as principal columnist on the *Workers Press* (2nd series) in the late 1980s and early 1990s, Fryer commented on these events. The stark contrast between his honest memories and the self-serving and misleading, but much better known, 'recollections' of the celebrated historian Eric Hobsbawm, CH, comes out in two of Fryer's columns republished in *Workers International Press*, vol. 2, nos. 1-2 (winter and spring, 1997-98), pp. 48-50.

[7] Terry Brotherstone, '1956: Tom Kemp and others', in Terry Brotherstone and Geoff Pilling (eds.), *History, Economic History and the Future of Marxism: essays in memory of Tom Kemp (1921-1992)* (London, 1996). This essay includes an account of Fryer's role in 1956.

[8] For a call for new work, and new thinking, on the miners' strike, see Terry Brotherstone and Simon Pirani, 'Were There Alternatives? Movements from Below in the Scottish Coalfield, the Communist Party and Thatcherism, 1981-85', *Critique*, nos. 36-7 (2005), pp. 99-123.

[9] Norman Harding, my Yorkshire comrade, has recently published *Staying Red: Why I remain a Socialist* (London, 2005). In my view, this is the only serious, autobiographical-historical, sustained approach to the story of the Socialist Labour League/ Workers Revolutionary Party so far.

[10] Cliff Slaughter, 'Where to Begin? New Thinking on the Old Idea of Socialist Internationalism', *Critique*, vol. 36-7 (2005), pp. 187-215.

[11] See the work reflected in the appendices below, and in the duplicated journal *Work in Progress*, no. 1, that appeared in 2000.

[12] See Karl Marx, *Capital*, vol. 3.

[13] István Mészáros, *Beyond Capital: towards a theory of transition* (London, 1995), p. 349.

[14] *Observer*, 11 September 2005. Hurricane Rita followed after this was written. President George W. Bush showed much greater concern for his rich fellow-Texans.

1

UNIVERSAL INTERCOURSE

Marx's approach

'A spectre is haunting Europe, the spectre of communism.' With these famous words Karl Marx and Frederick Engels opened *The Communist Manifesto*, first published in 1848.

At the outset of the 21st century, what Marx called a 'practical consciousness' of the possibility of communism must face up to the overshadowing threat of another spectre – the spectre of the destruction of humanity and of nature. A century has passed since Rosa Luxemburg's stark warning: 'socialism or barbarism!' She perceived the barbarians at the gates of human civilisation: today, a creeping barbarism is already within the gates. The deadly work – for the sake of profit and the accumulation of capital – of sabotaging the elementary natural and cultural conditions of the future socialist society is already well under way. And it is worldwide. The Europe of 1847 in which Marx and Engels were writing their *Manifesto* has become the world. More than ever do its words ring true:

> Modern bourgeois society with its relations of production, of exchange and of property, a society that has conjured up such gigantic means of production and of exchange, is like the sorcerer, who is no longer able to control the powers of the nether world whom he has called up by his spells.[1]

Socialism – or communism[2] – could not be confined to narrow national limits but would need, as its basic conditions, advanced productive forces and 'universal intercourse'. These conditions would be prepared by capitalism itself, with 'universal intercourse' taking the form of the world market.

In *The German Ideology* Marx and Engels anticipated the scope of the task facing us in today's 'globalised' world:

> Thus things have now come to such a pass that the individuals must appropriate the existing totality of productive forces, not only to achieve self-activity [i.e. to overcome alienation/exploitation - CS], but, also, merely *to safeguard their very existence.* [Emphasis added]
>
> This appropriation is first determined by the object to be appropriated, the productive forces, which have been developed to a totality and which only exist within a universal intercourse. Even from this aspect alone, therefore, this appropriation must have a universal character corresponding to the productive forces and the intercourse.[3]

And, they go on: 'Modern universal intercourse cannot be controlled by individuals unless it is controlled by all.'[4]

Only the control of productive forces and universal intercourse by all, then, could overcome the 'estrangement' of human beings from their own activity which capital imposed. And:

> This 'estrangement' ... can ... only be abolished given two *practical* premises. In order to become an 'unendurable power', i.e., a power against which men [*have*] to make a revolution, it must necessarily have rendered the great mass of humanity 'propertyless', and moreover in contradiction to an existing world of wealth and culture; both these premises presuppose a great increase in productive power, a high degree of its development.
>
> And, on the other hand, this development of productive forces (which at the same time implies the actual empirical existence of men in their *world-historical*, instead of local, being) is an absolutely necessary practical premise, because without it privation, *want*, is merely made general; and with *want* the struggle for necessities would begin again, all the old filthy business would necessarily be restored; and furthermore, because only with this universal development of productive forces is a *universal* human intercourse between men established, which on the one side produces in *all* nations simultaneously the phenomenon of the 'propertyless' mass (universal

> competition), making each nation dependent on the revolutions of the others, and finally puts *world-historical*, empirically universal individuals in place of local ones.[5]

Marx's early writings have often been criticised by would-be 'scientific Marxists' as abstractly 'humanist'. Yet clearly his 'world-historical, empirically universal individuals in place of local ones' is far from abstract. Similarly, his insistence (quoted above) on developed productive forces and universal intercourse as the preconditions for communism is followed immediately by the statement that:

> The appropriation of these forces is itself nothing more than the development of the individual capacities corresponding to the material instruments of production. The appropriation of a totality of instruments of production is, for this reason, the development of a totality of capacities in the individuals themselves...
>
> Only at this stage does self-activity coincide with material life, which corresponds to the development of individuals into complete individuals and the casting-off of all natural limitations.

We shall see later – in looking at the notes Marx made when he was working on his *Capital* (eventually published as *Grundrisse*) – that the oft-repeated assertion that Marx's later writings left behind these ideas is quite without foundation.

In this book, my emphasis is on the dangers now posed to the basic foundations of the future socialist society by capital's 'destructive self-reproduction'. Not the least of these dangers is the destruction wrought by the debasement of culture and its effects on individuals. To fight against that in every field is an essential part of any effective struggle against capital and for the future.

This calls to mind the dictum of the pioneering left-wing American historians, Charles and Mary Beard, who wrote: 'If, as [is] claimed, some form of socialism, based on machine industry, lies beyond the present regime, it will certainly take a civilised people to operate it'.[6] The Beards here echoed Marx's own insistence that socialism depends not only on developed productive forces and universal intercourse but also on 'the all-round development of individuals'.

In the preparation of *Capital* – that is to say his 'mature' work – Marx returns to his early stress on the relation between universal intercourse and free, cultured individuals, in a manner that entirely undermines those crudely ideological critics who oppose communism to individuality. Capital, he insists, itself drives towards a historical stage

> ... where the labouring society relates scientifically to the process of its progressive reproduction, its reproduction in a constantly greater abundance; hence where labour in which a human being does what a thing could do has ceased. ... Capital's ceaseless striving towards the general form of wealth drives labour beyond the limits of its natural paltriness, *and thus creates the material elements for the development of the rich individuality which is as all-sided in its production as in its consumption, and whose labour also therefore appears no longer as labour, but as the full development of activity itself, in which natural necessity in its direct form has disappeared ...*[7] [Emphasis added]

These 'material conditions' creating the potential of an abundance of free time ('the creation of a large quantity of disposable time') for use by culturally developed individuals take on an inhuman, negative aspect so long as the rule of capital persists. Marx is scathing in demonstrating that for millions 'free time' means unemployment. It means, under capital, an excess of idleness and of waste, on the one hand; on the other, of luxury, lavish spending. It creates a subservient servant class, providing a variety of the sort of 'services' that lead Marx to remark: 'From whore to pope, there is a mass of such rabble.'[8]

Marx asserts that on the basis of the material conquests of the capitalist mode of production, it is possible to look forward to

> the cultivation of all the qualities of the social human being, production of the same in a form as rich as possible in needs, because rich in qualities and relations – production of this being as the most total and universal social product, for, in order to take gratification in a many-sided way, he must be capable of many pleasures, hence cultured to a high degree...[9]

The contrast with the outcome of this availability of free time so long as the sway of capital prevails could hardly be more marked. In addition to the production of masses of waste and innumerable artificial wants, as well as unemployment and deprivation of all kinds, we have today's so-called 'leisure industry', with the time devoted to its vacuities and the 'products' designed for it. All this is delivered to a populace condemned to a minimal education and a culturally corrupted diet of entertainment. Those commentators who lecture us about youth crime, 'hooliganism', 'yob culture' would do well to reflect on the causes of these phenomena.

A caveat. One must be careful not to interpret 'intercourse' in Marx's text as only the technical means of communication and 'economic' relations (the world market). Marx seems to mean more than this by 'social forms of intercourse'. He wrote that his 'conception of history' relied not only 'on examining the real process of production – starting from the material production of life itself', but also on 'comprehending the form of intercourse connected with and created by this mode of production', that is 'civil society in its various stages'. This was 'the basis of all history'.

One of the most striking – and tragic – manifestations of the capital system's barrier to the truly human development of the already existing means of universal intercourse is at the very centre of its 'world market' – that is, today's world labour market.

Capital's consequences in Asia, Africa, Latin America and, increasingly since 1990, Eastern Europe, drive millions into forced emigration to seek work. Clearly it is not for technical reasons – as in the past when there were inadequate means of transport – that they are not free to move to, and work, where they wish.

Never were those means of transport more efficient. The simple reality is that state apparatuses serving capital prevent free movement (except for those workers for whom they have a particular need of their own). All those capitalists and their political servants who impose these oppressive restrictions and controls on men and women who must sell their labour-power are of course without exception enthusiastic 'neo-liberal' advocates of 'free' trade.

The case of Information Technology

Do we have the technical means of 'universal intercourse' for large numbers now, under capitalism? Yes, undoubtedly we do, but we have the means at the cost of being exploited by their possessors. Computers, the internet – in a certain sense and to a certain degree – overcome limitations of time and space. They surely complete the material/technical conditions for that 'universal intercourse' necessary for communism, already in large part laid down, as Marx emphasised, by capital's creation of a world market.

But universal intercourse *for what* and *for whom*? Communism will mean production for use, to meet the human needs defined and developed by freely cooperating individuals, and not production of exchange-values, as is fundamental to the rule of capital. As Mészáros puts it, such a concentration on use-values

> ... is inseparable from the question of all-sided development of the social individual's needs and productive capacities. For such a development is feasible only within the unrestricted – i.e. no longer class-interest-and-class-conflict-determined – framework of 'universal intercourse' and 'universal exchange' of human capacities and accomplishments as opposed to universally dominant exchange-value.[10]

This truly was Marx's conception. In *Grundrisse* we find:

> What is wealth other than the universality of individual needs, capacities, pleasures, productive forces etc., created through universal exchange? The full development of human mastery over the forces of nature, those of so-called nature as well as of humanity's own nature, the absolute working-out of his creative potentialities...[11]

What is required is

> [a] radical restructuring ... tantamount to elaborating a qualitatively different form of social metabolic control. The nature of the new form can be summed up, quoting Marx's words, as a system based on 'a general plan of freely combined individuals'. This means in simplest terms the replacement of labour's chains imposed by capital with the *cooperative ties* of the individuals and

> the various groups to which the individuals belong. Through this qualitative change they are enabled to establish a far superior and potentially more productive form of *overall coordination* than what is feasible on the basis of the authoritarian control of labour in capital's chain-gang system.
>
> In other words, the social metabolic control of freely combined individuals – instituted and constantly developed by the freely combined individuals themselves – makes possible the sustainability of a new productive order. For *sustainability equals the conscious control of the social metabolic process of reproduction by the freely associated producers* (which is, of course, the only feasible form of *self-control*) in contrast to the untenable, structurally entrenched, adversariality and ultimate destructiveness of capital's reproductive order.[12]

In the hands of capital, the means of communication transmit corruption, the destruction of culture and the debasement of humanity, as well as exploitation – the perverted forms, that is, taken under the rule of capital by 'universal intercourse' in the realm of social relations and culture.

The trade in such things as paedophilia (and not only through images) and pornography is well known, and there are ever-new threats. Racism and anti-Semitism has proliferated on the internet, spawning more than 2,100 websites, the European Union's racism monitoring unit reported some years ago. Most of the sites are based in the United States, but in Germany too, the internal security service has been registering growing numbers of hate websites.

'What was proscribed, undercover, shameful and liable to prosecution in the past is today readily available on the Net,' the European monitoring centre said in the annual report it published in 2000: 'movements which were in decline in both Europe and the US have received a new lease of life thanks to the sites they have created.' There is even a long-standing site offering the full text of Hitler's *Mein Kampf*.

Jason Burke writing in the *Observer*, November 13, 2005, discussed the dangers of right-wing opposition to immigration: 'This discourse is potentially dangerous. The conservatives, be they French Republican diehards, extremist mullahs or newspaper columnists, are likely to find in the age of the internet, satellite TV, communites of second-or-third generation immigrants that number in their tens of millions, not to mention massive and growing pressure from migrants beyond European borders, huge flows of capital and ever greater movements of cultural exchange, that it is impossible to try to turn back the clock. Pulling up the drawbridge will not work. History is flowing in the wrong direction. This means their actions are likely to get more desperate, their logic more twisted and their rhetoric more rabid. The paradox is that the faster globalisation moves, the more radical and possibly more numerous they'll become.'

In Chapter 6 some of the implications of the 'information revolution', and in particular electronic communication, for the re-foundation of the working-class movement are briefly discussed. Here the intention is only to provide some examples of the fate of these scientific conquests under the rule of capital.

The following is an extract from the article 'Mayday, Mayday' by Jeremy Rifkin in the *Guardian*, April 28, 2001:

> Question: what is the single most valuable piece of property worth owning at the dawn of the information age? Answer: the radio frequencies – the electromagnetic spectrum – over which an increasing amount of communication and commercial activity will be broadcast in the era of wireless communications. Our PCs, palm pilots, wireless internet, cellular phones, pagers, radios and television all rely on the radio frequencies of the spectrum to send and receive messages, pictures, audio, data, etc.
>
> But now powerful commercial media are seeking to gain total control over the airwaves. Imagine a world in which a handful of global media conglomerates like Vivendi, Sony, BSkyB, Disney and News Corporation own literally all of the planet's airwaves, and trade them back and forth as 'private electronic real estate'. A strategy is beginning to unfold in Washington DC to make that happen.
>
> On February 7 [2001], 37 leading US economists signed a joint letter asking the Federal communications commission to allow broadcasters to lease spectrum they currently license from the government in secondary markets. The letter, which went virtually unnoticed by the general public, is the opening salvo in a radical plan

> to wrest control of the entire spectrum from governments around the world, and make the radio frequencies a private preserve of global media giants. If they succeed, the nation state will have lost one of its last remaining vestiges of real power – the ability to regulate access to broadcast communications within its own geographical borders. …
>
> If the radio frequencies of the planet were owned and controlled by global media corporations, how would the billions who live on earth guarantee their most basic right to communicate with one another? In an era where more and more of our daily communications take place in cyberspace, access to the airwaves becomes critical. Of course, those who can pay will be connected. But what about the 62 per cent of people who have never made a telephone call, and the 40 per cent who have no electricity? How will they ever secure access to cyberspace in a world where the admission fee is controlled by a few global media giants?
>
> If the flow of human communications is controlled by global media companies,[13] how do we ensure that social and cultural points of view that may differ from those of the companies who own the frequencies will be allowed to flow over the spectrum?… How do we prevent these companies from exerting undue influence over commercial life itself, because of their control over the channels of communication through which business is conducted? And finally, in the new era, when everyone is connected with everyone else in commercial information and telecommunications networks, how do we prevent corporate owners of the radio frequencies from exploiting the data on people's lives that flows through cyberspace? What safeguards will people have over their privacy when every aspect of their life story is accessible as data bits travelling over corporate-owned and controlled communications channels?

Good questions! They are perhaps best summarised as: what price 'universal intercourse' under the rule of capital? On the question which is our concern here, namely the contradiction between the new means of communication/production, vastly intensifying and accelerating 'universal intercourse', on the one hand, and the nature of capital on the other, there is surely nothing to add. Clearly (monopoly) competition in this field means not only depriving us of this 'free good', but also the tearing of pieces of the world market away from each other. We await a progress report on Tony Blair's November 2000 claim to be:

> preparing for an ambitious partnership with some of the world's top IT companies to ensure that the benefits of the information revolution reach developing countries, by using new technology to train teachers in Africa.

The *Guardian Weekly*, reporting this noble aspiration, said:

> Mr Blair believes that education is the long-term key to tackling poverty and boosting economic development, and that teachers are vital in delivering the benefits of new technology to poor children. The Imfundo project is at the forefront of the UK government's drive [*sic*] to bridge the 'digital divide' between computer-literate people with access to the internet and new technology, and those who are being left behind by the high-tech revolution.

Blair's pretensions mirror the naïve illusions held by many, such as those answered by this letter to the *Guardian* from Arturo Robledo, Mexico City:

> Stephen Buckley and Anthony Faiola claim the internet can act as an equaliser in the developing world. They must be commended for their optimism. In Mexico, ten years after privatisation of the state phone company, there are only ten lines for every 100 inhabitants. To get a new line you pay $170 dollars fee plus the $20 monthly rent; the majority of the population earns only $1 a day. Meanwhile the owner of the phone monopoly, and main internet provider, has an estimated wealth, according to Forbes, of $7.9bn.

And, on the same theme, Microsoft owner Bill Gates,

> ... speaking in Seattle at a conference on using computers to help the third world, said he still had faith in the ideal that technology could bring about a better world, but he doubted that computers – or global capitalism – could solve the most immediate catastrophes facing the world's poorest people. People who thought that developing countries could benefit from the e-economy had no idea what it meant to live on $1 a day with no electricity, he said. 'You're just buying food; you're trying to stay alive.'
>
> The billionaire technologist became positively vitriolic about the idea of using computers in the third world: 'Mothers are gong to walk right up to that computer and say, "My children are dying, what can

you do?" They're not going to sit there and, like, browse eBay or something. What they want is for their children to live. Do you really have to put in computers to figure that out?'[14]

Considering the 'IT revolution' in the context of the capital system's destructive self-reproduction, it is understandable that Fidel Castro was led to say, at the UNESCO conference on Culture and Development in June 1999, in Havana: 'Internet? Yes, we can use it – to tell the 80 per cent of Americans online that they have to stop and realise the Earth is on the edge of an abyss.'

Increasingly, commercial use of the internet threatens the individual and his/her privacy:

> Keith Little, a computer technician who makes house calls on the apple farms of central Washington state, says more and more of his clients are asking him to take steps to protect their online privacy. So he scans their computers for any mischievous programs and installs security software. What surprises people is how often Little finds programs designed to funnel bits of their personal information from their computers and into giant corporate databases. He says more than half of the 20 or so computers he inspects each week are running stealthy programs he calls 'spyware'....
>
> 'Your tax records, what medical sites you've been looking at, your online banking – if someone has spyware on your machine, they would have access to that data and it would be next to impossible to tell if it was leaving,' said Travis Haymore, a former federal government computer security investigator.... 'Right now it's a free-for-all. Anything goes,' says Montreal computer consultant Gilles Lalonde.
>
> This is the kind of environment that permits these kinds of intrusive behaviours, allows them to flourish. If we don't start to define some ethical rules, before long people will lose their trust in all online companies and this great technological revolution just stops.[15]

Does IT contribute to prosperity? Ignacio Ramonet wrote the following in the April 2000 edition of *Le Monde Diplomatique*:

> Marx once said: 'Give me the windmill and I'll give you the Middle Ages.' We could add 'Give me the steam engine and I'll give you the Industrial Revolution' and then update that as 'Give me the computer

> and I'll give you globalisation'. This might be deterministic, but the basic idea is useful. At any historical turning-point, a key invention appears, and never by accident: it transforms the status quo, and takes society in a new direction.

Imperceptibly, over a decade or more, we have been moving into such a phase. At the end of the eighteenth century, the invention of the steam engine led to the Industrial Revolution, changing the world with the growth of capitalism, the creation of the working class, the birth of socialist ideas and movements, and new possibilities for colonialism. Yet as machinery, the steam engine was only designed to replace muscle power. The role of the computer is to replace brain power – so the changes are even more radical. This era's main characteristics are instantaneous transfer of intangible data, and a proliferation of electronic interconnections. The internet is the heart, the crossroads and the synthesis of this. Information highways are to our era what railways were to the industrial era: a powerful factor in promoting trade and commerce.

The Nasdaq index, which covers most high-technology shares in New York, registered a gain of 85.6 per cent in 1999. Even though the index fell sharply in March 2000, it had still gained over 20 per cent overall just since the beginning of 2000. But this get-rich-quick easy money, involving neither work nor effort, seems a mirage. In the United States, the inequality gap has widened and is reaching levels not seen since the Depression of the 1930s.

The real possibilities promised by Information Technology are very different indeed, and are realisable only when humans have freed themselves and the technology from the grip of capital. As already noted, the time involved in production and communication (computerisation makes the means of production and the means of communication more and more coincide) is greatly reduced and in some cases virtually eliminated by information technology. If indeed, as Marx wrote, 'Economy of time, to this all economy ultimately reduces itself',[16] then the implications of this reduction are enormous, and Marx's work on the question of time in capitalism and in communism surely now takes on added significance. Marx devoted much attention to the importance of machinery in capitalist production. He wrote that when machine production '... increase[d] the relation of surplus labour to necessary labour, by enabling labour, through increase in its productive power, to create a greater mass of the products required for the maintenance of living labour capacity in a shorter time', this meant that capital thereby 'reduces human labour, expenditure of energy, to a minimum' (NB, *a minimum* – CS), and concluded: 'This will redound to the benefit of emancipated labour, and is the condition of its emancipation.'[17]

The imperatives fundamental to production in the capital system have driven that system to utilise ruthlessly information technology, just as capital has in the course of its development inexorably opened up the planet's resources of every kind. But it is clear that what is involved here is an unprecedented acceleration of that *socialisation of production* which comes more and more into contradiction with the social metabolic process based on accumulation of capital through the 'theft of alienated labour time':

> To the degree that labour time – the mere quantity of labour – is posited by capital as the sole determinant element, to that degree does direct labour and its quantity disappear as the determinant principle of production – of the creation of use values – and is reduced both quantitatively, to a smaller proportion, and qualitatively, as an, of course, indispensable but subordinate moment, compared to general scientific labour, technological application of natural sciences, on one side, and to the general productive force arising from ... social combination in total production on the other side – a combination which appears as a natural fruit of social labour (although it is a historic product). Capital thus works towards its own dissolution as the form dominating production.[18]

Once large-scale machine production comes into existence, the individual worker's contribution to the value of the product becomes, as against 'the value objectified in machinery, ... an infinitesimal, vanishing magnitude'[19]. Governing of production processes and communication by the machines called computers and the whole field of Information Technology have carried this development to unimagined lengths. In these machines resides the 'social brain', through which can be programmed and coordinated the labours of individuals separated by thousands of miles:

> The development of fixed capital indicates to what degree general social knowledge has become a *direct force of production*, and to what degree, hence, the conditions of the process of social life itself have come under the control of the general intellect and been transformed in accordance with it.[20]

But until now the capacities of this social brain are appropriated by competing capitals. In parenthesis, we may refer back to Marx:

> The accumulation of knowledge and of skill, of the general productive forces of the social brain, is thus absorbed into capital, as opposed to labour, and hence appears as an attribute of capital, and more specifically of *fixed capital*, insofar as it enters into the production process as a means of production proper.[21]

They are not at the disposal of the producing social individuals, but are alienated from them, and are used to exploit them, purely for the purpose of creating exchange-values on the sale of which surplus value can be 'realised' and capital thereby accumulated. This capital is dead, stored-up labour, which returns to the scene to further exploit the producers. Against this, Marx posited

> [the] true concept of the process of social production.... The saving of labour time is equal to an increase of free time, i.e. time for the full development of the individual, which in turn reacts back upon the productive power of labour as itself the greatest productive power.[22]

The great advances contained in the 'information revolution' are precious preconditions for the future socialist society. It is surely not difficult to see that all possible efforts must be made to oppose the perversion of our 'social brain', our social 'general intellect', its use for capital's destructive self-reproduction, and even to utilise information technology itself to organise against capital.

Indicating the possibilities

In his paper entitled 'New Technology and the Learning Revolution'[23], and elsewhere, the researcher on sustainability, David Hookes has indicated the liberating potential of the new technology. The gap between this potential and today's global reality is awesome. In December 2003 the United Nations World Summit on the Information Society was attended mainly by delegates from the poor countries of the world. They were confronted by a startling statistic:

> Only 1 per cent of people in the world's poorest countries are connected to the Internet. The 400,000 residents of Luxemburg have more Internet capacity than all of Africa's 760 million inhabitants.[24]

The 176 delegates gathered to discuss the Information Society surely deserve the century's prize for optimism. They

> formally adopted a plan aimed at ensuring access to television and radio services for all of the world's population by 2015 and ensuring that half of all people will have access to some form of information and communication technology.

However, the world's poor must hold their breath just a little longer: 'Progress [was] to be measured at a follow-up summit meeting in Tunis in 2005.'

It is crystal-clear that the 'globalisation' now reached by the development of capitalism is hardly the universalism anticipated by Marx; indeed it is in a very meaningful sense its opposite. No one can any longer entertain the idea that each society would go through predictable and similar stages of evolution, let alone the bogus theories of 'developing societies' of the last half-century. The evolution of society and culture differs fundamentally from that of natural species, and all theories depending on analogies with the latter are fatally flawed. In nature, as Stephen Jay Gould has so succinctly put it:

> ... since any well-defined taxonomic group can trace its origin to a single common ancestor, an evolutionary tree must have a unique

> basal trunk. Second, all branches of the same tree either die or ramify further. Separation is irrevocable; distinct branches do not join.[25]

In the history of humanity, distinct branches (societies, cultures) do 'join'! The different human societies (branches) connect and re-connect in various ways. There have been simple theories of combination, diffusion, subjection by conquest and so on. The latest of these processes of connection and combined development has brought 'globalisation'. This should be seen not just as a completion of the capitalist world market (as in Immanuel Wallerstein's 'capitalist world system'),[26] but – returning to Gould's terminology – as the restoration of the 'trunk' at the highest (world) level.

It is from this standpoint that I approach the themes of this book. The necessary social revolution will necessarily take in, learn from, advance on and subsume the contributions of all past cultures, from primitive societies and their relation to nature onwards. The great question confronting us is this. Can human individuals master this globalised society and culture that they and their ancestors have created?

Capitalism is no exception to the formulation Marx and Engels used in *The Communist Manifesto*: 'The history of all hitherto existing societies is a history of class struggle.' Was Marx right in seeing the working class as the revolutionary force raised up by capital? The revolutionary content of 'globalisation' and the great increase in productivity of labour is a massive socialisation of production within the shell of capitalist private property and accumulation. What are the problems and prospects for a proletarian internationalism in response?

The internet itself epitomises both the problems and the possibilities. On the worldwide web there are 600 billion pages; to which something like a billion people have access. Potentially – and actually for millions of them already – there is free and instantaneous mutual exchange of information, opinion and creative work. As Rafael Behr wrote recently:

> In an era whose triumphant idea is capitalism, where success is generally measured in the accumulation of wealth, it is hard to

> conceive of a parallel society established and self-governed on principles of trust and common ownership. But it exists. The biggest aggregation of human experience and knowledge ever created belongs to everyone, it is available on demand and it is free. But for how long?

How long, indeed? The government of China has already cut millions of its citizens off from the internet. As this book goes to press, it is reported that 'dissidents' in China have been imprisoned as a result of Yahoo's supplying their details to the Chinese government. This fact brings us face to face with one of the main themes of this book. The conquests of human culture, as well as of nature itself – the preconditions of a future truly human society – must be defended, protected and used *now*, against the destructiveness of capital. And this must include the protection and development of the new means of universal intercourse. Behr cites Noam Chomsky, who summarises well the threat:

> Major efforts are being made by the corporate owners and advertisers to shape the internet so that it will be mostly used for commerce, diversion and so on. Those who wish to use it for information, political organising and other such activities will have a harder time.[27]

The key questions posed in the following chapters encompass this critical concern.

---

[1] See K. Marx and F. Engels, *The Communist Manifesto* (many editions).

[2] For Marx and Engels there was no essential difference: 'communism' merely distinguished their socialism from utopianism.

[3] K. Marx and F. Engels, *The German Ideology* (written 1845-6, first published in full, Moscow, 1932) in *K. Marx and F. Engels, Collected Works*, V (London, 1976), p. 87.

[4] Marx and Engels, *German Ideology*, p. 88.

[5] Marx and Engels, *German Ideology*, pp. 48-9.

[6] See Charles A. Beard and Mary R. Beard, *The Rise of American Civilization* (first published, London, 1927).

[7] Karl Marx, *Grundrisse*: foundations of the critique of of political economy (rough draft), tr. Mark Nicolaus (London, 1973), p. 325.

[8] Marx, *Grundrisse*, p. 272.

[9] Marx, *Grundrisse*, p. 408.

[10] István Mészáros, *Beyond Capital*, p. 526.

[11] Marx, *Grundrisse*, p. 488.

[12] 'Introduction' to the Indian edition of István Mészáros, *The Power of Ideology* (Kolkata, 2004).

[13] The most valuable media groups:-

1: Time Warner (US) £44 billion

2: Viacom (US) £33.8 billion

3: Disney (US) £31.1 billion

4: Google (US) £30.6 billion

5: News Corporation (US)£26.8 billion

6: Yahoo! (US) £26 billion

7: Vivendi Universal (France)£18.1 billion

Source: Bloomberg (Values by market capitalisation, excludes conglomerates with media subsidiaries)

[14] The *Guardian Weekly*, November 9-15, 2000.

[15] Reference regrettably mislaid.

[16] Marx, *Grundrisse*. p. 172.

[17] Marx, *Grundrisse*, p. 398.

[18] Marx, *Grundrisse*, p. 700.

[19] Marx, *Grundrisse*, p. 694.

[20] Marx,*Grundrisse*, p. 704.

[21] Marx, *Grundrisse*, p. 694.

[22] Marx, *Grundrisse*, p. 711.

[23] At web site http://hometown.aol.co.uk/davehookes/moscow1.pdf

[24] *International Herald Tribune*, 15 December 2003.

[25] Stephen Jay Gould, *Wonderful Life: the Burgess Shale and the nature of history* (London, 2000, first published, 1990), p. 38.

[26] Immanuel Wallerstein, *The Modern World-System: mercantilism and the consolidation of the European world-economy 1600-1750* (New York and London, 1980); and many other works.

[27] For the facts and quotations in this paragraph, see Rafael Behr's article in the *Observer*, 11 September 2005.

2

GLOBALISATION

Countless examples could be given of the destructive consequences of the operations of globalised capital, and of the threat to humankind of its continued rule. I have assembled some of them in this chapter; but space dictates that it can only be a fraction of the whole.

Section 1: Introductory

A few preliminary remarks are in order. Certain misconceptions about capital's 'globalisation' are common. The term is often used to imply that the unevenness of economic and social conditions characteristic of capitalism's development has been overcome. In reality, the polarisation of economic power, of wealth and of conditions of life has vastly increased and continues to do so. Uneven development, and the explosive 'combined development' of unevenly developed economic, social and political processes, are more and more pronounced. And it is not only in the 'underdeveloped countries' that the consequences are negative. For example, the law section of the London *Times* reported on 11 May 2004:

> Behind the rhetoric of a globally integrated, knowledge-based economy is a more sobering reality. Many corporations will 'shop

> around' jurisdictions to identify those where workers are cheapest and unions are weakest. In the United States, which is predicted to lose millions of jobs to India and China in the next few years, surveys have suggested that this issue ranks in the minds of voters above the handling of the war in Iraq.

Such evidence surely excuses us from the need to take seriously those who answer the anti-globalisation protesters by saying that only globalised big business can 'save the world', a variation on Margaret Thatcher's mantra that 'there is no alternative'. I hope I will be forgiven for thinking them unworthy of comment (though two examples are given below).

Then there are would-be socialists, and even former self-professed Marxists, who hold that, from the past successes of capitalism in postponing and displacing its contradictions, we must conclude that the system is capable of overcoming any and every contradiction and crisis. It should occur to them that if in the past contradictions were displaced (not of course overcome at all) by 'exporting' them, then globalisation means that those avenues are closed, and not that capital has proved itself capable of 'business as usual'.

Last of all, there are committed socialists who see the contradictions and evils of the capital system in its latest phase ('globalisation') as 'nothing new' for a system which after all established the world market and has always been a 'world system' Certainly there is nothing new about its basic contradictions and structural antagonisms, but it is imperative to go further, and recognise that the system as such reaches its structural limits. We owe to Mészáros the most powerful clarification of this central point:

> [The] crisis of capitalism perceived by Marx in the mid-19th century in the 'European little corner of the world' failed to become for a long time a general crisis. Instead, the continued historical ascendancy of the bourgeois order on the 'much larger terrain' of the rest of the world dissipated for an entire historical period even the relatively limited European crisis. As a result, the socialist movement itself as first articulated by Marx and his intellectual and political comrades in arms could not help being fatefully premature. The Marxian theory

> was striving as it could at the time of its conception towards its realisation, but reality itself refused to strive towards it in a way hoped for and stipulated by its originator.
>
> Today the situation is radically different. In a significant sense it is even the diametrical opposite of what used to be the case in Marx's lifetime. For although the deepening structural crisis of capital means that 'reality is beginning to move towards thought', it seems that as a result of the defeats and failures of the socialist movement (especially in the recent past) thought itself – together with the necessary material and organisational forces without which even the most valid thought cannot 'grip the masses' and become effective material force – refuses to move towards reality and 'strive for realisation'. In the meantime the needs of the people remain frustrated and denied as ever before.
>
> However, despite the major defeats of the past the deciding issue is that the end of capital's historical ascendancy in our own age – through the extension of its domination even to the most distant and formerly isolated pockets of the planet – has brought with it the activation of the absolute limits of this system of social metabolic control. ... [The] margin of displacing the system's contradictions becomes ever narrower ... notwithstanding the once unimaginable destructive power at the disposal of its personifications. For through the exercise of such power capital can destroy humankind in general – and indeed it seems to be bent on doing just that (and with it, to be sure, also its own system of control) – but not selectively its historical antagonist.[1]

This is to say that all the misconceptions mentioned above miss the essential basis for approaching our problems, namely, the entry of the capital system in decline into its structural crisis – a crisis which brings with it real and present dangers to the survival of the human race and of the basic resources of the planet. We live in a historical situation where to satisfy oneself with the formulation that capitalism prepares the material foundations, i.e. productive forces, for socialism is the gravest of errors. Capital's 'destructive self-reproduction' now predominates. The destructiveness of capital towards the natural environment is by now a commonplace, and the very infrastructure of social life is ever more threatened. 'Old' problems like mass unemployment (now structural) and poverty, and permanent contradictory tendencies such as the falling rate of profit and industrial over-capacity now take more extreme forms, as the system becomes increasingly dominated by the need for massive funds of 'fictitious capital' to find profitable investment. (Between 1971 and 1995, the proportion of all foreign exchange transactions directed to trade in goods and services fell from 30 per cent to 1.5 per cent!).

'Globalisation' means not only spatial expansion to the geographical limits but also, and more importantly, immeasurably greater interrelatedness, mutual interconnectedness and reciprocal sensitivity of all processes and parts of the whole. The technological accompaniments of globalisation (above all, Information Technology) obviously heighten the efficiency and rapidity of communication but also the vulnerability of every part to problems in other parts. Information Technology will often provide the means to detect and attend promptly to problems, but detection is easier than repair, and in any case it is the vulnerability of each part of the system, and of the system as a whole, that predominates. Not even the fastest and biggest computer can assemble and comprehend every element and every interconnection and development, involved in any crisis, let alone resolve the emerging problems. But the problem is not a merely technical one. What all the 'experts' forget is that the process of production and realisation ruled by capital is by its very nature uncontrollable. The phrase 'intensification of contradictions' has become frighteningly appropriate. It indicates that we must anticipate – and as far as possible prepare for – new forms of the class struggle endemic to the capital system (endemic by reason of the structurally antagonistic relation between labour and capital), given the new and globally interconnected nature of capital's functioning.

The characterisation of developments in the global economy as 'neo-liberalism' is misleading to say the least. For all the talk about free enterprise, freedom from state interference and the efficiency of 'the market', the fact is that today's economic giants find the state indispensable economically as well as politically.[2] Rather than the reign of free-market competition and absence of state 'interference', we have monopolies sustained by the state machine:

> From the airline industry to the publishing business, from the railroads to telecommunications, American corporations have worked hard to avoid the rigours of the market by eliminating and absorbing their rivals. The strongest engines of American economic growth in the 1990s – the computer, software, aerospace, and satellite industries – have been heavily subsidised by the Pentagon for decades. Indeed, the US defence budget has long served as a form of industrial policy, a quasi-socialist system of planning that frequently yields unplanned results. The Internet at the heart of today's 'New Economy' began as the ARPANET, a military communications network created in the late 1970s. For better or worse, legislation passed by Congress has played a far more important role in shaping the economic history of the post-war era than any free market forces.[3]

Section 2: 'Global' politics

No one can any longer be unaware of the simple fact that US financial, political and military dominance and power make nonsense of the idea that globalisation is some sort of evening-out process. Before taking a few examples of the ongoing effects of globalisation of capital, it is worth considering the way in which US policy has been developing in line with its overwhelming economic dominance. *The Global Intelligence Report* of 25 February 2002 – i.e. *before* the second war on Iraq – circulated to corporate subscribers, while in some respects superficial, indicates this very clearly. Here is what it had to say about the so-called 'war on terror':

> From where the Bush administration sits, there is every reason to believe that the United States will be attacked by al-Qaida again. Even more important, the possibility that al-Qaida or some other anti-US organisation has obtained weapons of mass destruction cannot be excluded. If that turns out to be true, then millions of Americans may possibly be killed in the coming months or years.
>
> The most important goal for Washington must be to make absolutely certain that no further attacks, especially nuclear, chemical or biological, can be launched against the United States. There is no other comparable interest. The Bush Doctrine is based on the notion that the defence of the homeland from attacks represents an interest so fundamental that all other foreign policy interests must be completely subordinated.
>
> We might summarise the Bush Doctrine this way: The United

States faces an extraordinary danger. Washington is therefore prepared to take any action anywhere in the world to defend itself from this threat.

The defence of the homeland cannot be reduced to only defeating al-Qaida. The Bush administration has studied the lessons of the Israeli wars on Black September and other Palestinian groups and has drawn this conclusion: the defeat of any single group can disrupt and delay future attacks, but it cannot by itself eliminate them. Even if the United States were to utterly destroy al-Qaida, a new group would likely emerge. Therefore, the United States has three strategic goals:

1. Disrupt and defeat al-Qaida in order to buy time for a more thorough solution.
2. Prevent the emergence of follow-on groups by denying them sanctuaries in states where they can organise, train and plan.
3. Limit the threat posed by al-Qaida and follow-on groups by systematically eliminating weapons of mass destruction being held or developed by regimes that are favourably inclined toward them or in states where there is substantial sympathy for them.

Beginning with the last goal, there are a finite number of nations that have intensive programmes under way to develop weapons of mass destruction and delivery systems and that also might be prepared to aid al-Qaida. Three were named by US President Bush during the State of the Union speech: Iraq, Iran and North Korea. Another unnamed nation is Pakistan.

It must be assumed by the United States that the first three of these countries are developing WMD and/or delivery systems. It cannot be ruled out that either their governments or powerful factions within their borders might be inclined to provide al-Qaida or other groups with these weapons for use against the United States.

Washington requires that these and other nations that are identified demonstrably and verifiably abandon all attempts to build weapons of mass destruction and delivery systems. They should also convince the United States that they will under no circumstances transfer any technology to al-Qaida or any other group that intends covert action against the United States.

In the case of Iraq, for example, no assurances that might be made by Baghdad could possibly carry any weight. It would therefore follow that it is the intention of the United States to identify and directly attack any Iraqi facilities that might be developing WMD. The recent announcement that the United States reserves the right to use nuclear weapons if needed fits clearly into this strategy. If it is determined that there are facilities that cannot be destroyed by conventional means, Washington is prepared to use nuclear weapons.

Intelligence is always imperfect. It is possible that sites will be hit that do not produce WMD. This is something the United States is prepared to accept. More serious is the possibility that all WMD sites are not identified. So in order to minimise the risk the United States intends to destroy the Iraqi regime by overthrowing its leadership through a variety of military means, obviously including air strikes and special operations.

If Iraqi President Saddam Hussein is in a hardened facility, even the use of nuclear weapons is not out of the question. A secondary and highly desirable outcome will be replacing the Hussein regime with one that is prepared to both abandon the development of WMD and deny sanctuary to groups planning to attack the United States. *All other considerations, both humanitarian and geopolitical, are completely secondary to the primary goal.* [Emphasis added]

This account of the 'Emerging Bush Doctrine Reshaping US Strategy' (of course the 'doctrine' is now – and was at the time of writing – well past the 'emerging' stage) confirms the nature of today's historical/structural crisis as political and military as well as 'economic'. It prompts one to suggest the following roughly designed hypothesis. The US has sheer economic dominance world-wide (globally), and has to some extent solved for a considerable time the problem of assuring standards of living for millions of its citizens, including its workers – what with 'the consumer society' and the rest.[4] This is of course at the expense of billions of people outside the US, and millions of poverty-stricken people in the US itself. Reflecting on 9/11 and its aftermath: might it not be that the political cost of this plunder has now brought for the first time a dire threat to the security of the American people? The administration rightly expects more such attacks, and even fears atomic weapons being used against it. That is why the strategy outlined in the *Global Intelligence Report* has taken shape. Anything, even atomic warfare, will be used against anyone who is suspected of harbouring or arming al-Quaida, or indeed of posing any threat to American economic, or 'security', interests.

Instinctively, the Bush administration fears that, should the American people see that their rulers cannot defend them, all hell would be let loose – 'prosperity' or no prosperity. The reaction we saw to the defeat and deaths in Vietnam would pale into insignificance. A deadly development of the structural crisis is in prospect. Is it not just as likely that a major change in the relation between classes in the US and intensive class struggles will result from such a political/military deepening of the structural crisis as from an 'economic' one? And the anxieties of America's rulers I am hypothesising about here would assuredly be well placed. Even before the dreadful revelations in late April 2004 that US soldiers had brutally tortured and murdered Iraqi prisoners, polls in America were showing that voters were increasingly doubtful about the Administration's handling of terror threats before the attacks of September 11, 2001 – now generally called 9/11. Six in ten said that the administration had underestimated the threat.

In 2004, furthermore, Europe provided direct evidence of an immanent crisis of confidence, when, on 11 March, 2,012 people were killed by bomb attacks in the Atocha and other Madrid underground stations. Spanish Interior Minister Angel Acebes declared: 'It is absolutely clear that the [Basque] terrorist organisation ETA was seeking an attack with wide repercussions.' A general election was to be held three days later, and all campaigning was stopped in the name of national mourning – the right-wing, Popular Party, government hoping to cash in on public feeling for 'strong' measures against ETA. In the event the massive demonstrations of the intervening days became increasingly dominated by demands for 'the truth!', as it became clear that the attack was perpetrated by Islamic terrorists. The Spanish people understood very well that it was directed against the Spanish regime's already-unpopular support for the policies of Bush and Blair in Iraq. The Socialist Party opposition duly won the elections, and its leader immediately promised withdrawal of Spanish troops from Iraq.

A year before 9/11, Noam Chomsky had already told us what to expect of US foreign policy. In a striking anticipation of the US decision to go to war with Iraq, he wrote a comment, in *Le Monde Diplomatique* of August 2000 (when Clinton was still President), that should give pause to those who see the behaviour of the Bush administration as something new.

> The most remarkable feature of the debate over rogue states and the Iraq crisis is that it never took place. True, many words were spoken and there was dispute about how to proceed. But discussion stayed within rigid bounds that excluded the obvious answer: the US and UK should act in accordance with their laws and treaty obligations.... The UN Charter states that 'the security council shall determine the existence of any threat to the peace, breach of the peace, or act of aggression, and shall make recommendations, or decide what measures shall be taken in accordance with Articles 41 and 42', which detail the preferred 'measures not involving the use of armed force' and permit the Security Council to take further action if it finds such measures inadequate.
>
> The only exception is Article 51, which permits 'the right of individual or collective self-defence' against 'armed attack ... until the Security Council has taken the measures necessary to maintain international peace and security'. Apart from these exceptions, member states 'shall refrain in their international relations from the use or threat of force'.... No state has the authority to make its own determinations on these matters and to act as it chooses. The US and the UK would have no such authority even if their own hands were clean, which is hardly the case. Neither outlaw states, like Saddam Hussein's Iraq, nor the US accept these conditions: the US position was made clear by Secretary of State Madeleine Albright, the ambassador to the UN, when she informed the Security Council, during an earlier US confrontation with Iraq, that Washington would act 'multilaterally when we can and unilaterally if we must', because 'we recognise this area as vital to US national interests'.
>
> Albright reiterated that stand when UN secretary general Kofi Annan undertook his February 1998 diplomatic mission: 'We wish him well,' she said, 'and when he comes back we will see what he has brought and how it fits with our national interest.' When Annan announced that an agreement had been reached with Saddam Hussein, President Clinton announced that if Iraq fails the test of conformity,

> as determined by Washington, 'Everyone will understand that then the US and hopefully all of our allies would have the unilateral right to respond at a time, place and manner of our own choosing.'
>
> When the International Court of Justice at the Hague in 1986 condemned the US for unlawful use of force against the Sandinistas in Nicaragua, demanding that reparations be made, Congress immediately voted new funds for the same unlawful purposes. Secretary of State George Shultz explained in April 1986 that: 'Negotiations are a euphemism for capitulation if the shadow of power is not cast across the bargaining table.'

This may fairly be taken as the US ruling class's view of diplomacy and of international institutions. It was to be expanded upon nine years later:

> A secret 1995 study made by the Strategic Command, which is responsible for the nuclear arsenal, outlines the basic thinking. The study, *Essentials of Post-Cold War Deterrence*, was released because of the Freedom of Information Act, and according to the Associated Press, shows how the US shifted its deterrent strategy from the defunct Soviet Union to so-called rogue states such as Iraq, Libya, Cuba and North Korea. The study advocates that the US exploit its nuclear arsenal to portray itself as 'irrational and vindictive if its vital interests are attacked'. That 'should be a part of the national persona we project to all adversaries', particularly the rogue states. 'It hurts to portray ourselves as too fully rational and cool-headed', let alone as committed to such silliness as international law and treaty obligations.

I now quote at length from an article describing one example of opposition to the then projected war on Iraq.

> On December 9, 2002, the San Francisco Labor Council (AFL-CIO) unanimously adopted the following resolution: 'Labor Needs to Take a Clear Stand Against the War.' The resolution also includes an endorsement of the January 18 National March in Washington DC and joint action in San Francisco, and of the People's Anti-War Referendum.
>
> Resolution of the San Francisco Labor Council: Labor Needs to Take a Clear Stand Against the War.
>
> Whereas, since the tragic events of September 11, 2001, we have seen the beginning of a relentless new assault on labor – from the

employers, and from the government acting on their behalf; and

Whereas, using the so-called 'war on terrorism' and 'national security' as a pretext, the Bush Administration has spearheaded a renewed assault on organized labor, starting with the use of Taft-Hartley (and threats to militarize the ports) against West Coast dockworkers ... wholesale threats to the job security and union rights of 170, 000 federal workers ... the racist firings of experienced airport screeners ... threats to curtail the right to strike and organize ... and the impending contracting out of hundreds of thousands of federal jobs. On more than one occasion, government spokespersons have referred to union actions defending our jobs, working conditions and living standards as akin to terrorism, or as 'aiding and abetting terrorists', or as a 'threat to national security'; and

Whereas, Bush's war (on Afghanistan, Iraq, Colombia, the Philippines, where next?) has become the main engine for the repression of labor. 'National security', in the hands of a thoroughly anti-labor Bush Administration, is being used as a bludgeon against labor, with the intent of rolling back all the gains workers have won since the 1930s, including collective bargaining itself, and including social programs championed by the labor movement like welfare, social security, unemployment insurance; and

Whereas, a strong fight-back requires that labor make it a priority to stake out a clear, forthright and fighting stance against Bush's war, and see the anti-war and anti-globalization movements as our strategic allies, needed if we are to defeat the assault on labor and move to the offensive. We got a glimpse of the potential power of this combination during the 1999 showdown in Seattle; and

Whereas, the Rev. Martin Luther King, Jr., embodied the coming together of the labor, anti-war and civil rights movements during the tremendous upsurge of the mass movement in the 1960s, and we need to revive this powerful combination of the people's forces to defeat Bush's war and the racism that underlies it and that it promotes; and

Whereas, our opposition to the Bush Administration's war on the Iraqi people, and to their attacks or threats against other smaller, sovereign countries around the globe, fits hand in glove with labor's fighting defense of the interests of the working people of all races and nationalities here at home; therefore be it

RESOLVED: That the San Francisco Labor Council, AFL-CIO, endorse the Martin Luther King weekend anti-war activities – the

> January 18, 2003 marches in San Francisco and Washington, DC in opposition to the war on Iraq, and the Grassroots Peace Congress being held in Washington, as well as the People's Anti-War Referendum ['VoteNoWar'] by which millions of Americans are casting their 'votes' against this war; and be it further
>
> RESOLVED: That this council work to ensure that organized labor and the national AFL-CIO take a clear and early stand against Bush's war.
>
> Adopted unanimously by the San Francisco Labor Council, December 9, 2002

It should be added here that Bin Laden and the terrorists' chiefs are themselves men of globalisation, with its predominance of finance-capital. In this they parallel the chiefs of the State Department, the IMF and the World Bank, not to mention George W Bush himself, whose family has been for some 25 years friends of the Bin Ladens – a relationship arising from their oil connections. Bush made sure that in the immediate aftermath of the 9/11 attack, Bin Laden family members in the US were taken to safety by a private jet, a favour the FBI did not rate highly as a contribution to the 'war against terror'. And Michael Moore, checking for 'Taliban' on the net, found that Taliban cadres had received training on a special course at university in Texas, the Governor of that state being at the time one George W Bush.

Noting that 'the change in mandate and objectives (of the IMF), while it may have been quiet, was hardly subtle: from serving global economic interests to serving the interest of global finance', Joseph Stiglitz writes:

> The billions of dollars in the Cayman Islands and other such centres are not there because those islands provide better banking services than Wall Street, London or Frankfurt; they are there because the secrecy allows them to engage in tax evasion, money laundering, and other nefarious activities. Only after September 11 was it recognised that among those other nefarious activities was the financing of terrorism.[5]

Another 'revelation' after 9/11 (some two years after) concerns in particular that intrepid enemy of Saddam's tyranny and hunter of weapons of mass destruction Donald Rumsfeld. Elaine Monaghan wrote in the London *Times* of 20 December 2003:

> Washington: The US played down objections to Saddam's use of chemical weapons in the 1980s in talks with his Government. In 1984, President Reagan ordered Donald Rumsfeld, his personal envoy to the Middle East, to dilute condemnations of the weapons Saddam was using in its war with Iran, a newly revealed memo shows. The Iraqi leader was told that Washington's public criticism would not derail attempts to forge a better relationship.
>
> In the briefing paper for Mr Rumsfeld's trip to Baghdad in March 1984, he was told to remind the Iraqis that the criticisms of chemical weapons use were made 'strictly out of our opposition' to the lethal arms 'wherever it occurs'. He was to emphasise the US desire to stop Iran winning its war with Iraq and improve ties 'at a pace of Iraq's choosing'.
>
> The National Security Archive of George Washington University obtained the memo using the US Freedom of Information Act. Malcolm Byrne, of the archive, said that had the US maintained its stance in private, 'at least we could have prevented ourselves from falling into a moral pit'.

It seems germane at this point to record my own reaction to 9/11. Shortly after the attacks, I circulated, on an email discussion list, the following notes which I had made for a contribution to a discussion at a joint meeting in London of the two groups, Movement for Socialism and Workers Left Unity (Iran). They are dated 3 November 2001.

> After the September 11 attack, are we any wiser?
>
> These notes are not about 'what happens next?' or 'what should we be doing now?', but a different question. I was foolhardy enough to suggest as title for the discussion: are we any wiser after September 11? Please take my introduction not as claiming to answer that question, but only to pose it as sharply as I can, and hoping to learn from the exchange. So, I shall not be providing 'information' (there's plenty of that) but only ideas, suggestions. Can we after September 11 recognise inadequacies and mistakes in our thinking about the historical period we live in, or is it 'only a confirmation of our perspectives', as some of us used to say (even if it is, then it's time to

rethink)? Are we faced with a review of the way we see our responsibilities?

I don't intend here to get into the arguments about what we should be doing politically in reaction to the events on September 11 and after, except insofar as ideas about that are relevant to the question I'm addressing, viz., is September 11 an event which insists we change our thinking? Can we base our reactions and prescriptions on precedents, e.g. 'the main enemy is at home'? There are those on the left who seem to think that 'the enemy is at home' means that it is enough to march in demonstrations of protest against the war in Afghanistan. Naturally the class enemy is quite unmoved by protest. The internationalists of 1914-18 would have been amused to hear that 'the enemy is at home' was an injunction to voice 'anti-war protests'. Of course the principal content of 'the enemy is at home' is that the class struggle continues, and that there must be an implacable struggle against 'patriotic' and 'responsible' class-collaboration in the 'national interest'. In every country the capitalist class and its state take advantage of the 'difficulties' caused by September 11 and the costs of war to pursue their attacks on jobs, on working conditions and on civil liberties. Far from acquiescing, as the trade union bureaucracy and leaders of the 'socialist' and 'social-democratic' parties do, the workers' movement needs to take every possible advantage of the ruling class's concerns and problems.

As for those who are content to remind us how in another period Trotsky insisted, 'defend Haile Selassie's Ethiopia against Mussolini's Italy', it is necessary to underline one of the main lessons we have had to learn in the last few years, i.e., that with the structural crisis and globalisation of capital and the collapse of the Soviet Union and Stalinism a whole historical period (and the slogans appropriate to it) came to an end. Remember what happened to the proverbial guest who sang funeral hymns at a wedding 'and received a sound thrashing for his pains'.

There is of course much to be said about the fraudulent 'war against terrorism' conducted by a ruling class which in the last few decades has inflicted untold terror on millions, from Vietnam through Nicaragua, Honduras, Guatemala, Chile, Angola, Iraq and many other countries. Similarly, there is much to be said about the absence of any direct evidence produced against the supposed culprit, Bin Laden, whose presence in Afghanistan is used as the pretext for the murderous bombing attacks. And much to be said about the American ruling class's own use and financing of Bin Laden and others like him in the past. Chomsky and others have already piled up the arguments on those questions, which in this company don't need to be debated.

It may well be some time before we can begin to answer the question I'm asking, because the causes and consequences of September 11 will only be clarified in the subsequent developments. And of course the September 11 attack is most likely only one of a new sequence of attacks and responses. So my suggestions are tentative – and we should not be diverted from serious discussion and analysis by those who say we must above all be getting on and doing something.

All of us have changed our thinking a great deal over the past ten or fifteen years. The question is: did we change it enough, or always direct our questionings at the most important issues? I shall not be saying much more than this: perhaps we can now see that we did not take seriously enough, or far enough, the new things we found ourselves having to learn; perhaps we did not realise just how far behind reality our previous conceptions had fallen.

In particular: some things about structural crisis (i.e. the rule of capital having only now reached the global scale and the stage of its truly historical crisis). We had learned that the continued rule of capital threatens not only the 'socialism or barbarism' defined by Rosa Luxemburg at the beginning of the twentieth century, but now 'socialism or the very destruction of humanity'. Reflecting on what produced September 11, I believe: (a) we did not take seriously enough the fact that this historical crisis of the system is not only 'economic' but is deeply embedded in the whole of politics and ideology; (b) we underestimated the fact that globalisation, far from 'evening out' economic and social conditions, brings with it increased unevenness and inequality, which inevitably must produce new and unanticipated phenomena of 'combined development', including, now most strikingly, the turn of millions to religious dogma dredged up for 'modern' reactionary purposes. Clearly, this unevenness has created a world where at least two-thirds of humanity is more and more impoverished and oppressed, super-exploited, and US capital and its state are more and more confirmed as dominant economically and politically.

In consequence, the threatening and already begun destruction inherent in capital's continued 'destructive self-reproduction' is not only 'economic' but has a 'fall-out' throughout culture and society, with intensive and insoluble conflicts and conditions of social life which drive people to seek desperate solutions. That is why religious fundamentalists can appeal to millions, even though forces recruited on this basis have in the name of god themselves perpetrated unspeakable atrocities on the peoples of Algeria, Iran, and Afghanistan. An inexhaustible reservoir of irrepressible revolt has been created by the conditions of the 'new world order'; and upon this these reactionary forces draw.

They are all the more able to do so because of the historic betrayals and collapse of Stalinism and of social-democratic reformism, which have left millions without any hope or prospect of a political solution. And so once again religion is both 'the sigh of the oppressed creature, the heart of a heartless world' and at the same time a powerful weapon in the hands of reactionary forces who manipulate the oppressed.

And the commanders and paymasters of these reactionary forces are a new breed – not just corrupt nationalist leaders in a particular country or local mafia or hoodlums or mercenaries at the service of regional landlords and bosses, but big-time gangsters and a new type of politician who does not need or depend on some ability to exploit a particular national constituency or take advantage of a particular national crisis and/or political vacuum, like say Hitler or Mussolini. They are the 'new men' of globalisation, no less than today's bank chairmen or Bill Gates, if you like. They operate at the global level and can command the resources (financial and operational) to do so. Thus these men, resting on people made desperate by the demands of globalised capital and turning to the most backward and archaic of ideologies (religion), yet have at their fingertips the products (IT and weaponry) of the most developed means of production and communication (the two more and more coincide today). They have that possibility because they have placed themselves, in earlier situations, at the service of big capital, in particular the US, for massive financial rewards.

Thus the prerequisites of a future positive social order, a communist order – I mean what Marx called 'universal intercourse', highly developed and socialised forces of production, and 'all-round development of individuals' – are completely and destructively perverted, not only in the field of material production as such, but throughout the social organism, throughout today's culture.

This leads directly to the issue I want most to stress. September 11 and all that it entails surely now makes it clearer than we had seen, that the change from the rule of capital to a socialist order of life will face, and faces now, great problems not only in the mode of material production but in the whole fabric of culture, ideological, political, moral. Do we not have to return to Marx's insistence that for the social revolution there would be necessary a 'mass communist consciousness', and ask if the achievement of this does not today present new problems created by today's structural crisis of capital? These problems face us not in some future revolutionary period but have to be addressed now and throughout the transition to socialism. I think that this is the point of concentration for our thinking. The picture of collusion and opportunistic collaboration between the US ruling class, the oil-rich rulers of the Middle East, the fundamentalist organisations, the bourgeoisie of Pakistan, Indonesia, etc., and, more and more, the ex-bureaucrat capitalists of Russia and China has its importance in this context and not simply as the field of conflict over imperialist economic and strategic interests or as a propaganda illustration of the evils of imperialism.

What follows from this, for any steps towards the re-founding of a truly internationalist workers' movement? We had all begun to understand that in the light of capital's now 'destructive self-reproduction', the workers' movement has the responsibility to defend and protect now the endangered natural and cultural elements of any future positive social metabolism. This very important aspect surely now needs a lot of new thinking and new initiatives at every level from the global to the local.

One last consideration, which I have not been able to integrate satisfactorily with what I've already said. The depth and universality of the crisis (which we have to remember is essentially global) has political 'fall-out' which is, despite US power and dominance, not under the control of that power – the ruling class, the 'personifications of capital', also experience it as a profound crisis. I don't need to go over what innumerable observers have shown to be the ineptitude of the US idea of a war against Afghanistan. And 'everyone' knows since September 11 that a massive US retaliation brings nearer and more certain the repetition of such attacks. We surely should add that the search to create their 'alliance' against terrorism is producing intense political instability, endangering the present regimes in Pakistan, Indonesia, etc., bringing them into conflict with the masses, despite Blair's mantra that 'this is not a war against Islam' (note however the hapless George W Bush's talk of a 'crusade'!). And what will be the eventual effects inside the United States where, after all, from the socialist standpoint, the power of capital must ultimately be decisively confronted?

Some people among the opponents of capital find Negri and Hardt's book *Empire* a theoretical guide One reason for its appeal is that it

> tries to show that globalisation, notwithstanding its negative consequences, provides in fact the very basis of the necessary new socialist social order; it is, as they say, 'positive'. I think that this notion retains the picture of a capitalism which develops the productive forces for socialism and does not take sufficient account of the fact that capital's self-reproduction, as always uncontrollable, is now a destructive one, with all the attendant dangers. Negri and Hardt also tell us that 'Empire' is the new 'subject' or driving force of today's history, that 'Empire' dictates and controls what happens. While they do pay attention to what they call the 'corruption' or social/cultural breakdown that develops, they tend all the same to give a picture of a new world order of control by capital. I think we have to return to, reinforce and develop the fundamental point that capital is, yes, the rule of dead over living labour, but that its overriding imperative of accumulation is not subject to control or plan. Not only are the 'economic' consequences essentially uncontrollable but also, equally important, the political consequences of this uncontrollability, which all the time intensify the unevenness and explosiveness of the situation globally and in every country.

Section 3: How globalised capital helps 'develop' the 'underdeveloped'

a: Oil

To say that the outpourings of 'economics correspondents' in liberal as well as openly conservative journals about the positive and unique benefits to mankind of global big business contradict the facts would be the understatement of the epoch. Of the myriad available examples, perhaps the most 'globally' manifest is that of the operations of the transnational oil companies. The following paragraphs are taken from Roland Pierre Paringaux's article 'Should Corporations Care', in *Le Monde Diplomatique*.

> The case of Shell in Nigeria is the best known. In Africa's biggest oil-producing country, where the people are still among the poorest in the continent, the manna extracted by the Western oil giants has for decades enriched tyrannical elites and their corrupt clients, and helped them to hold on to power. Some of the beneficiaries in a system in which Shell held the lion's share, amassed considerable fortunes (General Sani Abacha, who died in 1998, and his close associates are

believed to have accumulated $3bn between 1993 and 1998 in accounts at 19 Swiss and French banks in Switzerland). In the early 1990s the oil-rich Niger delta became the scene of violent confrontations between the local ethnic minorities, who accused Shell of damaging their environment and their culture, and the Nigerian security forces that had orders to protect the oil installations.

In 1993 the Movement for the Survival of the Ogoni people, led by writer Ken Saro-Wiwa, mobilised tens of thousands of people against Shell. It became an international issue, prominent enough to force the world's leading oil company to stop production. To get it started again, General Sani Abacha's government unleashed a murderous repression. Hundreds of Ogoni were arrested, imprisoned and summarily executed. Two years later Saro-Wiwa and eight Ogoni activists were executed in spite of international protests. There was tremendous outrage. Since then the company has admitted that it had been 'forced' to pay the Nigerian security forces directly on at least one occasion in 1993.

In 1998 BP came under fire when it was revealed that it had signed agreements with the Colombian army to protect its installations in a guerrilla zone. Shortly afterwards its security arm, Defence Systems of Colombia (DSC), was accused by Human Rights Watch of importing weapons and training the Colombian police, who were well known for their brutality. When an inquiry was launched, DSC refused to cooperate.

Recently *Business Week* accused Mobil Oil of complicity with the Indonesian armed forces in massacres perpetrated close to the US company's installations in Aceh province. Since 1980, when Aceh Liberation Movement separatists began attacking Mobil's installations and martial law was imposed, there have been constant rumours of disappearances and mass executions. After the fall of the Suharto regime (itself installed after the US-inspired bloody overthrow of Soekarno) in 1998, the Indonesian Human Rights Committee uncovered a dozen mass graves containing hundreds of bodies. Many had been tortured. Mobil denied any involvement. But, according to *Business Week*, the company admits having supplied food, fuel and equipment to the soldiers protecting its installations. ...

Oil and human rights do not mix in Sudan either. The Islamist leadership in Khartoum, at war with the Sudan People's Liberation Army guerrillas in the black, partly Christian south, is regularly accused of atrocities, forced displacement and tolerance of slavery practised by the militia in its pay.

Against this background Amnesty International has published a report in which it states that foreign oil companies 'turn a blind eye' to these human rights abuses. It provides a list of oil companies operating in the Upper Nile region. They include, with a greater or lesser degree of involvement, the China National Petroleum Corporation (China), Petronas (Malaysia), BP Amoco (Anglo-American), Talisman Energy (Canada), the International Petroleum Corporation (Sweden), Agip (Italy), TotalFinaElf (France), the Gulf Petroleum Company (Qatar), the National Iranian Gas Company (Iran) and Shell (Netherlands).

In Angola oil revenues are feeding an endless civil war that has claimed several hundred thousand lives. NGOs report that in 1999 more than half the $900m paid by international oil companies in operating rights was used to fund yet another military offensive against Joseph Savimbi's Unita rebels. The rest was used to feed corruption. Last year the British organisation Global Witness accused high-ranking Angolan officials of using oil royalties to buy arms from the Russian underworld through 'front' companies at inflated prices. In a hard-hitting report it also accused the oil multinationals and Western banks of complicity in Angola's 'humanitarian disaster'. Some 20 oil companies, including BP (now part of BP-Amoco), Exxon, Gulf and TotalFinaElf, operate in Angola and plan to invest billions of dollars there in the next few years.

In January 1999, Human Rights Watch accused the Enron conglomerate, a US energy giant, of complicity in serious human rights violations in India. The organisation wrote that the Dabhol Power Corporation, which is 50 per cent Enron-owned, 'employs security forces who routinely beat and harass people demonstrating peacefully against the power plant'; it accused the US and Indian governments of 'looking the other way'. The biggest foreign investment in India, Dabhol is a joint venture between Enron, two of the largest companies in the US, General Electric and Bechtel, and the Maharashtra State Electricity Board.

Since December 1996 a third of Iraq's $11bn export income has been collected to compensate companies and individuals claiming for losses during the invasion and occupation of Kuwait and during the Gulf war. The collection and awards are made discreetly by an organisation with a dubious legal basis, the United Nations Compensation Committee (UNCC), dominated by the United States, which still believes that Iraq must pay reparations for Saddam Hussein's ambitions. This year the Kuwait Petroleum Company, and

> a few others, were awarded $15.9bn in a single payment, which is double the amount the Baghdad government received between 1996 and 2000 to feed and care for 17m people. That figure is almost equal to the total compensation due to 2.6m private claimants.[6]

The reality of the 'victory' in Iraq provided a suitable afternote. This, from the *Guardian* newspaper, 18 April 2003:

> An engineering firm with close links to the Bush administration won the main contract for the reconstruction of Iraq's infrastructure last night, sealing a deal worth up to $680m to rebuild the country's electrical, water and sewage systems. ... Only a handful of firms were invited to bid for the first set of eight US aid contracts and, like several of the others, Bechtel has faced allegations of conflicts of interest. Its senior vice-president, Jack Sheehan, is a member of the Defence Policy Board, a Pentagon advisory group whose members are approved by the secretary of defence, Donald Rumsfeld. George Shultz, the former secretary of state, is on Bechtel's board, and also chairs the advisory group of the pro-war Committee for the Liberation of Iraq. ... An earlier $7bn contract for fighting oil fires became the focus of controversy when it was awarded to Kellogg, Brown and Root, a division of Halliburton, once (1995-2000) run by vice-president Dick Cheney.

That is how democracy works. And of course – one of the problems about writing this book is that it is bound, in respect of many of its details, to be out of date well before it is published – much more is emerging all the time.

The London *Times* of 8 May 2003 reported Henry Waxman, a Californian Democrat, who accused Bush of hiding the role played in Iraq by the company once run by Vice-President Dick Cheney, as saying that: 'Only now, more than five weeks after the contract was first disclosed, are members of Congress and the public learning that Halliburton may be asked to pump and distribute Iraqi oil.' By October 2003, the United Nations and the World Bank calculated the cost of Iraq's 'reconstruction' at $56bn, money that will end up in the coffers of American contracting firms like Bechtel and Halliburton. Fair reward for Bechtel and Halliburton having disbursed respectively $769,221 and $673,331 respectively for George W Bush's Republican Party between 1999 and 2002!

While oil companies undoubtedly will profit mightily from the defeat of Saddam's regime, it would of course be an oversimplification to see the war on Iraq as just a war to seize oil resources. At the root is the fact that the capital system in decline imperatively requires massive state expenditure on destruction and war; and the US ruling class and its state is inexorably bent on establishing its political and military domination worldwide. The wars on Iraq provide an awesomely clear example of one of the basic premises of this book. More than 50 years ago, as students of anthropology we learned about the 'transition from barbarism to civilisation'. Now we are obliged to study, and hopefully learn to reverse, a transition from civilisation to the new barbarism.

To quote once again from my own notes, this time made in April 2003:

> Ancient Mesopotamia, now Iraq, was the birthplace of our civilisation more than 5,000 years ago, when the toil and ingenuity of the forefathers of the people of today's Iraq harnessed the waters of the Tigris and Euphrates. But today the peoples of Iraq are suffering thousands of dead and maimed men, women and children, the victims of the barbarism perpetrated by the latest product of that civilisation's history – the globalised capital system, represented directly by the economic, political and military power of the ruling class of the United States.
>
> Having supported, maintained and armed the oppressive regime of Saddam Hussein, enabling his forces to torture and butcher hundreds of thousands of Iraqis and Kurds, the US regime, driven by its need for total global domination, now undertakes a bloody war for control of the strategically vital region and its natural resources. The overthrow of Saddam is a life-and-death necessity for the peoples of Iraq; but it is their task and theirs alone, with whatever support is possible from the working class internationally.
>
> This war will mean the death of thousands of men, women and children and the impoverishment of countless others. Here is the mirror of the future of the peoples of the world unless the capital system is overcome by the self-organisation and solidarity of all working people, integrating a socialist Iraq into a world society in

> which exploitation is abolished. The US juggernaut is rolling over the peoples of Iraq precisely in order to further the establishment of a world order that can prevent humanity from achieving socialism and preserving its future.
>
> Here, a century later, is the meaning of Rosa Luxemburg's 'socialism or barbarism': the terrible blood price paid by the descendants of the world's first civilisation for the globalisation of capital and the delay in opposing it through the re-founding of working-class internationalism.

One week after I had written that, the famous Baghdad museum of Mesopotamian civilisation was ransacked and looted in the disorder sparked by the US 'victory'. Nabhal Amin, joint director of the museum, was in tears as he said to the Reuter correspondent in Baghdad:

> They have looted and destroyed 170,000 ancient objects dating back thousands of years. ... That represents billions of dollars. The Americans were supposed to protect the museum. If they had posted just a single tank and two soldiers, nothing like this would have happened. I hold the American troops responsible for what happened at the museum.

On the same day, participating in the Paris anti-war demonstration, Iraqi exile Adil, interviewed by the newspaper *Libération*, was brief and bitter: 'The Americans knew how to protect the oil wells, but not humanity's heritage.' He could not have been more right. On 17 April two senior cultural advisers to President Bush resigned. Chairman of the advisory committee Martin Sullivan said: 'It didn't have to happen. In a pre-emptive war that's the kind of thing you should have planned for.' And his colleague Gary Vikan: 'If we understood the value of Sumerian cuneiform tablets to our past, as we do with oil getting us somewhere in our cars, I don't think this would have happened.' 'If', indeed!

In the brutal days of capital's primary accumulation, colonisation and imperialist division of the world between the great powers, every society of hunter-gatherers and subsistence cultivators was mercilessly destroyed, from the American Indians – or native Americans – and Australian aborigines to the peoples of Africa and Asia. Now, in the epoch of capital's structural crisis, we are witness to the cynical and ruthless destruction by capital of anything that stands in its way, including the very birthplace of our civilisation and those who live in its homeland. The barbarians have entered Mesopotamia.

Samuel Holder's comments at much the same time (see *Carré Rouge*, no. 25, April 2003), referring to the differences between the US and the French and German bourgeoisies, ring true:

> The one point on which they all remain in agreement is to wage war against the ordinary people and to use all means to extract the maximum surplus value from the world working class still in work. It is on this exploitation front that the imperialist bourgeoisies keep, for the time being, more opportunities and room for margins for manoeuvre. So long as the working class has not built up an arsenal of coordinated defences against their offensives, the wars in the Middle East, in Colombia, in Chechnya and other parts of the world will continue to rage and provoke many and varied changes in relations between states, without endangering the imperialist system. The strategic class for the future of the world remains, more than ever, the working class which produces everything and ensures all the exchanges and all the services in every continent.

Perhaps the most fitting last word on 9/11 and what followed can be found in that picaresque story of globalisation, Salman Rushdie's wonderful *The Moor's Last Sigh*:

> But a darker time came upon you, and just as Boabdil, the last Nasrid Sultan, was too weak to defend his great treasure, so we, too, were proved wanting. For the barbarians were not only at our gates but within our skins. ... We were both the bombers and the bombs. The explosions were our own evil – no need to look for foreign explanations. We have chopped away our own legs, we engineered our own fall. And now can only weep, at the last, for what we were too enfeebled, too corrupt, too little, too contemptible to defend. – Excuse, please, the outburst. Got carried away. Old Moor will sigh no more.

And, as for Bush and Blair and those who stood by them in perpetrating their barbarism: 'Once, indeed, there were giants on our stage; but at the fag-end of an age, Modern History must make do with what she can get.'

b: On Africa – War

Those who attribute the genocidal conflicts of the last 20 years in Africa to 'underdevelopment', 'tribal enmities' and so on, are well answered by Marxist anthropologist Claude Meillassoux in the following contribution made to the 'Alternative Davos' organised by the political group *Attac Suisse* in Zurich in January 2001.

> The effects of globalisation and privatisation of the war-massacres in Africa
>
> Preliminary remark
>
> I would like to point to the paucity of information on African conflicts in the media reputed to give objective reporting, in particular *Le Monde* and *Le Monde Diplomatique,* and particularly the inadequacy of information on the successive conflicts which stained Congo Brazzaville with blood in 1997 and 1999.
>
> 1. Introduction
>
> It is a commonplace to repeat that the riches of Africa have never ceased to make the continent the prey of Western powers. War has continuously raged there at the instigation of one or other of those powers. Today's wars take place in the framework of privatisation and globalisation, reaching the heights of horror. Events taking place in Africa today, the carnage and the famines, the setting up of successive mafia powers for warlike exploitation of the mineral resources of ex-Zaire, illustrate dramatically the deleterious effects on victims from the most vulnerable regions of the world.
>
> 2. A general definition of war
>
> War, as such, has always been a morally more than doubtful enterprise, and only very debatable reasons have been found to justify it. It is the pursuit of an objective by means which question the rules of civilisation, in particular, respect for human life. This practice, when offensive, approaches the criminal, through the use of murder, massacre, torture, and every other sort of physical and mental/moral

brutality, all justified in the name of the end to be achieved. It is this end which is used to distinguish offensive war from mafia practices. ... In reality the decision to wage offensive war always comes from the side which estimates that it will be the winner in a confrontation, i.e., the stronger party. Its outcome depends not on morality but on this force.

3. The privatisation of war

Throughout the centuries war has been perpetuated under a pseudo-moral banner – if not God, then King, Country. However, war economy has never ceased to be present, because war necessitates the organisation of a kind of production: of weapons, of circulation and transport of this special product, its stocking, its maintenance, and above all its replacement, given the destructiveness of the enterprise. Thus resort to investment and a treasury is obligatory. Because of the need to mobilise a large number of men to use the weapons, war quickly came under the control of political powers sufficiently centralised to be capable of this mobilisation. The state in each country thus quickly became the principal instigator and manager of wars. When the aristocratic state, with its economic prerogatives, disappeared, war production fell under the aegis of capitalism, and then under that of its most corrupt form: mafia.

Given the lawless state prevailing in an Africa dismantled by the aggression of private interests, privatisation has evolved towards its natural outlets: savage capitalism and 'mafia-isation'. In the capitalist framework, the war economy is shared between public arsenals and private companies. The former find themselves confronted by the laws of the market. Weapons for the exercise of force are still the object of legal commercial restrictions, making them even more precious, more desirable, for those with access to them, since their use goes along with a quasi-monopoly for a longer or shorter period, which can militarily favour the buyer.

Because of this, the arms trade becomes one of the most profitable businesses by reason of the added 'premiums' going with it. Parallel to common or garden selling, these 'premiums' feed complementary transactions, profitable for those who understand the transactions essential to clearing obstacles in this special market. These intermediaries thus 'render service' just as much to the buyers as to the sellers by marking out the tortuous circuits necessary for their transactions. Shady intermediaries are plugged into these parallel transactions, drawing large commissions, and persuading themselves that their intervention is necessary for the benefit of all partners. For whom are these weapons destined today? They are useful to corrupt individuals, men who have arrived by all sorts of means to positions of authority and who need these weapons to reinforce their power and to exploit the wealth to which these weapons give them access, on condition that they can also recruit the human forces necessary to wield the weapons.

4. The wars in Africa

Only recently has the truth begun to filter through about the horrors committed in countries where war has long been summarily explained either by the psychology of the inhabitants or by 'ethnic conflicts'. For a whole period ethnic differences have been almost unanimously pointed to as the principal factor causing war, not only in supposedly tribal countries, but today even in Europe.

Very often, current discourse confuses individual, spontaneous, ill-controlled, sporadic behaviour with the deliberate, organised and continuous use of force, in particular through war. So what most often results from political ventures can be attributed to supposedly uncontrollable and irrational human passions (which can be unleashed in the ultra-permissive context of a war). Every one of us carries a dose of ferociousness, but only certain circumstances are conducive to its being expressed; war is one of these. The present onslaught on Africa is the worst sort of re-colonisation. The proliferation of independent proto-states, ready to sell their stolen booty or sacrifice their people to foreign powers, of which we have seen many examples, contributes to the multiplication of these murderous conflicts.

Like everywhere else, belligerency has existed between African populations. But if we examine this more closely, apart from minor clashes between neighbouring groups, the more far-reaching wars have their origin in interventions from outside, beginning with slave wars instigated by slave-traders and continuing to wars provoked by colonisation, leading to the mobilisation of Africans against Africans. The factors generally put forward to explain wars in this context (racial hatred or ethnic hostility) seem to me very slight compared with external factors, as much economic as military.

Before 1914, the boundaries of African states had been drawn by the colonial conflicts between rival European great powers. The size of the colonies was more or less in proportion to the strength of these powers. Today, the attacks on Africa still come from these colonial powers, but also from enterprises playing an analogous role. The new division of states tends to develop according to big business and corporations. When I was a student at the University of Michigan, I read in *Michigan Review*, the journal published by the Department of Economics, an article which gave the Mafia as an example of a good form of business organisation! This opinion has found an excellent application in the African situation among others. The settling of accounts between the present godfathers of ex-Zaire (like the assassination of Kabila on 18 January 2001) clearly shows the mafia-like character of the economic relations which reign today in this part of the world and the nature of the 'wars' fought on their basis.

5. Mercenaries

It is well known that the 'renting' of mercenaries is today a flourishing business in Africa and I shan't dwell on it. But the 'mercenariat' has gone on in such proportions, reaching to the very heart of civil society, that we must briefly examine its causes. The recruiting of armed personnel, capable of the worst horrors, as in Sierra Leone, touches even children. The principal causes are economic. Cilliers and Mason write: 'The IMF and the World Bank, through their structural adjustment programmes, have led to the privatisation of services which were the only protection of the state,' and 'foreign policy and the army are the latest additions to the list of privatisations' (*Peace, Profit or Plunder*, Johannesburg 1999).

The two main financial development agencies created at Bretton Woods, the IMF and the World Bank, have practised a so-called 'development' policy whose sole aim – or at least the sole result – has been to bring down the price of labour-power everywhere. Although the expressly Christian ideology of their leader is verbally hostile to the 'class struggle', their 'structural adjustments' have favoured and aggravated social inequalities and thrown an increasing proportion of Africa's population into such poverty that they are driven to look for any possible way out. The outcome is the individual solution: the gun or the hoe; enlistment in armed bands, whatever they may be. From this point of view, the economic responsibility of the so-called development agencies and their leaders is crushing. In this economic climate, recruitment of mercenaries and war auxiliaries becomes simple.

Weapons, by reason of their mafia destination, act not as a means of combat, but to inspire terror in the civilian population. The simple possession of cheap weapons gives the owners the means of paying themselves from a civilian population terrorised by their exactions and permits the merchants of death to take control of regions propitious to the exploitation of mineral and other riches – and to appropriate the product.

6. Ex-Zaire: a vast region completely pillaged

The United States, allied to South Africa, helped Rwanda and Kabila to get rid of Mobutu (1996-7). US 'special forces' trained the Rwandan units which put Kabila in command. ... They used Uganda and Eritrea to aid the rebel forces in Sudan. They have major mining interests in Congo-Kinshasa. Private companies are now tearing the continent apart according to their financial needs, trying to ensure resources at the least organisational cost, with no concern, not even a hypocritical one, for 'spreading civilisation' as the colonialists used to pretend. On the contrary, these new conquests are made by professional belligerents recruited and paid on the spot. All this at the price of thousands of lives paid by the local populations. To get themselves engaged, the warlike bands outbid each other in atrocities to show their effectiveness to their commanders. This butchery, by many competing bands, multiplies yet again the causes of conflict. Millions of refugees trying to escape the many dangers, wander in the bush, condemned to famine and in the very worst material and sanitary conditions.

Western business is far from innocent in all this. Observations concerning the implications of this extreme form of exploitation have been brought together by Colette Braekman (a Belgian journalist working for many years in Africa) in a well-informed article ('The Democratic Republic of Congo dismantled by its neighbours' in *Le Monde Diplomatique*, October 1999). She draws attention to the fact that, according to the peace signed in Lusaka in July 1999 under the control of the Organisation of African Unity, a mixed military commission was to be designated to exercise its authority on the Congo. Since then, no such thing has come about. In 1997, Kabila made an agreement with the firm America Mineral Fields, who were to provide him with funds to prosecute the war. The country was infested with 'rebels' of all kinds, pillaging the local population. There was no respected central authority. Local resources were pillaged to finance wars and to enrich the 'elites'. Mineral resources were seized by Rwandan and Ugandan soldiers. New provinces were created *ex nihilo*, such as that of Kibale-Ituri, whose governor was named as a certain 'commandant Kazini'. Links between politicians and foreign companies were numerous. The lands of Kivu, a Congolese province, produce rare minerals coveted by international firms such as Kenrow International of Gaitherburg, Tenfield Holdings Ltd, Collier Venture Ltd, Sparora Mining Ltd. The Vice-president of Tanzania is said to be the owner of shares in the company Littlerock Mining Ltd.

Colette Braekman mentions other enterprises having financed military operations in exchange for profitable contracts, such as Barrick Gold Corp. (of which George Bush is a shareholder); Russell Resources (Australian) directed by the ex-general David Agmon; Krall (also Australian). Also cited: Banro American Resources; the Chinese Company of Non-ferrous metals. Among the most coveted resources are diamonds. A few companies merchandise the stones. (De Beers is believed to have remained engaged in the Congo to control the diamond market.) The wars instigated in Angola against the government of president Dos Santos by the rebel movement Unita, led by Jonas Savimbi, were carried on for a long time thanks to the sale of uncut diamonds which increased to more than $3bn from 1992 to 1999. De Beers agreed not to buy Angolan diamonds from Savimbi, nor from Foday Sanko (British-trained officer, executioner of Sierra Leone; responsible for ordering the cutting off of the hands and arms of civilians in Sierra Leone when an opposition party advocated voting 'to take their destiny into their own hands').

But so what! Relief was already assured by an internationally notorious mafioso, Arkadi Gaidamek, cited in the framework of the Falcone affair. And Jean-Christophe Mitterand is today legally associated with an Israeli diamond dealer (Lev Levaev) for the trafficking of Jonas Savimbi's Angolan diamonds. Lev Levaev, a fugitive from justice, is nonetheless authorised to pursue a defamation case against two editors of the 'Survie' society.

7. On other 'African' wars

Add to the especially devastating Zaire war, the one financed by the French firm TotalElfina between three bloodstained politicians, among them the present president N'guesso, which has sacked and pillaged Brazzaville. (This murderous conflict has been passed over in complete silence by the French and international press.)

I remind you of killings instigated by the West that are happening now: the bloody repression against the Ogoni people in Nigeria, undertaken by Nigeria's military government with the material assistance of the Anglo-Dutch company Royal Dutch Shell. This crushing of a people is accompanied by capital punishment by hanging (with the help of false witnesses), as in the case of the writer Ken Saro-Wiwa. Let us not forget the atrocities committed in the Horn of Africa in the conflict between Ethiopia and Eritrea. Four hundred inhabitants of a village were exterminated by deliberate crushing under two tanks. But there are no tank-making factories in Africa. Finally, the case of the genocide in Rwanda, inspired by Nazi doctrine and carried out by a Christian population and by certain of their priests. The intervention of the French Army in 'Operation Emerald' was to protect the killers against the troops of the FPR (Rwanda Patriotic Front). Some of those politically responsible, including French and Swiss, were found refuge thanks to official intervention.

8. New causes of wars

Other causes of conflicts and wars take shape in numerous parts of Africa.Thus an aggravation of land conflicts can be seen. Land has become a coveted object. In Nigeria, the dictator Obasanjo took land for himself during his time in power, 1976-9. Land expropriation is in process throughout the whole length of the Senegal valley. Because of the construction of the Manantali Dam, the Mauretanian Army has expropriated the residents, who cannot use the rise and fall of the river to irrigate their fields. They are replaced by new owners using petrol-driven pumps. Some of the expropriated cultivators, refugees in Mali, are accused of going over to banditry in the Nioro region. Such conflicts quickly take on an ethnic aspect between the refugees considered as 'peuls' and the local Soninke population. *Le Républicain* (Bamako) also points to bloody conflicts in the Mopti and Kayes regions and in the Fifth and First Regions between herders and cultivators.

According to some, the object of the horrific massacres perpetrated in Algeria is to provoke terror and drive the peasants off their land. Attempts to appropriate water also feed conflict. Diverting the waters of the river Senegal (which the Senegal government is accused of) to irrigate the fossil valleys is provoking numerous explosive tensions. Better known is the unresolved conflict between Israel and Jordan over the waters of the Jordan.

9. Conclusion

> Competition, driven on by the globalisation of the world economy, is calculated to be terrifyingly destructive towards a continent already gravely weakened by 'structural adjustments' and hit by the worst sanitary disasters. The conflicts and killings contribute greatly to the worsening of the living conditions of the people. For some, living conditions disappear in suffering. For survivors, they often end in the dispossession of their land, that is, of their means of life, bringing endless migrations, often in overpowering and sometimes fatal conditions. They provoke mortal famines, especially for children.
>
> Stop the sale and traffic of weapons, condemn the profitability of this deadly business, punish severely those who engage in it, no matter who they are and what their origins – this is a task which must be urgently accomplished.

A suitable footnote to Claude Meillassoux's analysis was provided by the arrest on 7 March 2004 at Zimbabwe's Harare airport of 64 mercenaries (South African, Namibian, Angolan, Congolese and Zimbabwean). Also arrested was Simon Mann, ex-SAS soldier, leader of the group. Harare was a stopping place for the mercenaries, on their way to an attempted overthrow of the government of oil-rich Equatorial Guinea. Two days later 15 men (from South Africa, Armenia, Kazakhstan and Germany) were arrested in that republic and charged with plotting a coup. The leader of the group claimed they were acting for one Ely Calil, Lebanese businessman, an associate of Severo Moto, head of the self-proclaimed government-in-exile. Simon Mann had previously helped found the South African company Executive Outcomes and its British associate Sandline, the outfit which helped the Sierra Leone government defeat the rebel group RUF. The Zimbabwe Home Affairs Minister claimed that Mann and the mercenaries had been hired by Moto and that Mann had been promised oil mining rights and a cash payment of £1m.

c: Child labour

Even on the restricted definition used by the United Nations, more than 200 million of the world's children are working – doing everything from stone-breaking to tailoring. Child labour is exploited on an infinitely more massive scale today than ever before. And to see this as a problem of the customary practices of 'underdeveloped societies' would be the greatest possible mistake. What must be understood are the economic and political imperatives of globalised capital – imperatives that, as Claude Meillassoux has explained, have shattered all traditional family and working relations.

Examination of the modes of circulation of services in the domestic community and its transformations and disintegration under the impact of wage-labour shows the organic links between its members, which ensured in the domestic community a structural reconstitution from generation to generation, have been broken. This break directly provokes a global economic transfer to the capitalist sector of a part of the labour-power produced in the domestic sector, which, under the impact of this extraction, is degraded. This break goes on from generation to generation in the proletarianised classes of rural origin, causing a social decomposition which could be curbed only by a programme of public aid. This break, being at the root of a demographic explosion, gives rise in international business circles to fear of a social overflow, a fear of invasion by costly surplus population, which today inspires the so-called 'liberal' policy imposed by the IMF and the World Bank, the domestic social effects of which can end only in a severe attack on the physical and moral conditions of the proletarianised populations of the underdeveloped countries.

> The deterioration of social security conditions implied in the monetarist policies advocated by the two international institutions has the immediate consequence of encouraging the people affected to compensate for this insecurity through a higher birth rate. Thus they have an exactly opposite effect to that which was desired. In reality, it is in creating miserable living conditions for millions in the third world, that is, through disease and premature death for, above all, children and the old, that this policy reduces the population by disembarrassing it of its inactive elements, the old, the sick and infirm, but also the children. The UNICEF report on the circumstances of

> death through sickness and malnutrition of 12 million children in the third world in 1979 shows in tragic fashion the demographic results. No researcher in the human sciences can remain unaffected in the face of such a situation.[7]

And in a May 2000, *Carré Rouge* interview with Francois Chesnais, Meillassoux said:

> We have published a work in which we attempt to understand why child labour has become so widespread. Here too there exists a logic proper to capitalism but not necessarily to the society in which these children live. In these societies, children are not put to work to make profit; they are forced into it by the economic conditions to which they are subjected. What economic conditions? It is the lowering of wage-levels to so low a level that the children come into competition with their parents. The workings of exploitation and of the market mean that children eliminate their parents from the labour market; and so, since they have little protection, they are paid practically any sum the employer decides. Moreover, and this is very important, the advantage of having children work is that they have employment only so long as they remain children. From the moment they cease to be children, they are of no further interest to their employers. From the human point of view this is extremely serious, because the individual who ceases to be a child is no longer useful for anything: he/she has had no training, has never studied, and is thrown on the street. The child's 'retirement' is the streets, at some fifteen years of age. He/she has been used by the system under conditions extremely profitable for the employers during childhood and is then thrown on the scrap-heap.
>
> 'Developing' those countries not 'developed', means to lead peasant families or families of peasant origin to produce for the market or to be employed as wage-earners. Once labour-power becomes a commodity, the human being who secretes it and the woman who bears it are on the road to reification; they become 'human resources' and, like every other resource, mineral, vegetable or animal, good for exploitation.
>
> The high fecundity of rural families in the traditional framework of manual agricultural economy is explained by the necessity of keeping the number of those able to work as far as possible constant despite the food shortages and famines which periodically decimate the infant generations. During the phase of economic expansion, the

fecundity of families of rural origin continues in the towns, not to attenuate the effects of climatic hazards but (in the absence of a public social security system) to continue to ensure the security of the older generations and to prepare a network of material aid for the children. However, the combined effects of free exchange, reduction in social expenditure, and the falling international price of the primary materials provided by these countries have achieved the desired objective: a general lowering of the price of labour-power in the majority of the underdeveloped countries.

The growing unemployment among adults and the decline in wage-levels contributes to changing the direction of family policy towards the necessity of having children – from now on less and less to prepare for the future than to meet immediate needs. As the economic situation deteriorated, demography took on a new configuration with a diminishing number of unproductive members, through the fragility of the older generations and, still more serious, through putting the children to work at an earlier age. This harmful practice has developed in a number of the countries subjected to structural adjustment. Employing children between five and fifteen is increasingly common in commercial agriculture, mining and unskilled industrial and craft jobs. The lowering of the reward for work is thus accompanied by a displacement of many jobs occupied by adult men towards those social categories which are traditionally underpaid: women and children. We know that emigration and unemployment of men has already contributed in large measure to the multiplicity of single-parent families. The competition which children pose to adults of both sexes has had the effect of aggravating unemployment in their parents' generation, so that in many families the children have come to be the only breadwinners. But in such circumstances and to the extent that it lasts, young workers recruited because of their young age lose their jobs at the end of their adolescence, if they haven't died while still at work. The family (i.e. the mother) is thus constrained in order to survive to go on bearing the only commodity she is capable of putting on the market, i.e. the always cheap child labour-power. For these 'families', to have enough children so that they can follow one another on the labour market at the end of the few years their jobs last, becomes a tragic necessity.[8]

I return to the question of child labour in Chapter 5.

d: Drugs

An extract from George Winslow's *Capital Crimes*:[9]

> Just as post-war developments destroyed peasant economies in the developing world, they also pushed millions of whites, blacks and Hispanics off the land in the United States. Then, as these groups moved to large urban centres, major corporations reduced their investments in the older industrial cities (a trend that was encouraged by government policies), destroying the job base in many urban centres and leaving many communities increasingly vulnerable to the ravages of the drug trade. Heroin addiction began to rise dramatically in the 1950s and topped 750,000 by the end of the 1960s. Eventually, the flow of drugs out of Southeast Asia and Latin America created new economic and social problems – such as addiction, crime and disinvestment – which in turn were affected by changes in the structure of the global economy.
>
> For example, as the economic crisis of the 1970s convinced corporations to shut down more factories, the number of unskilled jobs in urban centres dropped dramatically, and the communities most buffeted by these changes witnessed an epidemic of violence in the 1980s. Many young men who might once have moved from petty gang violence in their teens to unskilled manufacturing jobs and families in their twenties were unable to find work in the legitimate economy, turning to crime or the drug trade to make a living. By the late 1980s the law-and-order policy, as it reduced millions of people to poverty, had created a vicious circle of violence. Global drug gangs could recruit millions of poor peasants in the developing world to grow and smuggle drugs, with millions of poor people consuming and peddling those drugs inside the United States.

As Winslow also indicates, the politics of the United States ruling class were hardly designed to ameliorate this situation:

> Even as Ronald and Nancy Reagan were touring the country telling teens to 'just say no' to drugs, the US continued to support pro-American allies that had dominated the Latin American drug trade for decades. In the 1960s much of the trade was controlled by anti-Castro guerrillas, who were heavily funded by the CIA, and in 1973 *Newsday* reported that 'at least 8 per cent of the 1,500-man (Bay of Pigs) invasion forces has subsequently been investigated for drug-

> dealing'. Later Noriega is believed to have received as much as $10 million in bribes from Colombian cartels to allow them to smuggle drugs and launder money in Panama while he was making millions from US government agencies for his help in supporting the contras in Nicaragua. ...
>
> A 1988 congressional investigation led by Senator John Kerry found 'there was substantial evidence of drug smuggling through the war zones on the part of individual Contras, Contra suppliers, Contra pilots, mercenaries who worked with the Contras and Contra supporters throughout the region' and that US officials 'failed to address the drug issue for fear of jeopardising the war efforts against Nicaragua'. Subsequent investigations, notably Peter Dale Scott and Jonathan Marshall's book *Cocaine Politics*, added more details, and in the summer of 1996 the *San Jose Mercury News* published an explosive series detailing contra leaders' sale of large amounts of crack cocaine to dealers in poor black neighbourhoods of San Francisco and Los Angeles.[10]

The ravages resulting from the sale and use of drugs, especially among the younger generation in all countries, are surely among the most compelling examples of the threat to humanity's future posed by the continued rule of capital. It cannot be said too often that Rosa Luxemburg's warning 'socialism or barbarism' a century ago has to be understood in a new way: the longer capital's rule persists, the more barbarism actually invades social life, and the necessity of finding ways to stem its destructiveness must be confronted by the working-class movement. This time, it is not a question of 'the barbarians at the gates' but of a barbarism eating at the heart of humanity. The same framework of thought is essential in considering the problem of crime.

e: Crime

My original intention was to include a chapter on 'social breakdown', with much of it devoted to the problem of crime. The publication of John Lea's excellent *Crime and Modernity*,[11] – written from a perspective similar to my own – makes such a chapter unnecessary. Here, however, are one or two examples Lea does not use.

From Winslow's *Capital Crimes* again:

> In the 1990s as the economy became more globalised, crime became a global industry that linked street addicts with peasants in Bolivia and bankers in Switzerland. Today only a few cartels supply virtually all the cocaine that reaches America. ... The modern political economy of crime is a kind of toxic byproduct of a global economy based on profits and high finance rather than on social justice, an economy dominated by large multinational corporations and financial institutions.[12]

What Winslow points to here is the manifestation on today's global scale of what was always an inescapable feature of capitalism's social consequences and its attitude to crime. One of the many nineteenth-century critical observers, John Ruskin, wrote powerfully:

> A great nation does not spend its entire national wits for a couple of months in weighing evidence of a single ruffian's having done a single murder; and for a couple of years, see its own children murder each other by their thousands a day, considering only what the effect is likely to be on the price of cotton, and caring nowise to determine which side of the battle is in the wrong. Neither does a great nation send its poor little boys to jail for stealing six walnuts; and allow its bankrupts to steal their hundreds of thousands with a bow, and its bankers, rich with poor men's savings, to close their doors 'under circumstances over which they have no control', with a 'by your leave'; and large landed estates to be bought by men who have made their money by going with armed steamers up and down the China Seas, selling opium at the cannon's mouth, and altering, for the benefit of the foreign nation, the common highwayman's demand of 'your money or your life' into that of 'your money and your life'. Neither does a great nation allow the lives of its innocent poor to be parched out of them by fog fever, and rotted out of them by dunghill plague, for the sake of sixpence a life extra a week to its landlords. ...
>
> Also, a great nation having made up its mind that hanging is quite the wholesomest process for its homicides in general, can yet with mercy distinguish between the degrees of guilt in homicides; and does not yelp like a pack of frost-pinched wolf-cubs on the blood-track of an unhappy crazed boy, or grey-haired clodpate Othello, 'perplex'd i' the extreme', at the very moment that it is sending a

> Minister of the Crown to make polite speeches to a man who is bayoneting young girls in their father's sight, and killing noble youths in cool blood, faster than a country butcher kills lambs in spring. And lastly, a great nation does not mock Heaven and its Powers, by pretending belief in a revelation which asserts the love of money to be the root of all evil, and declaring, at the same time, that it is actuated, and intends to be actuated, in all chief national deeds and measures, by no other love.[13]

Winslow continues:

> During the last 50 years, dramatic changes in the global economy, in which multinational companies enjoy new freedom to move goods and services anywhere in the world, have also created a fertile breeding-ground for violence by exacerbating many social problems and reducing social services that address the causes of crime. ... Unfortunately, the same global economic changes that have encouraged powerful corporations to move their operations wherever their costs are lowest, make the economics of local communities increasingly insecure. The communities that lose jobs and are starving for capital not only suffer some of the worst social problems and crime rates, but find it virtually impossible to attract the investment and capital they need to rebuild.

Winslow's introduction outlines the contents of his book:

> Part I, by tracing the Burmese heroin trade and particularly the activities of one drug lord, introduces the basic structures of globalisation that have allowed street and corporate crime to thrive. It shows how the spread of market economies (dominated by major multinationals) into Asia and Latin America impoverished many peasant communities and created a large reserve army of labour that was recruited into the drug trade.
>
> Part II ... uses an apparently senseless killing on the Brooklyn Bridge to demonstrate the vicious cycle of economic decay, social dislocation, and rising violence in urban centres. It looks at the movements of capital, jobs and factories that have bred street crime by destroying the economic and social fabric of local communities and explains how these economic changes have affected the politics of crime.
>
> Part III takes up the trillion-dollar business of corporate crime, beginning with the example of forests in the Pacific Northwest. It

> shows how the growing power of major corporations over society has subjected millions of Americans to dangerous work, inadequate health care, environmental damage, and poor government services. It explores some reasons why these large and expensive causes of violence are ignored, even encouraged, while various individual misdeeds draw increasingly harsh punishment.

Shades of Ruskin!

f: Are things getting better?

A London *Times* headline on 10 July 2001, over an article by one of their in-house commentators, Anatole Kaletsky, read: 'Developing countries will suffer without continued globalisation'. And again – on 16 August 2002, this time over a piece by Graham Searjeant – 'Only big business can save the planet'.

Contrast these now quite routine sentiments with another piece from the *Times* – on 9 September 2002 – 'Water: 1.2bn people lack access to safe drinking water; 2.4bn lack proper sanitation.... Energy: More than 2bn people have no access to modern energy, principally electricity....' And *Le Monde Diplomatique* (November 2000):

> Reports from international organisations remind us of the misfortunes of children in the third world. Six out of 100 babies do not survive for longer than a year; eight out of 100 die before the age of five. By 2025 there will be two billion new babies, nearly all of them (97 per cent) born in the poor countries of the south, where they will not have enough food, drinking water, housing, education or health care. In the former Soviet Union children have been abandoned and forced to fend for themselves as social structures have imploded.

Or the *Guardian* of 14 August 1999:

> Declaring that humanitarian catastrophes are reaching 'irrevocable crisis proportions' in several African countries, the United Nations secretary general is putting his weight behind a big ministerial meeting on Africa at UN headquarters in New York next month, a meeting meant to be 'a wake-up call' to a world which seems to be abandoning the troubled continent. 'We have had a very poor response to our

appeals for the crises in Africa. The needs are mounting, but we are not able to get those countries which have resources to give,' Kofi Annan said. In the face of Africa's natural disasters and long-running wars, he said, 'people talk of donor fatigue, but how can we be that insensitive when we see the pain? Is it that we are not telling the story effectively?'

The UN is almost the only organisation telling the stories of the 200 Angolans every day who die deaths related in some way to the war in a country where, in one besieged town, Malange, four children die of starvation daily; of the tens of thousands of Angolan, Congolese, Sudanese and Somali children who have lost all hope of living ordinary family lives or having access to schools or clinics; of the countless Sierra Leonean children who have lost hands and arms to the machetes of the rebel fighters who have tortured the country since 1991.

Even before Africa's war zones, desperation has become a norm. Last week two teenage boys from Guinea lost their lives when they stowed away under a plane flying to Belgium. They were trying to escape everyday lives without hope and get an education in the Europe so familiar to them from television. Angola was the country most affected by long-running conflict, Mr Annan said, with insecurity intensifying as Jonas Savimbi's Unita movement struggled to take over the Central Highlands. An estimated 600,000 Angolans are in acute need and there are fears for up to 3m more whose conditions cannot be ascertained because they live beyond the range within which UN agencies are able to operate in current conditions.

In Somalia 300,000 people face starvation now and another 1m are in a rapidly deteriorating condition. Burundi, Guinea-Bissau, Congo-Brazzaville, the Democratic Republic of Congo, Ethiopia, Eritrea, Uganda, Tanzania and Rwanda are also facing serious humanitarian need, according to the UN. 'My predecessor, Boutros Boutros-Ghali, used to call these 'orphan crises', and they still are,' Mr. Annan said – crises largely neglected and ignored by the world....

Mr. Annan's language is diplomatic, but among the many disheartened aid officials there is bitterness. 'The world spends $9bn a year on dog food,' said one, 'and cannot find less than one-tenth of that for the most dispossessed people in the world.'

And, as a bitter-sweet footnote one can add the following:

McDonald's has been accused of extreme insensitivity after releasing a new sandwich called the 'McAfrika' in Norway, one of the world's

> richest countries, at a time when 12 million people are facing starvation in southern Africa.... Nor has McDonald's agreed to withdraw the offending product from sale. However, it has offered to allow aid agencies to leave collection boxes and fundraising posters in Norwegian restaurants – but only in those selling McAfrika burgers and only for as long as the 'special promotional burger' remains on sale. In a statement yesterday, McDonald's said: 'All of the involved parties [including 12 million starving? – CS] are happy with this solution. We hope this will put a wider focus on the important job these organisations are doing, and McDonald's in Norway are pleased to be able to support this'[14]

g: Andhra Pradesh – a test case

In the shock election results in India in May 2004, one leader to fall from power was Chandrababu Naidu, chief minister of the state of Andhra Pradesh. His regime had for years been generously funded by the British state under Blair's Labour government, by the US administrations of Clinton and George W Bush, and by the World Bank. To keep these patrons happy, Naidu entrusted his economic policies to the American McKinsey consultancy, which provides a programme called 'Vision 2020'. The main planks of this programme were: privatisation of universities and state hospitals; repealing the laws that protect small businesses and substituting 'large corporations'; and the removal of some 20 million people from the land.

As George Monbiot put it, in the *Guardian* of 18 May 2004:

> Put all these – and the other proposals for privatisation, deregulation and the shrinking of the state – together, and you see that McKinsey has unwittingly developed a blueprint for mass starvation. You dispossess 20 million farmers just as the state is reducing its number of employees and foreign corporations are 'rationalising' the rest of the workforce, and you end up with millions without work or state support. 'The state's people,' McKinsey warns, 'will need to be enlightened about the benefits of change.'

On the insistence of the British Labour government, the secretariat implementing the programme is in the hands of the right-wing Adam Smith Institute, and its work is funded by the British government. It will be remembered that Blair's party had a friend and million-pound donor in Bernie Ecclestone, who received in return exemption from the ban on tobacco advertising on his Formula One Grand Prix motor-racing enterprise. The same Ecclestone was looking to Naidu for permission to take Formula One racing to Hyderabad. Interesting, then, that in January 2004, as Monbiot reports, McKinsey told Naidu's Cabinet that

> Hyderabad should be a 'world-class futuristic city with Formula One as a core component'. To make it viable, however, there would be a 'state support requirement of four to six billion rupees'. This means a state subsidy for Formula One of £50m-£75m a year. It is worth noting that in Andhra Pradesh thousands now die of malnutrition-related diseases because Naidu had previously cut the food subsidy.

As was soon to become well-known, legislation was prepared by Blair's government to exempt Ecclestone's Grand Prix circuit from the ban on tobacco advertising!

h: The IMF to the rescue

The London *Observer* correspondent, Gregory Pallast, studying IMF strategy for Ecuador in the context of the brilliant declaration by Professor Anthony Giddens – sociologist, former Director of the London School of Economics, and 'theoretical' guru to Prime Minister Blair – that 'globalisation is a fact', reported in October 2000 that he had:

> … found a secret (IMF) schedule. By 1 November, 2000, it says, its government is ordered to raise the price of cooking gas by 80 per cent. It must eliminate 26,000 jobs and halve real wages for the remaining workers in four steps in a few months specified by the IMF. It must begin to transfer ownership of its biggest water system to foreign operators by July 2001, and grant BP's Arco subsidiary the right to build and own an oil pipeline over the Andes. That's for starters. In all, the IMF's 167 loan conditions look less like an assistance plan and more like a blueprint for a financial coup d'etat. The IMF says it has no

> choice. Ecuador is broke, thanks to the implosion of its commercial banks. But how did Ecuador, an Opec member with resources to spare, get in such a pickle? For that, we have to go back to 1983, when the IMF forced its government to take over soured private debts owed by Ecuador's elite to foreign banks. For this bail-out of United States and local financiers, Ecuador borrowed $1.5bn. To repay this loan the IMF dictated price hikes for electricity and other necessities. And when that didn't drain off enough cash, yet another assistance plan required the state to eliminate 120,000 jobs. Furthermore, while trying to meet the mountain of IMF obligations, Ecuador foolishly 'liberalised' its tiny financial market, cutting local banks loose from government controls and letting private debt and interest rates explode.
>
> Who pushed Ecuador into this nutty romp with free-market banking? Hint: the initials are IMF. It made bank liberalisation a condition of another berserk assistance plan.

Pallast went on:

> In Tanzania today, 1.4m people are getting ready to die. They are the 8 per cent of the population who have the AIDS virus. The financial 'rescuers' found a brilliant neo-liberal solution: require Tanzania to charge for hospital visits, previously free. This cut the number of patients treated in the three big public hospitals in the capital, Dar-es-Salaam, by 53 per cent. The financial cures must be working.
>
> The IMF and World Bank told Tanzania to charge school fees. Now the bank expresses surprise that school enrolment is down from 80 per cent to 66 per cent. Altogether the Bank and IMF have 157 other helpful suggestions for Tanzania, and the Tanzanian government secretly agreed in April 2000 to adopt them all. It was sign or starve. No developing nation can borrow hard currency without IMF blessing (except China, whose output grows at 5 per cent a year thanks to following the reverse of IMF policies).
>
> The IMF and World Bank have effectively controlled Tanzania's economy since 1985. Admittedly, they found a socialist (*sic*) nation mired in poverty, disease and debt. Their experts wasted no time in cutting trade barriers, limiting government subsidies and selling off state industries. This worked wonders. According to Nancy Alexander of the Washington-based Globalisation Challenge Initiative, in 15 years Tanzania's GDP per capita has dropped from $309 to $210, the literacy rate is falling and the rate of abject poverty has jumped to 51 per cent of the population.

The World Bank and the IMF were born in 1944 with simple, laudable mandates: between them to fund post-war reconstruction and development projects and lend hard currency to nations left skint by temporary balance of payments deficits. But in 1980 they seemed to take on an alien form. In the early 80s third world nations, haemorrhaging after fivefold rises in oil prices and a similar jump in dollar interest payments, brought their begging bowls to the two bodies. But instead of debt relief, they received structural assistance plans listing an average of 114 'conditionalities' in return for capital. The particulars varied from nation to nation, but in every case they had to remove trade barriers, sell national assets to foreign investors, slash social spending and make labour 'flexible' (that is, crush unions).

So what have the free-market prescriptions accomplished? An article by Samuel Brittan in the *Financial Times* last week declared that the new world capital markets have 'brought about an unprecedented increase in world living standards'. Brittan cites the huge growth in GDP per capita, life expectancy and literacy in the less developed world from 1950 to 1995.

Now hold on a minute. Until 1980 virtually every nation in his survey was either socialist or welfare statist. In those dark ages of increasing national government control and ownership (1960-1980) per capita income grew by 73 per cent in Latin America and by 34 per cent in Africa. By comparison, since 1980, Latin American growth has come to a virtual halt, growing by less than 6 per cent over 20 years – and African incomes have declined by 23 per cent.

Now let's count the corpses. From 1950 to 1980 socialist and statist welfare policies added more than a decade of life expectancy to virtually every nation on the planet. From 1980 to today life under structural assistance has become brutish and shorter. Since 1985 the total number of illiterate people has risen, and life expectancy is falling in 15 African nations. Brittan attributes this to 'bad luck, (not) the international economic system'. In the former Soviet states, where IMF and World Bank plans hold sway, life expectancy has plunged, adding 1.4m a year to the death rate in Russia alone. Recently, the IMF admitted that 'in the recent decades, nearly one-fifth of the world population have regressed' – arguably 'one of the greatest economic failures of the 20th century'. And that, Professor Giddens, is a fact.

Claude Meillassoux was surely not far off the mark when he remarked in his *Le Monde de l'Homme*, of Parson Malthus' drastic prescriptions for population control:

> ... today they are put into operation throughout the world by the most powerful international agencies, the World Bank and the IMF. Let us add that more and more it seems that certain sections could envisage recourse to war, to massacres and to epidemics as still more radical means of influencing demography.

j: A note on education

Given that the reproduction of labour-power includes education, in this context a highly significant example has been provided by Gradoni: he notes that every year some 65 billion francs are sent by Mali workers working in France to their country, and 'in Mali all schools are built thanks to associations of relatives funded by migrant workers who send money to them.'[15] It might spring to mind that France would supply 'aid' to its ex-colony. The fact is that such aid is indeed offered by France but is rejected by the Mali government because France offers it only on condition that the Mali government reduces the number of migrants (which would of course cut down the amount sent back by migrant workers and put pressure on the regime to itself provide funds!). And so this manifestation of the (typical) relationship between the governments of the richer countries and those of African and Asian states provides what an American President might call a 'double whammy'.

> The international agencies, the IMF and the World Bank, provide no better outcome, even when their employees try to encourage local community 'self-help':
>
> After setting out as a matter of building and maintaining social infrastructures, the ban imposed on public sector recruitment by structural adjustment very soon led to rural communities themselves having to hire and pay their own teachers; and in the majority of cases, children have once again had to be put to work in the school fields in order to pay supply teachers' wages....
>
> 'Community' schools – set up and financed by parents – are in rapid expansion in most of the French-speaking countries of Africa as a response to the withdrawal of state funding.[16]

k: Forced emigration

In the celebrated 'free market', the freedom of movement afforded to capital does not of course extend to those who are compelled to put their labour power on the market. On the question of forced emigration, asylum seekers and the fate of the emigrants, it is perhaps enough to reproduce here an article by Semret Fesshaye – a nursery teacher from Asmara, Eritrea who had been in Britain for 10 months, and is a founder member of the Eritrean Women's Association[17] – published in the *Guardian* of 3 November 2003:

> I am an asylum seeker from Eritrea. At home I was placed in detention because I am a Jehovah's Witness, a religion that is unacceptable to practise in my country. In jail I was raped so badly that I still have problems walking. I fled to England when I was released for one reason only – I believed that here I would be safe. But for myself and thousands of other asylum seekers, England is no longer a safe place. The Home Secretary has announced that he is tightening the rules about who can claim asylum. Section 55 of the Nationality, Immigration and Asylum Act 2002 requires him to refuse to provide support for an asylum seeker if he is not satisfied the asylum claim was made as soon as reasonably practicable after the claimant's arrival in Britain.
>
> Asylum seekers who come here with false passports will be penalised. For those of us fleeing persecution in our countries it is almost impossible to leave with our own passports. The officials who beat us won't helpfully stamp our passports and give us their blessing to speak out in the West about human rights abuses. When the British government is on friendly terms with our governments it keeps silent about the persecution there. It is also almost impossible to reach Europe without paying an agent to smuggle us there and provide us with false papers. Agents breathe down our necks at the UK port or airport we arrive at and tell us to say nothing. It is not easy to disobey them and announce that we are here to claim asylum. I know of people who have claimed asylum the day after they arrived in the UK and been told they have left it too late and are therefore not entitled to any support.
>
> There is no doubt the Home Secretary's policy will reduce the asylum-seeker statistics dramatically. He will be able to boast to the sections of the media which portray us as scroungers that he is ridding

the UK of a scourge. On paper we will no longer exist. Our lowly status as asylum seekers is being replaced by an even lower one as non-people. We will have no right to a roof over our heads, no access to schools for our children, no legal advice and no opportunity to see a GP when we are sick. The Home Secretary wants to show that he is 'tough as boots' on this issue. A compassionate approach is seen as a vote loser. What he has failed to mention is that although many of us will officially cease to exist, we will still come here because we believe that in our own countries our lives are at risk. In Eritrea I was a nursery teacher. I would love to do that job here. I would be able to support myself. I do not want to be a drain on the state. I want to contribute to British society. But I am not allowed to work.

When I first arrived, my asylum claim was rejected and I was forced to sleep rough. Sometimes I slept at Victoria Station, sometimes on night buses. I was terrified of being attacked. I know of at least one woman who was raped by a man who offered to help her when she was homeless. Now the government has agreed to process my asylum claim and I have been given a small room in London to live temporarily. But many asylum seekers are still out on the streets, including pregnant women. I have seen people get sick from sleeping rough and going without food. Sometimes up to five women sleep on the floor of my small room. I know how hard it is to sleep rough and to have absolutely nothing.

Traditionally, asylum seekers in this country have remained silent for fear of deportation. We have allowed others to speak on our behalf, but because the situation we find ourselves in is so disastrous we are starting to speak up for ourselves. Women from Eritrea and other African countries have formed the Eritrean Women's Association to support one another. Other asylum seekers are forming support organisations too. Although they long to lead normal, law-abiding lives, as non-people some asylum seekers will feel they have no choice but to steal to survive. Without an address it is impossible for officials to keep track of people. Does the Home Office prefer us to disappear into the underbelly of British society? Not seen, not heard and working for shadowy bosses in the jobs many British people don't want to do for a fraction of the minimum wage? We are a useful source of cheap, unregulated labour that can boost the economy. The government has expended enormous effort in reducing the numbers of rough sleepers. But now a new wave of non-people will seek shelter in the doorways and stairways of central London.

In Eritrea I didn't know whether I would die by the knife or by the bullet. If this policy continues, some of us who hoped to find a safe haven in Britain risk dying of cold and hunger.

1: Keeping them in order – arming the controllers

1. This from the *Observer*:

British firms are involved in supplying torture equipment to third world countries responsible for gross human rights abuses. One Birmingham-based company, HPP, offered to help to arrange delivery of leg-irons and CS gas to a private security company in Rwanda, where tension between Hutu and Tutsi tribes is still simmering after up to 1m people died in the 1994 genocide.

In negotiations with an undercover reporter HPP faxed quotations for the consignment, and said the equipment would be flown to Rwanda by a Spanish-based company called Larrangua y Elorza. The cost for 35 hand-and-leg cuffs, 10 belly chains and 300 CS gas canisters was £1,720. HPP quoted the price in pesetas, but indicated it would be happy for the goods to be paid for with a sterling cheque drawn on a British high street bank.... After coming to power in 1997 the Blair government announced that anyone exporting leg irons would need licences(!). However, it is still easy for businesses based in Britain to arrange sales from overseas. The Metropolitan Police had to drop a recent investigation into a businessman alleged to have sold electric shock batons to the Cypriot police. The Crown Prosecution Service ruled that because the batons were bought in the US there was no case to answer, even though the deal was 'brokered' in the UK.

Leg irons and CS gas have a terrible history in Rwanda. CS gas was used at least once by the Interahamwe Hutu militia to flush sheltering Tutsi out of buildings before hacking them to death. Leg irons have been used by military intelligence officers in Rwanda in the torture of prisoners. Dozens of British companies have exploited legal loopholes and continued brokering. Customs officers are investigating a series of air freight specialists in London and Gatwick that organise transport for arms shipments from Eastern Europe to central and west Africa.

Britain is continuing to sell arms to countries involved in regional aggression or with poor human rights records, in spite of its

> commitment to an ethical foreign policy, according to the Government's annual report on arms exports. Two of the biggest buyers of British arms are Indonesia and Saudi Arabia, both with poor human rights records. The two account for 25 per cent of British arms sales. Other countries with scant regard for human rights, such as China and Bahrain, also receive British military equipment. ...The Foreign Secretary, Robin Cook, defended his policy, saying a tough line worked with some countries but 'there will be other times when critical engagement, dialogue and encouragement is more likely to produce results'.
>
> The United States increased its share of the international arms trade last year (1999), and now accounts for nearly 50 per cent of the $53.4bn annual market, according to the International Institute of Strategic Studies publication *The Military Balance.* Britain came second, selling nearly $10.5bn worth of weapons, while France was third at about $6.5bn. Much of these weapons systems were supplied to the Middle East, the world's biggest arms market. Saudi Arabia, the world's largest arms buyer, purchased more than $6bn worth of weapons last year.

2. When thieves fall out ...

From the *Guardian Weekly* of 28 September-4 October 2000:

> The CIA and the former head of the Chilean secret police are scrambling to blame each other for a series of murders at home and abroad, including a notorious 1976 car bombing in New York. In the rush to implicate one another, both sides are divulging an unprecedented number of previously secret documents, to the elation of historians and survivors of the Chilean military regime that ruled from 1973-90. The latest round of revelations began last week when the CIA submitted a report to the US Congress that included secret papers from the early 1970s. These documents gave details of extensive bribery of Chilean politicians, efforts to 'disorganise' the Chilean Socialist Party and a $35,000 payment to Chilean military officials said to be involved in the murder of General Rene Schneider, who opposed US plans to overthrow the government of Salvador Allende at its birth in 1970.
>
> For Chileans, the most explosive item was evidence that the head of the secret police under the military regime, Manuel Contreras – a senior adviser to the regime's leader, General Augusto Pinochet –

was a double agent and briefly on the CIA's payroll. Contreras immediately denied the CIA accusations. They were in retaliation, he maintained, for his action in passing a stack of documents to US investigators in April 2000. 'The FBI is working to establish the truth (about CIA collaboration with Pinochet's secret police).... The CIA is quite worried that the judicial investigation will reach them,' Contreras said in an interview from his cell at Punta Peuco, a prison for military officials convicted of human rights violations during the military regime.

Counter-attacking, Contreras gave details of an alleged proposal by the CIA deputy director general, Vernon Walters, to secure the help of five US senators in improving Chile's tarnished image under the dictatorship, in exchange for $2m a year. Contreras also alleged that Gen Pinochet ordered him to ask the CIA to help organise the repressive secret police known as the Dina.

3. 'Global rise in anti-union violence'

The *Guardian Weekly* also told us, in 2000, that:

> 'The number of trade unionists killed for organising workers around the world was 140 last year (1999), an increase of 17 on 1998, with torture, beatings and imprisonment also on the rise in an increasingly anti-union global environment, according to a survey by the International Confederation of Free Trade Unions. Latin America is the world's most dangerous region for trade unionists, with 90 killed in 1999 because of union activity, and the widespread jailing and torture of activists. Colombia is the undisputed capital of anti-union terror with 69 assassinations, often by government-linked paramilitaries – bringing to 1,336 the number of unionists murdered in the country since 1991 – and hundreds kidnapped or forced into exile.
>
> Among those murdered was Cesar Herrera Torreglosa, a leader of the agricultural workers, victim of a drive-by shooting last December. An organiser of banana workers, he had reported death threats to the police, who took no action. Killings of trade unionists during strikes took place in Guatemala, Nicaragua, Brazil, Argentina and Ecuador. Nearly 3,000 unionists were jailed in Latin America, and levels of exploitation are reported to be intensifying.
>
> In Asia last year 33 members of the Nepalese Teachers Union were murdered; a Turkish union leader died in police custody and

> another was assassinated; Indonesian union protests were broken up with beatings. In Burma the army shelled a village that was to host a union-sponsored human rights event. There was heavy anti-union repression across the continent, particularly in the export-processing zones used to attract foreign capital. Market reforms in China have given rise to strikes and protests, frequently broken up by force. In Saudi Arabia and the Gulf region, trade unions are banned.
>
> In Eastern Europe nine trade unionists were killed in 1999, including several in Russia. Disputes about unpaid wages and deteriorating working conditions attracted widespread violence against activists, as union rights were restricted. In Africa the ICFTU reports the death in prison of two teachers' leaders in Ethiopia last year, the beating of strikers in Kenya, the deaths of union leaders in Morocco, and the torture of union activists in Togo.

John Lea writes of the change, in this period of capital's destructive self-reproduction, 'from social integration to security and the management of risk'.[18] A telling generalisation and clearly no exaggeration.

m: Escaping from Stalinism to 'democracy'

The process of restoration of capitalism in the countries previously under Stalinist rule has borne little resemblance to the hopes of 'democracy' entertained by millions. Even less can it be compared to the origins of capitalism in Europe – with its system of 'free enterprise' and the 'market'. What has emerged, instead, is a deadly combination of a modern 'robber baron' capitalism and the persistence of the worst features of Stalinist bureaucratic power and corruption. The journal *New Internationalist* (April 2004), in an issue devoted to 'Life after Communism', included the following items:

> Throughout the entire Yeltsin period, flight of capital away from Russia totalled between $1 and $2 bn every month. Each year from 1989 to 2001 there was a fall of approximately 8 per cent in Russia's productive assets. Although Russia is largely an urban society, 3 out of every 4 people grow some of their own food in order to be able to survive. Male life expectancy went from 64.2 years in 1989 to 59.8

> in 1999. The drop in female life expectancy was less severe, from 74.5 to 72.8 years. The increase from 1990 to 1999 in the percentage of people living on less than $1 dollar a day was greater in the former communist countries (3.7 per cent) than anywhere else in the world. The number of people living in 'poverty' in the former Soviet Republics rose from 14 million to 14.7 million even prior to the crash of the rouble in 1998.
>
> Between 1993 and 1995, 20,000 out of 27,000 Russian state enterprises were privatised. The Government sold them for about 10 per cent of their true value. Despite its transition to a market economy the bureaucracy in Russia has grown dramatically. The Soviet bureaucracy under Brezhnev (Soviet centralism) made up about 12 million people. It ballooned to 18 million under Gorbachev (restructuring). Under Yeltsin (transition) the number of state functionaries in Russia alone exceeded that for the whole Soviet Union in Gorbachev's time.

I now turn to a tiny fraction of the myriad available examples of life after Stalinism. The first concerns the fate of Mao's China. The London *Times* of 12 November 2002 reported:

> Capitalists attending their first Communist Party congress might be nervous, but it is a measure of how China has changed that, when a group of millionaire delegates appeared yesterday, they acted as though they were the party's natural constituency. Shen Wenrong, China's third richest man, sporting a tie with gold spots and stripes at a congress forum, said: 'My dream is to do good. I don't care about being a millionaire; all I want is to do a good job for my country.' Struggling with so much humility and altruism, the steel mill owner added: 'I will build the world's biggest steel company for my country.' With estimated assets of more than 100 million pounds, Mr Shen is the richest member of the Communist Party, which has recently begun to admit capitalists. Beijing is presenting the step as a sign that the party is becoming more progressive.
>
> However, closer scrutiny reveals that all the capitalist delegates at the congress are managers-turned-owners of former state-owned enterprises. Often party members for decades, they became capitalists by virtue of privatisation. Genuine entrepreneurs who financed and built their own businesses were not invited to the congress. Yesterday's debut for the party's capitalists was like a gathering of the heads of New York crime families. Their mouthing of party slogans was

> punctuated by attempts at intimidation and the arrogance of the unaccountable. Mr Shen, clenching his vast hands as if strangling a small animal, launched into an attack on the compilers of the Forbes Rich List, who placed him third in China. Jiang Xipei, owner of a power cable company, when asked how he saw his position in the Communist Party, ran a hand over his slicked-back hair and said, ominously: 'According to a Chinese proverb, if you don't do evil things you won't be scared by ghosts.' The pock-marked face of Zan Shengda, a textile king, nodded in agreement.
>
> The three men paid about 250 pounds in Communist Party membership fees in 2001 – probably their best business investment of the year. As party members, they will have direct access to legislators, regulators, judges, police chiefs and ministers, all of whose careers depend on party membership.... The growing class of private business entrepreneurs is treating the party as China's version of the Rotary Club, where important contacts are nurtured in the name of philanthropy.... The new owners of former state-owned enterprises are least likely to challenge the primacy of the party or demand respect for human rights. As heads of autocratic institutions, they are familiar with the arsenal of control used by the party. Employees in Chinese industrial companies often work 16-hour days, seven days a week, without regard for health and safety regulations. Owners withhold wages and lock workers inside factories to prevent them changing jobs.

Then there is the Wen family. The *Times* of 9 September 2003 tells us that they:

> ... held out on their farm plot until a man wielding a hatchet threatened to kill them, one by one. The attacker was part of a gang hired by a property developer to turn the land on which they had built their mud-brick home outside Beijing into an industrial park and a housing complex for expatriate executives. The family had fought off tax collectors and other property speculators over the years, but the hatchet man frightened them sufficiently to make them agree to leave their land without compensation. Mr Wen said: 'We lost decades of work and the Government did nothing to protect us.' The Wens are not alone. Some 20 million farmers have been rendered landless by China's modernisation in the last decade. According to a new report by a state think-tank, this development has resulted in countless small-scale injustices which may end up posing a grave threat to social stability.

How many of the revolutionary followers of Mao ever thought they would see their party heading a government which would have to concern itself with the social and political consequences of this kind of 'reform'? No doubt in their cadre schools they learned about the English enclosures integral to the very birth of capitalism.[19] Now they see the dispossession of tens of millions in the age of the capital system's structural crisis, when speculation and parasitism predominate, and when the hoped-for free enterprise and democracy in the ex-Stalinist states turns out to be a gangster capitalism. The state apparatus is 'reformed' in the spirit of the suppression of Tianenmen Square. The London *Times* reported on 20 August 2005, under the headline 'China creates crack units to crush poverty protests':

> China has established elite police squads equipped with armoured vehicles and helicopters under orders to quell riots in a country where a protest erupts every seven minutes.... Zhou Yongkang, the Public Security Minister, said recently that the number of mass protests across China soared to more than 74,000 last year, with 3.76 million people taking part, up from 10,000 incidents a decade ago.... Acknowledging the problem of rising unrest, a vice-minister said last month that violent demonstrations were inevitable, given economic changes, and said that they were a sign of growing democracy (!).

What future for the Wen family and millions like them? The *Times* report continues:

> The crucial question is at what point popular unrest will become a systemic problem. Rick Baum of the University of California in Los Angeles said two ingredients were necessary for discontent to turn into turmoil. The first was connecting nodes; a single issue around which the disaffected could be galvanised. The second was some form of intellectual leadership, the emergence of a figure or group capable of articulating an alternative vision. So far, neither exists. But the more farmers and workers become disaffected the greater the potential that that might change.

In the context of the argument of *Not Without a Storm*, it is interesting, to say the least, to compare Baum's remarks with a commentary on recent struggles in France by Brigitte Salino in *Le Monde* of 9 July 2003:

> The passing days have seen the independent creation of collectives which escape any form of control by the trade unions, all over France and extremely determined. We have been hearing things which are increasingly radical and which, above all, go well beyond the framework of questioning of agreements. There are those who easily smile on hearing the casual workers on strike calling for a 'national insurrection' and linking the causes of their movement to the struggle against globalisation, to the defence of retirement pensions and the social security system, or to the desire to kick out a French Government judged to be 'authoritarian, indeed totalitarian'. But those who are smiling are forgetting the essential: those casual workers are sending a message, that of confusion, indeed despair.

In the *Times* of 30 September 2003, Rosemary Righter provided evidence of how at the heart of the much-lauded 'growth' of China's economy is a fateful combination of breakneck capitalist restoration and the persistence of the worst aspects of the old bureaucratic 'command economy'. She summarises:

> The country's progress is vitiated by the enduring command economy mindset, as 'wild East' market capitalism is lubricated by all-penetrating corruption between officialdom and entrepreneur. Investment remains politically charged and in consequence distorted. Sun Daun, an entrepreneur now jailed for raising capital by opening a cooperative bank for his workers after officials denied him loans because he refused to pay kickbacks, told the *Times* correspondent: 'Once you pay the right amount to the right person you can erect buildings anywhere except Tiananmen Square, but credit is denied to entrepreneurs who cannot pay the 10 to 15 per cent kickback on a loan.'
>
> Local bureaucrats, reckoning that high growth statistics are their keys to promotion, are pumping funds into manufacturing and construction with barely a thought for the marketability of products or the local demand for forests of new office blocks. If it turns sour, the hyperactive official reckons that by then he will have moved up.... 'Special' development zones have turned from a bright idea into a runaway national obsession. Every province and

> locality has them; in one Nanjing district they cover more than half its land area. Supply so far outstrips demand that, of the two million hectares of province-level development zones in China, about 1.7 million hectares are idle. The glut leads to land being leased at a fraction of its development cost, or given away.
>
> The 'vibrant' Chinese city centres 'are ringed with rusting "iron rice bowls" ' – the unviable, revenue-draining state-owned enterprises (SOEs) whose progressive closure is a key to market reform. China has shed 41 million SOE jobs and 21 million more from cooperatives. These 'iron rice bowls' provide not just jobs for life, but housing, healthcare (revealed in the SARS emergency to have broken down), education and pensions. ... Last year alone construction and service sectors absorbed ten million, but at least 30 million are jobless, up to 200 million peasants have no real work, and up to 200 million more subsist as day labourers. The *Beijing Review* highlighted automobiles, where there is buoyant demand from China's small middle class. However, with all but eight of China's provinces and regions getting in on the act, output is already 5.5 million cars a year, with 20 more plants soon to come on stream. So, to create room for 'their' cars, local officials freeze out competition. Shanghai recently moved to protect its market by imposing a 'settlement fee' of 80,000 yuan (£5,800) – about 40 per cent of purchase price – on Hubei-made Citroens: Hubei slapped an identical fee on Shanghai-made Santanas.

The same problems exist in agriculture. And they are responsible for an increasing polarisation:

> Enormous wealth is being created, but too much is being pocketed by too few. Officially, a fifth of Chinese hold 80 per cent of savings, but fewer than 10 per cent have significant disposable income.... Innumerable taxes, charges and official exactions squeeze the farmer or small factory owner so hard that his work becomes valueless.... Even with 75 per cent annual growth, prices are falling and unemployment rising.

Perhaps most important, in this context, are the ominous global implications of the changes taking place in China. The penetration of capital powered by the great transnational corporations will inevitably bring large-scale concentration of land-ownership and mechanisation/ modernisation/ commercialisation of agriculture. Countless millions of small farmers and their families – hundreds of millions of people – will be driven from the land. Beside this, the already massive migration of young people from the countryside, seeking the attractions of the cities, will pale into insignificance.

Here a simple historical comparison shows up the dimensions of the problem. There are some 2 billion people in China, more than the whole world's population when centuries ago the peasantry was driven from the land in Britain. That exodus from the land provided wave after wave of propertyless workers for the manufacturers of the industrial revolution. There is not even this prospect for the dispossessed peasants of China. They will confront a production system which needs an ever-decreasing number of manual workers, a system dominated by robotics and information technology. What then? Where to go? In the centuries-long process of enclosures, agricultural and industrial revolutions, urbanisation, movement from country to town was, from the 17th century onwards, paralleled by the opportunities offered to millions by the opening-up and colonisation of America. In our 21st century there is, certainly, mass emigration, but nothing like the American frontier.

The next example concerns Russia ... and Chelsea Football Club.

The *Times* of 3 July, 2003 reported that Chelsea FC, one of the oldest and most famous in Britain, was bought by a newcomer to the football business, the Russian entrepreneur Roman Abramovich. Where did Mr. Abramovich come from?

With the collapse of Stalinism and of the Soviet Union and the other ex-Soviet republics, governing bureaucrats and managers who had controlled the state-owned command economy set about privatisation with a vengeance, some of them becoming apprentice capitalists, others advancing their political careers by merging their destinies with the mafia-like entrepreneurs who quickly came to the top. One of these politicians was of course President Boris Yeltsin. In May 2005 (Abramovich's first important contact) Mr

Shvidler became chairman of Yukos-Sibneft, the fourth-largest oil company in the world, formed from Mikhail Khodorkovsky's Yukos and Mr Abramovich's Sibneft. His other crucial contact was Boris Berezovsky. In 1993-94 Mr Berezovsky was Russia's chief oligarch, a kingmaker who, with his own and other oligarchs' money, would go on to make 'Czar' Yeltsin the President in 1996. Mr Abramovich, then 26, was head of an oil trading firm in Omsk and was carefully cultivating local politicians who enabled his company to grow into the most powerful in the region. Mr Berezovsky spotted him and invited him to join the board of a new oil company that he was setting up called Sibneft, and later made him chairman. 'Yeltsin created Sibneft,' Mr Abramovich says, 'at the stroke of his pen.'

Abramovich has an asset management company in London. No doubt his acquisition of Chelsea football club for £140 million (he has a fortune of £3.8 billion) heralds many unforeseen changes not only in football's transfer market but also in the London capital market. He will certainly not be the last London visitor from Russia's new breed of ruthless robber barons who have emerged now that 'democracy' has been delivered to the people of Russia. They were oppressed and exploited by the Stalinist bureaucracy under the infamously misnamed 'socialism in one country'. Now the wealth created by their labour and the natural resources of their country are appropriated by the likes of Abramovich. Only a dozen years after the fall of Stalinism, this man has his hands on the oil and aluminium wealth of all Russia, and his asset management firm oversees his holdings in the automotive, food, consumer products and pharmaceuticals industries. He is a worthy recruit to the world of globalised capital:

> The Russian oligarch who has bought Chelsea football club has gone into business with people who have been accused of 'murder', 'bribery' and 'extortion' in US proceedings, the *Times* has learned. As Roman Abramovich, 36, an oil and aluminium magnate, flew into London, questions multiplied about his £3.8 billion business empire and its connections with dubious interests. The source of his fortune was the privatisation of Russia's economy after communism (*sic*) collapsed, a process which delivered precious natural resources to a small number

> of individuals. The most serious allegations brought to court involving Mr Abramovich's business interests emerge against the backdrop of Russia's 'aluminium wars'. In the turbulent aftermath of privatisation, smelter managers, metals traders and journalists were reported to have been killed as different interest groups battled for control of the multibillion-pound industry.[20]

The background to these developments, and to the representatives of globalised capital in large part responsible for them, is succinctly presented by that critical and acute observer 'from the inside', Joseph Stiglitz, until the year 2000 Chief Economist at the World Bank and before that Chairman of Clinton's Council of Economic Ministers. It is enough for present purposes to quote brief extracts, scathingly summarising the story, from his *Globalization and its Discontents.*

> For the majority of those living in the former Soviet Union, economic life under capitalism has been even worse than the old Communist leaders had said it would be. The middle class has been devastated, a system of crony and mafia capitalism has been created, and the one achievement, the creation of a democracy with meaningful freedoms, including a free press, appears fragile at best, particularly as formerly independent TV stations are shutdown one by one.
>
> The IMF radical reform strategy did not work: gross domestic product in post-1989 Russia fell, year after year. The devastation was greater than Russia had suffered in World War II. In the period 1940-46 the Soviet Union's industrial production fell 24 percent. In the period 1990-99, Russian industrial production fell by almost 60 percent – even greater than the fall in GDP (54%). Privatisation, accompanied by the opening of capital markets, led not to wealth creation but to asset stripping. It was perfectly logical. An oligarch who has just been able to use political influence to garner assets worth billions, after paying only a pittance, would naturally want to get his money out of the country. Anyone smart enough to be a winner in the privatisation sweepstakes would be smart enough to put their money in the booming US stock market, or into the safe haven of secretive offshore bank accounts. It was not even a close call; and not surprisingly, billions poured out of the country.
>
> Thus, at the time of the East Asia crisis, Russia was in a peculiar position. It had an abundance of natural resources, but its government

> was poor. The government was virtually giving away its valuable state assets, yet it was unable to provide pensions for the elderly or welfare payments to the poor. The government was borrowing billions from the IMF, becoming increasingly indebted, while the oligarchs, who had received such largess from the government, were taking billions out of the country. The IMF had encouraged the government to open up its capital accounts, allowing a free flow of capital. The policy was supposed to make the country more attractive for foreign investors; but it was virtually a one-way door that facilitated a rush of money out of the country. The IMF had lent Russia the dollars – funds that allowed Russia, in turn, to give its oligarchs the dollars to take out of the country. Some of us quipped that the IMF would have made life easier all around if it had simply sent the money directly into the Swiss and Cyprus bank accounts.
>
> In 1989, only 2 percent of those living in Russia were in poverty. By late 1998, that number had soared to 23.8 percent, using the $2 a day standard. More than 40 percent of the country had less than $4 a day, according to a survey conducted by the World Bank. The statistics for children revealed an even deeper problem, with more than 50 percent living in families in poverty. Other post-Communist countries have seen comparable, if not worse, increases in poverty.

It is almost a truism that whatever atrocities and bloodshed accompanied the birth of capitalist classes in modern Europe and North America, progress in social production, in law and politics and in culture were facilitated. Clearly, an emergent capitalist class in any nation in today's world will have a very different historical role, with the institutions proper to globalisation (offshore funds, Swiss bank accounts, etc., not to mention the IMF, the World Bank and the US State Department and the President's Council of Economic Advisers) at its disposal. Rather than becoming the bearers of democracy, the rule of law, productive enterprise and cultural enlightenment, they can only be active participants in the processes which constitute the structural-historical crisis of the capital system.

As for the mass cultural heritage of 'socialism in a single country' and 'the socialist camp' now that capitalism is restored, perhaps an appropriate footnote to this chapter on globalisation is the recent finding that in East Germany, approximately one-third of all young people today express support for neo-Nazi and extreme nationalist organisations.

---

1 Mészáros, *Beyond Capital*, pp. 144-5.

2 See François Chesnais, *La Mondialisation du Capita*l (nouvelle édition augmentée, Paris, 1998).

3 Eric Schlosser, *Fast Food Nation: what the all-American meal is doing to the world* (London, 2002), p. 260.

4 But note Gore Vidal's acid comments: 'It is corporate America ... that declared war on the Clintons in 1993 when the innocent couple tried to give the American people a national health service, something every civilized country has but we must never enjoy because the insurance companies now get one-third of the money spent on health care and the insurance companies are the piggy banks – the cash cows – of corporate America.
'In order to destroy the health service plan, insurance and pharmaceutical companies, in tandem with lively elements of the American Medical Association, conspired to raise a half-billion dollars to create and then air a barrage of TV advertisements to convince the electorate that such a service was Communist, not to mention an affront to the Darwinian principle that every American has the right to die unhelped by the state, which collects half his income in life with which to buy, thus far, $5.5 trillion's worth of military hardware at stupendous – to this day – cost... Nothing personal in this, by the way. But how else can the ownership of the country send a warning to other feckless politicians that the country and its people exist only to make money for corporations now so internationalised that they cannot be made to pay tax on much – if any – of their profits'. Gore Vidal, *The Last Empire: essays* (London, 2002), pp. 226-7.

5 Joseph E. Stiglitz, *Globalization and its Discontents* (London, 2002), pp. 207, 228.

6 This translation from *Le Monde Diplomatique* appeared in a December 2000 edition of the *Guardian Weekly*.

7 Claude Meillassoux, *L'Économie de la Vie: demographie du travail* (Paris, n.d.), pp. 64-5.

8 Meillassoux, *L'Économie*, pp. 148-50.

9 Winslow, *Capital Crimes*, pp. 304-5.

10 Winslow, *Capital Crimes*, pp. 177-8.

11 John Lea, *Crime and Modernity* (London, 2002).

12 Winslow, *Capital Crimes*, p. 10.

13 See John Ruskin, *Sesame and Lilies*, of which there is a recent edition (New Haven, Conn. and London, 2002).

14 Reference regrettably mislaid.

15 M. Gradoni, 'Paroles de sans-papiers, ballade', *Maintenant La Lettre*, 6/8, p. 32.

16 Marie-France Lange, 'The Demand for Labour within the Household: child labour in Togo', in Bernard Schlemmer (ed.), *The Exploited Child* (London, 2002), p. 274.

[17] See centre@crossroadswomen.net

[18] Lea, *Crime and Modernity*, p. 117.

[19] Ellen Meiksins Wood writes in her *The Origin of Capitalism: a longer view* (London, 2002; first published, New York, 1999), p. 109: 'Enclosure riots punctuated the sixteenth and seventeenth centuries, and enclosure surfaced as a major grievance in the English Civil War. In its earlier phases, the practice was to some degree resisted by the monarchical state, if only because of the threat to public order.'

[20] Behind the origin of Mr. Abramovich's aluminium wealth is 'globalisation', to be sure, managed by US capitalist interests. The story is scathingly summarised in *Globalisation and its Discontents*, by Joseph Stiglitz, Chief Economist of the World Bank until the year 2000. In 1994, Alcoa, the word's largest aluminium producer , combined with the US State Department and the National Economic Council, to create an international cartel on the spurious grounds that Russia was 'dumping' aluminium on the world market. After a year in which Alcoa 's profits greatly increased, the cartel collapsed: 'The story does not end there: in April 2000 news emerged about how a private monopoly was successfully created to control 75-80% of the Russian yearly production, creating the second largest aluminium company in the world (after Alcoa).' Stiglitz notes that 'President Yeltsin, with enormously greater powers than his counterparts in any Western democracy, was encouraged to circumvent the democratically elected Duma and to enact market reforms by decree.'

3

THE DESTRUCTION OF NATURE

A mountain of work has appeared in the last two decades on the dangers to the environment, on the exhaustion of the earth's resources and on the destruction of nature. What needs to be understood, however, is that these threats are the inevitable consequences of the essential functioning of capital, and are uncontrollable as long as the capital system prevails. Already in 1845, in *The German Ideology*, Marx and Engels were writing of capital's 'destructive forces' and of the necessity to 'appropriate the existing totality of productive forces ... merely to safeguard their very existence.'

The production and reproduction of the means of life, so long as capital rules, takes nature's resources 'for granted'. There is no overall social control of the husbanding of these resources; each capitalist enterprise plunders and sells, or buys for productive use that part of the natural resources relevant to its needs (i.e. production for profit), without any regard for the total result. The sole aim of production in the capital system is the appropriation and accumulation of value to reproduce and augment the capital invested. That capital is invested in raw materials, in fixed equipment and its maintenance, in overheads, and in the one commodity which when used creates an added or surplus value. That commodity is the labour-power bought from wage-workers.

The exploitation of this labour-power is the indispensable condition for the creation of surplus value and the accumulation of capital. That means that the working class is structurally essential to the capital system. This is a class relation that cannot be removed so long as capital rules. This is a social relation, the central one: like its inseparable antagonist, capital, labour-power must be daily produced and reproduced. The social system ruled by capital as a whole is, in the last analysis, a machine for that production and reproduction. The conservation of nature and its gifts is left to chance. Marx had already seen the dangers of this:

> Capitalist production disturbs the metabolic interaction between man and the earth, i.e., it prevents the return to the soil of its constituent elements consumed by man in the form of food and clothing, hence it hinders the operation of the eternal natural condition of the fertility of the soil, etc., etc.[1]

He also pointed to the regressive nature of capitalist production in this regard, in a passage which must be a motto for the society of the future:

> From the standpoint of a higher socio-economic formation, the private property of particular individuals in the earth will appear just as absurd as the private property of one man in other men. Even an entire society, a nation, or all simultaneously existing societies taken together, are not owners of the earth, they are simply its possessors, its beneficiaries, and have to bequeath it in an improved state to succeeding generations, as *boni patres familias* (good heads of the household).[2]

Today's wanton destruction and threat to the future of the planet itself raises the question: can a working-class movement fighting the rule of capital restrict itself to the traditional economic and political demands, given the inescapable truth of István Mészáros's assertion that 'potentially overreaching itself is the hallmark of capital's relationship ... to the elementary conditions of social metabolic reproduction, in the absolutely inescapable interchange of humankind with nature.'

The point being made here is summed up better than in anything I could write, in an interview given by a member of the 'other side'. Responding to questions by a journalist of the French magazine *L'Express* (27 June 2002), Condoleezza Rice, then National Security Adviser to President George W Bush (and now Secretary of State in the US Administration), was nothing if not straightforward!

> Question: '... What about Kyoto?'
> Answer: 'About the environment: friendships and alliances cannot oblige America to sign and ratify treaties which are not in its interests. The Kyoto agreements demanded a reduction of 30 per cent in our energy consumption, which would destroy our economy and also harm the European economy.'

The US produces 25 per cent of the world's carbon dioxide emissions.

One-and-a-half years earlier, clear warnings had been given, such as that of John Gray, writing in the *Guardian Weekly*:

> It seems almost inevitable that the Bush administration will be more inward-looking, and more hamstrung by Congress, than that led by Bill Clinton. If so, the future is bleak. To think that the rest of the world can go ahead and solve its environmental problems without the Americans is mere folly. It is not only that the US has itself an enormous impact on the global environment. The whole structure of global governance – the World Trade Organisation, the IMF, the World Bank and so on – is an American construction. Without active American involvement, nothing can be done to reform it. The risk is that it will become weak and irrelevant, as – led by the US – more and more countries try to solve their problems unilaterally.
>
> Some environmentalists welcome this outcome. Certainly the Washington consensus (the belief that the best framework for globalisation is a worldwide free market) has led to repeated disasters, as countries with differing needs and circumstances have been forced into implementing rigid, ineffective free-market policies. But, contrary to the fond hopes of some environmentalists, the break-up of the flawed Washington consensus does not mean that a wiser approach is on the horizon. It means that we are in for an anarchic free-for-all, in which globalisation will go on unchecked.
>
> The dangers of wild globalisation are legion. If world markets become more turbulent, pressures for protectionism may be irresistible, particularly in the US. Most worryingly, wars may be fought for shrinking resources such as oil and even, in some regions, water.[3]

And Alain Bihr writes cogently, in a recent *Carré Rouge*:

> In the context of a deepening ecological crisis, the working class cannot abandon to the bourgeoisie the task of managing the growth of the productive forces, contenting itself with putting pressure on it to obtain a more just division of the fruits of that growth, to re-adjust the sharing of the net product to the workers' benefit. The workers' movement today must put itself in the position of exerting its weight on the orientations of the social production process, that is to say on the ends assigned to the act of social labour in its totality, on the use made of society's productive forces in their entirety. Its objective must be to tear away these productive forces from the 'productivist logic' imposed upon them by capitalist relations of production, and this before the expropriation of the bourgeoisie.

I shall return below — in chapters 4, 6 and 7 — to this crucial issue: the imperative need for a refounded working-class movement to find ways of taking responsibility for protecting and advancing the elementary foundations of the social order that will replace the rule of capital which daily deepens the ecological crisis to which Bihr refers. Here I cite only a few of the thousands of possible examples, selected over a period of only months during the preparation of this book, of the destruction of these natural foundations when they and the people who depend on them are caught in the web of capital's operations.

1: Fishing

From the *Guardian Weekly* in the summer of 2000:

> Two years ago (1998) the United Nations estimated that nearly half the world's fish stocks were fully exploited, and if stocks were to have a chance of recovery one in three of the world's fishing boats would have to stop fishing. Nearly 70 per cent of the world's stocks are in need of urgent management, the UN Food and Agriculture Organisation said. In June 2000 all nine of the North Sea commercial fish stocks were described by European scientists as 'outside safe biological limits' and 67 per cent of all stocks in the North Atlantic were severely depleted or threatened.... The European Union has disguised its chronic inability to manage once abundant fish stocks

> by using its financial clout to ensure that in Europe there is always enough fish to meet consumer demand. Its fleets now deplete the fisheries of Africa and South America. They deprive people of food and work, and destroy once healthy stocks round the globe. More than half the fish consumed in Europe is now imported because of depleted home water stocks. The EU has 'bought' a share of the stocks of 14 African countries and is looking for more.

And some of the consequences?

> Arona Diagne, president of the Senegalese independent fishworkers' association CNPS, said that more than 300 men have been lost in accidents with trawlers in the waters around Mbour over the past two years.... Even if they do identify the boats fishing illegally, they are rarely penalised. 'The industrial boats are very powerful with a lot of money and they can buy their way out of trouble,' Mr Diagne said. 'They corrupt the persons who are meant to stop them. The bribe is everything.'
>
> The Centre of Research for the Development of Intermediary Fishing Technologies (Creditip), a non-governmental organisation set up to protect the rights of artisan fishermen throughout West Africa, wants to see the West African countries adopt a common policy to fishing agreements. For the governments of the region, however, ending the fishing agreements with the EU and other countries is not an option. Senegal is indebted to the World Bank to the tune of $3.8 billion and the money from the fishing contracts is a vital source of hard currency. Last year Senegal spent $323 million servicing its debts – $311 more than the EU pays to plunder one of the country's only resources.[4]

2: Genetic research

The *Guardian Weekly* again:

> The race for commercial control over the essence of life is threatening to spiral out of control, with private firms, universities and charities claiming development rights over natural processes in the human body at the rate of 34,500 a month. Research undertaken by Gene-Watch UK, an independent watchdog commissioned by the *Guardian* newspaper, reveals the scale of the gene rush, as investors, scientists, entrepreneurs and lawyers use powerful technology and obscure laws to

isolate and patent the genes that make us what we are – before they even understand what the genes do. Biotech firms say they need patent protection to recoup their investments. But the risk to society is that future medical researchers – private and public – will have to hack their way through forests of patents, paying out licence fees to a host of gene-squatters, before the drugs of the genetic revolution reach the market.

Patents are already pending or have been granted on more than 500,000 genes and partial gene sequences in living organisms. Concern is growing in Europe over a European Union directive adopted two years ago that makes it easier to patent genes. In June the French President, Jacques Chirac, wrote to the European Commissioner, Romano Prodi, saying that gene patenting should not be permitted. Much of the pressure to liberalise European gene patenting laws has come from the US. Last year the chairman of the US drugs firm Pfizer, William Steere, said: 'Europe seems to be entering a period of the dark ages, where witchcraft and sorcery are prevailing.'[5]

3: Destroying humans – tobacco

Under the headline 'University takes tobacco "blood money"', Kevin Maguire wrote in 2000 about a product which kills millions:

> A leading British university was asked this week to scrap plans to accept £3.8m from British American Tobacco, which is under investigation over smuggling allegations, to finance a school of business ethics [*sic*]. Nottingham University's decision triggered protests from a cancer charity and anti-smoking campaigners. BAT, the world's second biggest tobacco company, will help Nottingham create what is billed as Britain's first international centre for corporate social responsibility.
>
> Smoking is the biggest preventable cause of cancer in Britain, killing an estimated 120,000 people a year, and Nottingham University has a strict no-smoking policy. University officials said there had been a lot of 'soul searching', and that nationally agreed guidelines on commercial funding had been followed. BAT is the only big donor to agree to fund the corporate social responsibility centre, which will have a professorial chair or directorship as well as visiting professors from the developing world, and scholarships for students from developing countries. BAT, along with Philip Morris, is being sued in New York over allegations that it is actively involved in organised

crime. Ken Clarke, the former Tory Chancellor and Health Secretary now paid over £100,000 a year as BAT deputy chairman, who is a Nottinghamshire MP, supported the deal. Oxford University allows Rupert Murdoch to fund a chair in English and a visiting professorship in broadcast media while Cambridge has a Shell chair in chemical engineering, ICI a chair in applied thermodynamics, Glaxo a chair of molecular parasitology, PriceWaterhouseCoopers a chair of financial accounting and BP professorships in organic chemistry and petroleum science.[6]

The *Guardian Weekly* in August 2000 reported:

Operating profits in Latin America rose 42 per cent, but BAT admitted a growing sum – $225 a year – is being spent on legal work to fend off cases involoving smoking-related illnesses. ... Neil Withington, BAT's head of legal services ... dismissed suggestions that the company might face a growing number of smuggling cases (as in Ecuador). He believed the threats were part of a propaganda exercise being coordinated by the UK-based anti-smoking campaign group Ash. 'I would be surprised if there was a huge escalation (of legal action) in this area,' Mr Withington said.[7]

4: Patents – licence to kill

Monsanto offers patent waiver on 'golden rice' to aid poor

Monsanto Co. said last week that it would give away certain patent rights to speed the use of a genetically modified rice that could save millions of malnourished children in poor countries from dying or going blind. The company said it would grant patent licences at no charge to the developers of 'golden rice', a variety of genetically modified rice enriched in beta carotene, the building block of Vitamin A. More than a million children weakened by Vitamin A deficiency die every year, and at least half a million more go blind.

Under pressure to demonstrate that agricultural biotechnology is more than just a vehicle for raising profits, companies have been falling into line behind golden rice. Astra-Zeneca PLC of London negotiated a deal to give Potrykus (Professor at the Federal Institute of Technology in Switzerland) patent rights for use in poor countries in exchange for the right to sell golden rice to farmers in wealthy countries. But Monsanto is the first big company to waive its rights unconditionally. Groups sceptical of agricultural biotechnology have been suspicious of golden rice, arguing that it is a convenient tool for Western corporations to burnish their image. 'Critics are concerned that the advent of golden rice's "quick fix" for Vitamin-A deficiency could kneecap other low-tech and more cost-effective initiatives, among them, to reintroduce the many vitamin-rich food plants that were once cheap and available,' the Rural Advancement Foundation International said in a statement. 'Rather than nurture a strategy that encourages biodiversity, golden rice could promote monocultures and genetic uniformity. This is the wrong strategy.'[8]

5: The Forests

The destruction of the Amazon rainforest is well documented and well known. There has been equally wanton plunder of the forest in the United States, with tragic consequences. 'It always annoys me,' Harry Merlo, President of Louisiana Pacific, was quoted as saying,

> We don't log a 10-inch top, we don't log to an 8-inch top or a 6-inch top. We log to infinity. It's out there, it's ours, and we want it all. Now.[9]

And, writes Winslow:

> Measured in terms of biomass, biologists claim that the temperate rainforests of northern California, Oregon, Washington, British Columbia and Alaska were the largest in the world, bigger than the tropical rainforests of the Amazon or Southeast Asia.[10]

These forests were the basis of work for loggers, truck drivers and millworkers. They also protected rich salmon spawning grounds and made for a climate favouring a prosperous dairy industry.

> In the late 1970s and 1980s, double-digit interest rates, the product of a global economic crisis, put a crimp on farmers and slowed the housing industry, thus plunging the timber industry into the worst depression since the 1930s. Meanwhile, overfishing and the destruction of salmon spawning grounds by dams and clear-cutting wreaked havoc on the fishing industries: the salmon harvest in the lower Columbia river dropped by nearly 70 per cent between 1981

and 1995. Many mills shut down, and employment in Oregon fell from 85,000 in 1961 to 60,000 in 1996. In some heavily logged areas, the problems were even worse. In Tillamook country on the North Coast of Oregon, the annual timber harvest fell from 262 trillion board feet in 1978 to 115 trillion in 1995, and the number of jobs in the sector declined by 32 per cent between 1977 and 1996, producing a number of serious social problems. Between 1979 and 1989, median household income declined by nearly 10 per cent to only $21,965.

6: The ex-Soviet Union

There have been many examples of the environmental damage (Chernobyl the best-known) under the Stalinist regime which, under the false banner of 'socialism in a single country', attempted 'peaceful competition' with capitalism. There will be more, with the current restoration of capitalism, while the environmental consequences of the earlier system persist.

The *Guardian Weekly* again in late 2000:

> 'Shocking' radioactive leaks found in Siberia
>
> Radioactive contamination of rivers around a top-secret Russian nuclear weapons complex in Siberia have reached 'staggering' levels, the worst monitored, and is out of 'rational control', a joint team of Russian and American monitors said last week. Following a monitoring expedition in July and August 2000 to the closed plutonium complex at Seversk, near Tomsk in western Siberia, the Russian and American nuclear watchdogs said they had registered alarming levels of radioactivity in tributaries of the Ob river, a key Siberian waterway. They said they found caesium and strontium-90 vastly exceeding safety levels in the rivers Tom and Romashka, close to the Siberian Chemical Complex, a sprawling plant established by the Soviet Union in the 1950s to make weapons-grade plutonium for warheads.
>
> But even more disturbing, said Prof Pashchenkno, plant life in the rivers contained high levels of phosphorus-32, which decays within a couple of weeks, meaning that the radioactive effluent was of very recent origin whereas the strontium and the caesium could date back to the 1960s. The closed nuclear town of Seversk is effectively a suburb of Tomsk, a city with a population of 500,000. Seversk was

created in 1949, at the onset of the superpowers' nuclear arms race. Mr Forofontov said lethal amounts of radioactivity were leaking into the soil and water in the region because of the practice of storing waste from the reactors in liquid form, which was then pumped deep below ground.[11]

And the same paper a month later:

Village children poisoned by Russian space junk.

Every time a Russian rocket lifts off from its launch pad at Baikonour, residents in the tiny Siberian village of Ploskoye, more than 1,500km away, are shaken by a terrible explosion. If it is dark, firework flashes are visible in the sky above their homes, with streaking flames burning through the air as fuel falls to earth. During the day a misty, yellowish cloud sometimes hangs over the region. Villagers say that the noise of the blast sets dogs howling for hours. In the days after each launch, rocket fragments from the shuttles ferrying astronauts and equipment to Mir, or to the international space station, can be found in the hills and forests nearby. Occasionally local farmers discover massive, shining metal cylinders – up to seven metres long and three metres wide – which have in the past been seized with delight and converted into chicken coops, hunting huts or grain storage tanks.

Recently, however, as more information emerges about the poisonous fuels lining the wreckage, the local people have started to regard the debris with mounting alarm. Village doctors have charted a growth in illnesses among their patients – from cancer to bronchial spasms to defects in new-born children – and concluded they are connected to the scattering of cosmic litter on the region.

Viktor Pakhomov, 55, head of the Ploskoye administration, is seeking to discover why, in his village of 1,000, people are becoming more and more unwell. For 40 years, little research has been done into the connections between illness and the space programme, so Mr Pakhomov has catalogued its effects himself. In his attempts to collect and identify toxic fuel remnants, he has burnt his retinas to the point of near-blindness, suffered temporary paralysis in his hands and scorched his lungs by breathing in poisonous fluids.

A Ploskoye doctor, Olga Vorova, is besieged by new patients every time a rocket is launched. 'We have people complaining of nausea, vomiting, headaches and finding it hard to breathe,' she said. 'But more worrying are what appear to be the cumulative effects of the pollution. In the past five years not one child in the village has been born completely fit – each baby has been diagnosed with blood problems or nervous system complaints.'[12]

7: Water

This section is the work of Steve Drury. It is dated 10 April 2000.

Water and solidarity

Two thirds of the world's population lacks sanitation that is adequate for healthy living. Of them, one billion people, including the majority of Africans, have no access to safe drinking water. Poor water supplies form the main contributor to the death of children under five years old. For hundreds of millions of people, getting water for domestic use consumes much of their daily labour, which involves mainly women and children trudging to distant water sources and carrying it home, on average twice each day.

Hardly a month goes by without a conference, often at ministerial level, that restates the elementary goal of giving every person on the planet an adequate and safe supply of water. UNICEF and FAO, and the 'aid' ministries of every advanced country, like the Department for International Development (DfID) in Britain and USAID, speak of little else with regard to Africa than water resources, food security and 'sustainable' development. They are noble words, yet there is no sign of improvement, and the plight of up to 15 million people in the Horn of Africa, where rains have failed for three successive years, bears witness to empty rhetoric. Of course, UN agencies, the EU's various 'Third World' Commissions and individual government bodies can, in the manner of Stalin's satraps, point to model developments and congratulate themselves.

Water privatisation

In her statement to the International Conference on Water and Sustainable Development in Paris (March 1998) Clare Short (the British minister heading DfID) included many fine 'visions' of the 'mission' of such bodies. Included in it was the reason why they come to nothing for the billions of people condemned to non-existent sanitation and polluted drinking water. 'Partnerships among governments, the private sector and civil society [I wonder what that might be] are critical to sustainable development [of water resources].'

Yes, indeed, the 'private sector' – read capital – is eager for such partnerships, provided they bring a rate of profit that its shareholders find agreeable. Throughout Europe, privatised water and sanitation utilities are hugely profitable, and are likely to remain so, for giving up water is not the first choice for most people falling on hard times. Since the removal of apartheid in South Africa, water utilities have been a prime target for privatisation and the strategic joint ventures of which Minister Short speaks. They are all in urban areas, involve water metering and a hike in water rates. Whole communities, particularly townships, are seeing family after family cut off from the most basic resource there is, as they find themselves unable to pay spiralling bills. Communities in the dry Transvaal in particular are rising up against the water pirates, and against the 'vision' and 'mission' of the likes of Clare Short. The latest protests are in Nelspruit, where a joint venture linking Biwater plc from Britain and the municipally-run Dutch water utility NUON (but now with a 50 per cent stake in Biwater) with government and 'civil society' sees a chance of an 'agreeable' rate of profit. South African urban areas are a favoured target, because they are the most numerous in sub-Saharan Africa and, despite the legacy of apartheid, people enjoy much higher average incomes than in the remainder. But unemployment runs at around 50 per cent in most urban areas.

Biwater was involved in the Tories' aid-for-trade programme during the 1980s, benefiting from dam and water distribution contracts in Malaysia and Thailand that were linked to arms supplies to the governments involved. Subsequently, Biwater has been criticised widely for failure of supply in Britain, Central America and India. Critical reporting of Biwater by GreenNet and the South African *Mail & Guardian* newspaper drew legal threats to the web service providers that host their archives (*LabourNet* and *SangoNet*), following earlier successful actions against the *Independent* and *Private Eye* in London. Campaigns against Biwater's privatisations, unsurprisingly, are not widely reported by the world's press for fear of legal repercussions in Britain. Biwater's bids to privatise water and waste services in South Africa total 12 billion rand.

The South African Municipal Workers Union (SAMWU) is appealing to NUON, as a participant still in the state sector in the Netherlands, to break from Biwater, seeking help from the Dutch public sector union Abvakabo. SAMWU has publicised widely the poor environmental and ethical record of Biwater in a number of joint ventures in India, central America and even Britain. The recent

World Water Forum in The Hague, sponsored by 130 governments and the World Bank, and attended by over 1,000 bureaucrats and executives, aimed at reviewing and refining a programme to privatise the world's water systems. SAMWU was able to make a presentation there on public alternatives to privatisation. Representatives of Lyonnaise des Eaux, a major French 'player' in water privatisation, walked out of that session. SAMWU's proposal is for 'twinning' between municipal water authorities on a no-profits basis, modelled on the Dutch public ownership of water utilities. NUON, a potential participant in such 'twinning', seems set to become part of the private sector itself. The Nelspruit issue clearly shows the inevitable need for internationalization of the fight against transnational capital by organised labour, and SAMWU has taken an important step along that road. The Declaration issued by the World Water Forum at The Hague in March 2000 included the following clause:

'Valuing water: to manage water in a way that reflects its economic, social, environmental and cultural values for all its uses, and to move towards pricing water services to reflect the cost of their provision. This approach should take account of the need for equity and the basic needs of the poor and the vulnerable.'

Throughout the Declaration, between its unarguable words regarding the problems linking water with poverty, poor health, women's issues, environmental pollution, drought and flooding, are threaded many references to 'stakeholders'. Just what this term means in reality, as regards governments and the World Bank, is brought out starkly by news emerging from Bolivia.

Bolivian trades unionists demonstrated on 6 April 2000 against a 35 per cent rise in water prices imposed on the city of Cochabamba. Military forces opened fire, killing six demonstrators, following the arrest of its organiser Oscar Olivera. On 12 April Hugo Banzer, former dictator and now elected president of Bolivia, declared a nationwide state of siege, abolishing civil liberties. The price hike stems from the new owner of the region's water system – International Waters Ltd. (IWL) of London, itself controlled by the transnational construction giant Bechtel, based in San Francisco. IWL's Bolivian operation is called Aguas de Altuni, and centres on the Misicuni dam project. Water from the dam will cost six times more than it would from alternative sources. The increased water charges are to recover the cost of the dam, with one problem: the dam has not yet been built by IWL and Bechtel, and neither has put any funds into the construction project. Clearly, the intention is that water users should come up with the necessary capital, so making Misicuni probably the most profitable project on the planet – for IWL. There is growing evidence for a corrupt relationship between IWL and the Bolivian authorities, involving IWL's getting the entire franchise for nothing. Even the World Bank's hydrologists are dubious about the project, having themselves devised an alternative project at a fraction of the dam's cost. Yet the World Bank director, James Wolfensohn, acquiesces over the growing fiasco, for good reason.

The World Bank and IMF, together with the EU, force 'master plans' on indebted countries through the structural adjustment programmes. Into these are written sell-offs of formerly public assets, such as water utilities. Consortia, like IWL, were formed solely to capture these assets. One of the first water privatisations in South America was the water supply to Buenos Aires, whose new operators immediately shed 7,500 workers and upped prices. One member of the consortium for Buenos Aires is Anglia Water of Britain.

Drought and famine

Nowhere is the obscenity of water privatization more thrown into sharp relief than in rural Africa. The spectre of catastrophic drought, famine and epidemic once more roams its poorest areas, as in the Horn at this moment. Despite drought and crop failure repeatedly see-sawing between semi-arid lands north and south of the Equator roughly every four to five years, there has barely been any investment from any source in strategic, high-yield wells, or developing means of water storage during wet periods. Both would give a measure of security to the people who live there, for them to store surplus food from increased harvests when conditions are good and to preserve the livestock on which most of them depend for an income. Most important, such simple improvements would put the means of survival in the hands of rural people themselves. Instead, massive funds, paid mainly to various consulting companies, have been invested in famine early-warning technology, based principally on advanced information gathered by satellite. No Somali or Afar needs to be warned of drought and famine. Both are foreordained by a single failure of the seasonal rains. The beneficiary of such early warnings is transnational agrobusiness that supplies the vast, though always inadequate food-aid, at an 'agreeable' rate of profit. Despite the fact that the south-eastern Ethiopian region of the Ogaden has been known to need 1.2 million metric tons of food aid over the last year or more, the major donors (the EU, the World Food Programme and USAID) have fallen short of their 'pledges' by more than 50 per cent. Grain that they have supplied has in many cases been months late in arriving. The cynical excuse has been that the war between Ethiopia and Eritrea would mean that such aid would prolong the war.

The private sector ventures into rural areas only where fat consultancy fees are to be had from UN agencies, the World Bank and the EU. Put out to tender, various 'Sector Studies' on water resources generate vicious competition that pits transnational consortia of private and state sector engineering and survey experts, usually under the umbrella of a 'lead agency' and its 'country counterpart' (usually a branch of a ministry). Whether or not successful tenders involve bribery, and whether or not they result in useful information, once the contracts and the funding are finished, the transnational consortia pull up sticks. They are the only beneficiaries. Nationalist regimes in power have repeatedly failed to make provision for water security on any scale that would allow the people of the affected areas to continue the lives that they choose. Instead, developments focus on joint-venture agriculture on the large scale, involving capital-intensive mechanisation. They use drought conditions to corral destitute people into such ventures, forcing them to break unwillingly from their traditional lives and culture to become low-paid agricultural labourers. The most notorious example of this was the shipment of thousands of people from the famine areas of northern Ethiopia in 1984-6 to the humid lowlands of south-west Ethiopia, by the regime of Mengistu Haile Mariam. These unfortunate families went from the frying pan into the fire, facing conditions and diseases of which they had no experience or resistance.

Pitted against extremes of climate, poor soils and the high costs of fertilizers, mechanization and fuels, Africa's farmers are the world's poorest people. Yet they are also the most resourceful and ingenious. Individual and communal farmers regularly produce higher and more diverse yields than capital-intensive farming on the large scale in Africa, when water is available.

Scientists and engineers for solidarity and co-operation

The bureaucrats of the World Bank, the UN agencies, the EU and individual governments, bundled in self-serving bodies, such as the World Commission on Water for the 21st Century and World Water Forum, with transnational capital seeking the highest rate of profit and corrupt nationalist regimes seeking their cut, have a common slogan. Following Margaret Thatcher, they say, 'there is no alternative' to privatising the most basic means of life. We say that there is an alternative. Break free of globalized capital, corruption and bureaucracy. Restore water supply and sanitation to community control, for development and use by a free association of producers.

Working co-operatively with rural and urban African communities, scientists and engineers can potentially make a dramatic difference to security, to productivity and to health. The immediate needs of millions of impoverished and dispossessed Africans hinge on resolving water-related problems: providing clean domestic supplies; those for livestock; and means of harvesting, storing and distributing rainfall for efficient irrigation. All other means of sustaining people's livelihoods stem from water-related issues: alternative sources of fuel and power (bio-fuels, wind and solar power) to the now vanished stocks of fuel wood and the valuable fertiliser consumed by burning dried animal dung; soil conservation and restoration measures; improved sanitation; low-cost, easily maintained pumps; affordable and efficient vehicles to transport surplus produce to market, thereby cutting out the middlemen and establishing fair prices and fair incomes. A developing co-operation with workers in the countries involved and internationally is central to bringing these potentials to fruition. Problems in the engineering, construction, transport and mining industries world-wide mean that increasing numbers of workers no longer have jobs that fit their skills and experience, if indeed they have jobs at all. That huge pool of collective skills, experience and self-organising ability, allied with the dispossessed rural producers and with scientists and engineers committed to transforming society, is the basis for a system of truly human relations that breaks from the stranglehold of markets and capital.

8: Towards a socialist environmental perspective

A further contribution from Steve Drury. These are extracts from a document dated 8 August 2001.

The working class and their communities, rural labourers, peasants and the dispossessed face growing environmental problems and deteriorating conditions of life daily. It is often said that all humanity is in the same boat, on 'Spaceship Earth', but it is clear that a tiny number have life rafts, while the majority travel in steerage and face the risks directly. The same applies to health issues that arise from the drive to maintain the rate of agricultural and retail profits by unwholesome means that have brought on BSE/vCJD, increasing risk of tuberculosis, enteritis and so on.

Environmental problems span all scales, from those affecting individuals, such as deteriorating housing, to the global issues of climatic warming and pollution of atmosphere and oceans. Most of such problems generally cannot be resolved by individual or community actions. Many are insidious, with consequences that show themselves only many years on; or distortions in natural processes build imperceptibly, suddenly to make themselves felt when they pass some natural threshold. Reporting of such issues is piecemeal, often giving such simplified coverage as to trivialise them. They are never set in their wider context, nor are details fully publicised. The many scientists researching environmental change, because of their specialisation and the level of detail that they accumulate, rarely are able to 'see the wood for the trees'. At all levels the reality of the problems and means of overcoming them are fogged by confusion that arises from ignorance, from dissimulation, but principally from separation of the problems from their context. This article aims at outlining that context.

Growing impact on the environment

Except for a few oddball scientists, often sponsored directly by transnational corporations, everyone recognises that human actions now have an all-pervading influence over every aspect of the rest of nature. There is a huge number of types of these so-called 'anthropogenic' changes to our world. They disrupt natural processes, drive species of plants and animals into premature extinction, pose threats of many kinds to human health, disturb the stability of land and impose a wide variety of shifts in the climate, that otherwise would be in a period of stability relative to the repeated upheavals during ice-age conditions. Various 'Green' groups do not exaggerate when they campaign against the growing likelihood of a catastrophic rebound of these changes on the whole of human society. None poses a greater threat than destabilisation of climate by emissions of the 'greenhouse' gas, carbon dioxide, from burning of coal, oil and natural gas, signs of which are now repeatedly confirmed. World climate governs patterns of vegetation on which growing human populations have depended entirely since the rise of agriculture and domestication of animals about 10,000 years ago. The present population is vastly larger than that which formerly subsisted by 'living off the land' as gatherer-hunters. Before about 10,000 years ago the estimated global population was little more than the attendance at Premier League football matches on a winter Saturday afternoon. It is quite probable that the current 6 billion world population would enter a period of famine whose magnitude would dwarf all human experience, should climate belts shift suddenly. According to recent analyses of how the climate system functioned in the not-so-distant past (before 10,000 years ago), which show how it can 'flip' from warm to cold in a matter of a decade or less because of quite small changes, that is increasingly probable.

The destruction and transformation of the world's diversity also impoverish culture. This is not some sentimental issue, for the very heart of culture, the combined wealth of human understanding, began with our gatherer-hunter ancestors' encyclopaedic knowledge of their surroundings, on which their fate depended. It also forms the main plank for our own spiritual life. Respect and awe for the natural world are not the exclusive province of intellectual aesthetes, but lie deep within the experience and yearnings of workers, peasants and the dispossessed, most clearly among young people. Moreover, not a month passes without some useful compound being extracted from rare and often insignificant-looking species, nor likewise without some vital lesson about how the natural world works. As well as its cultural aspects, the environment's diversity is, as it always has been, a vast bank of potential use-values for us.

Modern industry increasingly produces wastes that are so complex as to thwart any kind of safe disposal. These include artificial radioactive isotopes and complex organic chemicals. The first are indestructible and the second pose further threats in attempting to destroy them. Both form potential hazards for long into the future. Industrial capital has increased degradation of landscapes and urban areas on all scales. True wilderness, even in Antarctica, is vanishing. Access to those remaining areas in Britain least affected by agricultural capital becomes increasingly hindered by landowners, who block rights of public access to defend their 'sporting' or commercial privileges. The victories won after major battles for general rights of free access to open land, led mainly by working-class youth since the mid-20th century, have largely been overturned by 'anti-trespass' legislation in Britain. In fact, the issues of access and trespass at the heart of recent legislation are stalking horses aimed not merely at free movement in pleasing landscape, but at occupation of workplaces and unused buildings and urban land.

Capital and the environment

While capital remains at the root of production, nature becomes a passive collection of things that is solely the object of profit. The relation of humanity to nature is thereby a one-sided set of conditions to allow labour to be set in motion to generate profit. This one-sidedness is the source of growing human misery in every conceivable form and equally of the destabilisation of the environment. The Green movement proposes positive policies to deal with global warming and associated problems. In suggesting these measures, the Green movement is absolutely correct. However, the issue is the fundamental conflict between science, technology and human knowledge on the one hand, and a mode of production with capital, exchange value and the market at its core on the other. This is where Marxists part from most Greens. The basis of 'Green' policies in the parliamentary arena fails to recognise this conflict. Instead it appeals, through 'world leaders' and 'policy makers' for the self-reform of capital. It calls for co-operation between nation states – the advanced capitalist countries, the crisis-ridden former Stalinist states and the ex- and semi-colonial poor countries. To achieve success for these appeals it focuses on individual action to adopt Green lifestyles and to pressure the 'policy makers'. Leaving aside the fact that 'world leaders' and 'policy makers' have proved themselves totally incapable of taking a single decision that benefits humanity in the past, rather the opposite, we must concentrate on the economic implications for capital of these measures. In this way it becomes clear that self-reform as regards environmental problems is a totally utopian concept, as it is for any other social or economic issue.

Introducing anti-pollution measures demands not just the adoption of Green lifestyles at the level of the individual, but the introduction of the most advanced technology to avoid pollution, to reduce emissions that are inevitable in the course of manufacture and to clean up the mess that already exists, of which more later. In addition, attempting to resolve ecological crises means vastly increased investment in scientific research about the functioning of the Earth system, and in the search for 'environmentally friendly' means of production, particularly in energy generation. There is no escape from the fact that this entails a general and enormous increase in fixed capital. That, of course, fuels the tendency for the rate of profit to decrease. Such measures are therefore impossible under capitalism or any other of capital's guises without a corresponding decrease in necessary labour – for capital to resolve the problems that it has created means driving up general impoverishment globally.

Another utopian wing of the Greens, principally among aid and development agencies and nationalist governments in the so-called 'Third World', seeks to improve the lot of the poor by 'sustainable development'. However such is the gap between the average consumption of commodities by people in the developed world and that of the poor two-thirds of humanity that any significant improvement in their standards implies a massive increase in production of energy, metals, food and much else besides, with a redoubled boost to ecological destabilisation. 'Sustainable development' under present global conditions is utopian from an economic standpoint too. It demands input of capital to function in a market economy, and that is the particular lack within the 'Third World'. Its only source is inflow from either developed states or international bodies, such as the World Bank. That is possible only if it generates a rate of profit that is attractive, and that demands fiercely increasing exploitation of 'Third World' labour.

In the parliamentary arena, the Greens are trapped in the contradictions of globalised capital, and in those of their own world outlook. Their conclusions are based entirely on the experience of industrial capital. They accept the lie that the working class cannot organise technology and science to serve humanity and defend natural balances. Inevitably they deny that advanced standards of life can be sustained and extended to the whole of humanity. By orienting to 'world leaders' they rule out the mass of people having a choice in their own fate and their own self-advancement. As well as failing to grasp or even consider the dynamics of political economy, such Greens are philosophically bogged down as regards the relationship between humanity and nature, and its evolution. They are in crisis, equally as deep as that in which defenders of capital's world order find themselves.

Towards a socialist perspective on ecology

What does Marxism have to offer? How might a socialist world society tackle the grave problems inherited from the present stage of human evolution under capital? How does it consider the human-nature relationship? Looking to the appalling environmental problems of the former Soviet Union, Eastern Europe and China, that in many ways far transcend those of capitalism, many might say that socialised production is even less capable than that organised by capital. But this would be to identify bureaucratic state planning and Stalinism with socialism, and to disregard the irresistible pressure of capital on Soviet affairs. Indeed, Istvan Meszaros, in his book *Beyond Capital*, argues forcefully that Soviet economics was permeated by a market based on exchange value; a 'personification' of capital following the overthrow of capitalism in Russia.[13]

Marxists have neglected the dialectics of nature and the human-nature interrelationship since posthumous publication of Engels' *Dialectics of Nature*. Engels makes an important statement that anticipated the growing realisation today of the totality of nature in all its interconnections, in particular that with humanity.

'Let us not, however, flatter ourselves overmuch on account of our human victories over nature. For each such victory nature takes its revenge on us. Each victory, it is true, in the first place brings about the results we expected, but in the second and third places it has quite different, unforeseen effects which only too often cancel the first. Thus at every step we are reminded that we by no means rule over nature like a conqueror over a foreign people, like someone standing outside nature – but that we, with flesh, blood and brain, belong to nature, and exist in its midst, and that all our mastery of it consists in the fact that we have the advantage over all other creatures of being able to learn its laws and apply them correctly.'

The essence of the materialist world view is our indivisibility from nature as the source of our development and the thoughts in our heads. The relationship unifies us with wider nature, from which we emerged, but increasingly involves our conflict with it, both in surviving the conditions under which humans exist and our seeking consciously to bring parts of nature under our control. This is neither some fixed opposition, nor is the relationship's continual motion and change a never-ending, mechanical cycle. The relationship itself changes in the course of evolution of both human society and the rest of nature. Changes in nature carry the seeds of change in society, while social changes inevitably seek to transform nature too. In this respect we are at one with all other organisms that inhabit our planet, and indeed with those that lived on it in the distant past. Whatever the changes in the rest of nature that have been involved in the development of human society and economy, and whatever the reasons why, Marxists insist that they are inseparable from the entire course of inorganic and organic evolution of the universe and our home planet. To say otherwise would be indulging in the most absurd metaphysics. But just to state that axiom does not get us very far.

What characterises the peculiar interaction between humans and nature? Marx's position was that the unity is the exchange of materials between the rest of nature and a particular species. In the case of humanity this is through conscious material production; through labour. Within this unity are also the seeds of conflict with nature, part with the struggle to overcome the dangers of natural forces, part with that to understand, master and exploit those forces, and part flowing back to nature, both negatively and positively, as a result of the use of natural forces and materials.

Necessary steps

Many environmental problems are truly global, and lesser ones are essentially similar for workers, the rural masses and the dispossessed wherever they live. While capital and its representatives belatedly recognise many of the problems, they are organically incapable of tackling them without driving globalised capital deeper into crisis. Not only do they 'fiddle while Rome burns', but their fiddling accelerates the onset of ecological problems from which there may be no escape. Any beginning of a solution needs actions that are independent of capital. Socialist accountancy based on quality implies the greatest attention to the negative and positive influences on the environment of production and consumption, and seeking means of avoiding damaging rebounds on society. That is incompatible with any form of exchange which implies quantity, money and market, and the content of necessary labour; i.e. with the very essence of capital. It implies the eradication of exchange through markets; i.e. those of capital, commodities and labour, which are the crippling constraints on life – liberation from the tyranny of exchange-value and the negation of all past relationships.

However, passively waiting for some notional overthrow of capital on a global scale merely allows the environmental situation to become worse at a pace about which we can only guess. Moreover, capital's decline seems set to drive up the exploitation of labour and to abandon to their own devices increasingly large numbers of people, both the unemployed, sick and old of its developed parts as well as people in the 'Third World'. There can be no social revolution without workers and their potential allies first seeking ways of organising their lives and those of their communities to ward off more and more problems stemming from capital at its global limit. Whatever strategies emerge, it will become increasingly clear that economics outside and beyond that of capital are essential. Today it becomes more obvious that defence of past gains won from capital is no longer sufficient to resolve crisis conditions of all kinds. Transforming the class struggle to include offensive action on all fronts, opens a road to development of a 'mass communist consciousness' – by setting out to change the world people will change themselves and their consciousness.

How and when the self-organisation of the working class will transcend defence is, of course, unpredictable except in the broadest sense. It seems likely to emerge in individual communities, and local environmental problems will figure on the agenda – in some cases they could dominate it. Currently, the twinned issues of price and quality of basic foodstuffs, involving increasingly worrying matters of health, are of immediate concern at all levels in working class communities. So too are the growing areas of abandoned industrial land, many of which pose toxic threats to drinking water, and all represent capital's assault on the natural world and destruction of aesthetic resources. Setting out to resolve them will bring community after community together in recognising the need for a broader approach. The largest scale environmental destabilization, affecting the entire planet, will grow to pose general threats, and more obviously unwelcome changes in everyday life. These increasingly clearly will demand unified efforts linking broad associations of communities from country to country and continent to continent. Those scientists who have researched environmental change and issued increasingly detailed warnings, sooner or later will see the futility of addressing them to capital and its representatives. They will be drawn to put their knowledge and skills at the disposal of community movements that have taken initiatives. Such a unification, allied to community action that seeks to ensure sustainable employment, independent means of trading fairly with other groups and revitalisation of culture is likely to witness explosive development covering all aspects of human life, with rapid exchange and advance of knowledge.

Increasing independence from capital of action and reflection by workers and their allies, encompassing ever-broadening aspects of life, necessarily poses the issue of dual power and its resolution through the organisation of social revolution and the abolition of capital. In moving towards this situation, every aspect of existing science, technology and culture will have begun to be questioned. It will become increasingly clear that science and art have not only been held from the masses by capital, but have developed under it in an increasingly perverted way. It will become appropriate to question the extent to which they are truly useful, and to seek entirely new avenues to enrich culture.

---

[1] Marx, *Capital*, vol. I, chap. 15.

[2] Marx, *Capital*, vol. III, chap. 46.

[3] The *Guardian Weekly*, 28 December 2000–3 January 2001.

[4] The *Guardian Weekly*, 17-23 August 2000.

[5] The *Guardian Weekly*, 23-29 November 2000.

[6] The *Guardian Weekly*, 7-13 December 2000.

[7] The *Guardian Weekly*, 10-16 August 2000.

[8] The *Guardian Weekly*, 10-16 August 2000.

[9] Winslow, *Capital Crimes*, p. 200.

[10] Winslow, *Capital Crimes*, p. 199.

[11] The *Guardian Weekly*, 9-15 November 2000.

[12] The *Guardian Weekly*, 14-20 December 2000.

[13] Mészáros, *Beyond Capital*, p. 171.

4

WHERE TO BEGIN?

> For a long time, the forces of socialist emancipation were greatly handicapped by capital's ability to assume a conflict-attenuating transnational mode of functioning while denying its equivalent to its labour force trapped within the confines of various particularistic determinations and divisions. The necessity to overcome such determinations and divisions through the reconstitution of materially anchored international solidarity represents the greatest challenge to labour for the foreseeable future.
>
> István Mészáros, *Beyond Capital*

Introductory

The whole purpose of this book is to make a contribution to refounding working-class, socialist internationalism. And central to my approach is that this requires a radically different emphasis from that informing the thinking of almost all the twentieth-century Marxists. 'Globalisation', with its attendant threats – not only of barbarism but also of the very destruction of nature and of humanity – makes it necessary to begin afresh by revisiting Marx's insistence on the difference between the proletarian and all earlier revolutions. Let us briefly summarise his argument.

In earlier epochs, when the rule of one class was overthrown and replaced by that of another, it meant the advent of that new class's own particular mode of exploitation of other classes. The proletariat – propertyless except for the labour-power it is forced to sell in order to survive – does not have any such interest or mode of exploitation to impose on other classes. Its revolution means the end of class-divided society. Henceforth the relation between labouring humanity and the rest of nature will be a direct, collective one, unmediated by class divisions.

Confronting today's globalised capital and its present and future consequences, the working class, and those socialists who join with it, can no longer restrict their practice and theory to the winning of political power from the bourgeoisie. The assumption used to be that the overthrow of the capitalist state and the transfer of capitalist property to social ownership would guarantee the transition to a socialist order. Today, however, we have to recognise that it has become an inescapable necessity for the working-class, and the socialist movement, to defend, preserve, protect and nurture *now*, in existing conditions, the natural and cultural conditions of the future positive 'social metabolism' that is the true objective of the proletarian revolution. No socialist movement that ignores the responsibility of this defence and protection is now worthy of the name. If we in the 21st century are to take seriously Marx's and Engels' description of the communists as the most far-seeing section of the working class, that section most conscious of the necessary line of march, this must be our focus. The fact that, under the continued rule of capital, the *destructiveness* of capital's self-reproduction now predominates gives new and heightened significance to the concept that the working class in *its* revolution represents no particular, exclusive interest of its own, but the interests of all humanity.[1]

I deliberately refer to the *refoundation* of working-class, socialist internationalism, rather than use a term such as 'reconstruction'. The organisational and political forms previously taken by working-class internationalism necessarily rested upon the stages then reached by the capital system, by the condition of the working class, and by the development of the working-class movement in each country. To conceive of the present tasks in terms of 'reconstruction' of those forms would be profoundly mistaken.[2] It is indeed necessary to build the movement on the new foundations that now exist. The globalisation of capital, drawing the whole of the world's population into its orbit, achieves in a perverted and destructive way the basis for that 'universal intercourse' necessary for socialism. At the same time, it brings about the subjection of billions of men and women – and children – to wage-slavery. Thus the polarisation of society into two classes – proletarians on the one hand and the 'personifications of capital' on the other – is being completed on a world scale. This takes place, however, under conditions in which there are increased inequalities, and even conflicts of immediate interest, between the impoverished masses of Asia, Africa and Latin America and the better-off workers in the powerful capitalist countries. It is through overcoming in practice these and other attendant contradictions that the necessary 're-foundation' will be achieved.

Anti-capitalism and Marx

This leads immediately to a question for all those taking part in the recent massive demonstrations against the institutions of global capital. What does it mean to be anti-capitalist? Even at the risk of losing the attention of some of the new generations of activists straight away, it is necessary to insist that the starting-points for an answer (not of course the answer itself) are to be found in the writings of Karl Marx. In the 1850s, Marx was making notes for what was to become *Capital*. They are today published as *Grundrisse* – a book of over 800 pages. What follows here is written around some key extracts, passages that are very accessibly presented and explained in Chapter 28 of Roman Rosdolsky's *The Making of Marx's* Capital.[3] Marx wrote:

> The private exchange of all products of labour, all activities and all wealth [as under the rule of capital – CS] stands in antithesis to ... free exchange among individuals who are associated on the basis of common appropriation and control of the means of production. (The latter form of association [socialism/communism – CS] is not arbitrary; it presupposes the development of material and cultural conditions which are not to be examined further at this point.)[4]

So far, so good. This amounts to a summary of the well-known Marxist idea that socialism is not a utopia but requires objective conditions, which develop under capitalism. But does this suffice for our concerns today?

In addition to 'universal intercourse' in the form of the world market, Marx saw modern industry based on the use of machines as the foundation of the necessary 'material conditions'. The capitalists turned to machine industry in search of an increase in the rate of exploitation through reduction of necessary labour-time. This drive for 'relative surplus value' (as against absolute surplus value through increase of the labourer's hours) takes away from the worker any autonomy in the labour-process, so that he or she becomes at best a mere supervisor of the machine, and at worst its appendage, and always deprived of any part in the conception or planning of the work as a whole. But hidden behind this degradation is the potential for a higher form of production and culture. The labourer's job, instead of being an individual task, which is linked to others' work in a production process alien to him and commanded by others, and linked to the total social production only *ex post facto*, through the market, has become part of the application of society's accumulated science and technique. So long as capital rules, this accumulated knowledge and its application confronts the workers as an alien force. In capitalist production, machinery is a form of capital: 'Objectified labour (capital) confronts labour as a ruling power.'[5] Dead labour (capital) rules over living labour. However, as Rosdolsky summarises Marx's conclusion:

> The result of this is that the development of machinery offers, in fact, the surest prospect for their future liberation, by facilitating that radical reduction of working time, without which the abolition of class society would remain mere words.

Marx's own words are worth quoting at length, since they address the question we are concerned with. Are there objective conditions (contradictions) which are, so to speak, 'anti-capitalist'?

> Capital ... calls to life all the powers of science and of nature, as of social combination and of social intercourse in order to make the creation of wealth independent (relatively) of the labour-time employed on it. On the other side, it wants to use labour-time as the measuring rod for the giant forces thereby created, and to confine them within the limits required to maintain the already created value

> as value. *Forces of production and social relations – two different sides of the social individual – appear to capital as mere means, and are merely means for it to produce on its limited foundation. In fact, however, they are the material conditions to blow this foundation sky-high.* [6] [Emphasis added]

But again we must ask: does this suffice for our concerns today? How do the 'material and cultural conditions' develop *now*? Have we not reached a point where their development is being severely damaged and mortally threatened even as they continue to develop? And does not this imply that now the 'development' of the material and cultural conditions necessary for socialism is more than a purely objective consequence of capitalist production and reproduction, and requires revolutionary-practical activity?

To put it another way. If the development of these conditions for overcoming the rule of capital is left to their objective maturation under that rule, then capital's destructive side more and more predominates, and will actually destroy the necessary conditions for its overcoming. These conditions, it follows, have to be actively defended, protected and developed by capital's 'structural antagonist', the working class, together with all those who – as *The Communist Manifesto* says – 'go over to it'.[7] And, to the working class and its socialist allies, we have today to add the countless millions of subsistence cultivators and super-exploited workers and poor peasants of Asia, Africa and Latin America impoverished by globalised capital.

Marx went on to say that capitalism cannot overcome its own contradictions: they are inherent in it. It is capital itself that must be overcome. He had earlier pointed to 'the mass of antithetical forms of the social unity, whose antithetical character can never be abolished through quiet metamorphosis'[8] It is necessary, if we are to understand how to work for this 'abolition', to *re-work* what Marx wrote – as in the following passage – about the preparation of the conditions for socialism through capitalist development.

> The general bond and all-round interdependence in production and consumption increase together with the independence and indifference of the consumers and producers to one another.... Their own exchange and their own production confront individuals as an

> *objective* relation which is *independent* of them. In the case of the *world market*, the *connection of the individual* with all, but at the same time also the *independence of this connection from the individual*, have developed to such a high level that the formation of the world market already at the same time contains the conditions for going beyond it. *Comparison* [prices etc. – CS] in place of real communality and generality.[9]

The key words, 'contains the conditions for going beyond it', allow Marx to go on:

> Individuals cannot gain mastery over their own social interconnections before they have created them. Individuals are still engaged in the creation of the conditions of their social life, and ... have not yet begun, on the basis of these conditions, to live it.[10]

The sense in which capitalism/the market/competition 'prepares' for socialism is a matter much more profound than just a development of productive forces – thought of as 'means of production'. Thus, in *Grundrisse*, Marx asks: 'Do we never find in antiquity an inquiry into which form of landed property etc. is the most productive, creates the greatest wealth?' He answers: 'Wealth does not appear as the aim of production.... The question is always which mode of property creates the best citizens.' Contrast the capitalist mode of production:

> Now, wealth is on one side a thing, realised in things, material products, which a human being confronts as subject; on the other side, as value, wealth is merely command over alien labour not with the aim of ruling [i.e., as in previous modes – CS], but with the aim of private consumption, etc. It appears in all forms in the shape of a thing, be it an object or be it a relation mediated through the object, which is external and accidental to the individual.[11]

However this does not mean that Marx is celebrating a more human relationship in ancient society, and he adds:

> Thus the old view, in which the human being appears as the aim of production, regardless of his limited national, religious, political character, seems to be very lofty when contrasted to the modern world, where production appears as the aim of mankind and wealth as the aim of production. In fact, however, when the limited bourgeois

> form is stripped away, what is wealth other than the universality of human needs, capacities, pleasures, productive forces etc., created through universal exchange? The full development of human mastery over the forces of nature, those of so-called nature as well as of humanity's own nature? The absolute working-out of his creative potentialities ...?

In the capitalist mode of production and in bourgeois economics, this wealth as human creativity is imprisoned:

> This complete working-out of the human content appears as a complete emptying-out, this universal objectification as total alienation, and the tearing-down of all limited, one-sided aims (appears as) sacrifice of the human end-in-itself to an entirely external end. This is why the childish world of antiquity appears on one side as loftier.

Here, then, Marx is saying a little more about the 'material and cultural conditions' necessary for socialism. He is stressing the fact that it is capital which develops universal intercourse in the form of the world market and that capital by its nature drives unremittingly to the production of wealth, thus creating the potential of all-round development of human individuals.

This 'universal development of the individuals' will be a 'real development as a constant overcoming of the barrier' to 'the general development of the forces of production' and 'universal intercourse', says Marx. This is the opposite of humanity's subjection to the rule of capital, where development depends on and is limited by the 'needs' of capital not of humanity. Only with this transformation (as has been argued above) will humans begin to 'live' their social life rather than only creating the conditions for it. In such a social order, based on, and consciously pursuing, this free development, man will achieve 'recognition of nature (equally present as practical power over nature) as his real body.' Clearly, Marx's argument is that such a true relation to the rest of nature depends upon the overcoming of capital's barrier to the development of humanity's forces of production and universal intercourse, and not, of course, on trying to somehow halt that development.

The barrier to a truly human relation with the rest of nature, then – like the barrier to a truly human relation between human beings – is not blindness or ruthlessness. It is the totality of the restrictions on humanity's development of, and mastery over, the conditions its own labour has created over generations. These restrictions are, precisely, the barrier formed by the capitalist mode of production or 'social-metabolic order', with its unalterable imperative of the accumulation of capital. By its nature uncontrollable, capital stands in stark contradiction to what today's reality requires. Control by society as a whole over the resources and processes of the planet has become a life-and-death matter – and this becomes patently obvious to ever-growing thousands of people each day. It has been well said that

> ... the positive outcome depends not on the recognition by intellectuals that the historical justification of the capital system is over, but on the material force of a conscious social agency capable of eradicating capital from the social metabolic process, superseding thereby the rule of 'alien wealth' over society. If that agency proves to be unequal to the task, there can be no hope for the socialist project. But then, there can be no hope for the survival of humanity either.[12]

Put this in another way. Defenders of the environment should not be 'anti-growth' etc. (and certainly should not be seeking for capitalism to somehow be tamed), but truly 'anti-capitalist', in the sense that capitalism must be *overcome*, not just protested against, harassed, reformed, domesticated. This is because the truly human relationship between humanity and nature is not only disrupted – and in danger of destruction – by capital. It has also become *possible* and *necessary* because of the fact that capital's rule did bring development of productive forces and world market (universal intercourse). The sign standing above our own times, with the unbearable tension of the present threat from capital, is that the life-or-death limits of the 'antithetical unity' described by Marx nearly a century and a half ago are now inexorably being articulated.

> International solidarity ... is not an ideological imperative addressed to politically alert groups of workers. ... It is the necessary response

> to the objective challenge posed by the global articulation and integration of capital that in the course of the twentieth century (and particularly in the last few decades) acquired a most effective transnational dimension against its workforce. At the same time, it is a response made not only necessary but also materially feasible by the selfsame material structures of capital's transnational articulation which – in the absence of international solidarity – can be easily and with great efficacy used against the workers.[13]

Recognition of this is the precondition for, and the spur to, effective action. Of course, this does not mean that we live in a constant state of potentially successful socialist revolution provided only that international solidarity is achieved. It is nothing new for the interests of capital to constitute a barrier to mankind's further development. Certainly we now face 'destructive self-reproduction' as capital's mode of existence, but for the conditions of capital's overthrow to come about, there must occur an economic-social-political crisis resulting from capital's no longer being able to ensure – economically or politically – the displacement of its contradictions. It is in such a general crisis, under today's 'globalised' conditions, that the working class will make the experiences necessary for success. Preparation for those experiences, in practice and in theory, is the historic responsibility facing the working-class movement and all socialists.

Capital's 'structural antagonist'

It is clear that protest is necessary and legitimate but it is not enough. Protesters should not mistake their protest, as they so often do, for 'resistance'. What, then, to do? A century and a half ago, Marx and Engels saw the newly formed proletariat as the agency of real change, the force for socialist revolution. What is the situation today?

This role of the proletariat as the agent of a qualitative change is determined by the very nature of the mode of production dominated by capital. Marx noted that 'social wealth [capital] confronts labour in more powerful portions as an alien and dominant power … [and] the monstrous objective power which social labour itself erected opposite itself as one of its moments belongs not to the worker, but to the personified conditions of production, i.e., to capital.'[14]

It is on the basis of this understanding that Marx provided the theoretical basis for seeing the working class as the *structural antagonist* of capital as a whole. The point is that the antagonism is indeed inherent in and structurally constitutive of the capital system. Capital depends absolutely on wage-labour. It is itself 'dead' labour. The working class depends absolutely on capital. They define each other. Thus, in contrast to all other opposition, resistance or protest against this or that aspect of the system, or even against the system itself, the proletariat is an opposing force of a fundamental kind, carrying with it the necessity of a revolutionised social order:

> at the root of capital's historical constitution as (usurped but effectively ruling) subject we find nothing but social labour's own alienated subjectivity and potentially conscious power of control over its self-activity.[15]

And today? The piling up of the 'monstrous' alien power of the objective conditions of labour in the form of capital *has now become global*. This is the only content of what is called 'globalisation'. Herein is contained the essence of the foundations upon which proletarian internationalism must be refounded. The structural antagonism between capital and labour, which is the source of the potential overcoming of capital, is now patently global. How will the working class of this globalised antagonism move towards realising that 'potentially conscious power of control over its self-activity'? I take what some will no doubt dismiss as the old-fashioned view that the rule of capital must and will be overcome by communism. And by communism I mean, not some imagined ideal society, but the necessary unity, freedom and equality of all human beings made possible and necessary by today's productivity of labour and the accumulation of wealth created by it.

So much was already said more than 150 years ago in *The Communist Manifesto*. For present purposes, the argument can be summarised as follows. The class of owners of capital, the bourgeoisie, born in the European feudal society of the Middle

Ages, came to rule on the basis of a form of exploitation which surpassed and overcame the feudal limits and came to political power in England, France and then other countries. Under the rule of capital, the division and conflict between classes became simplified and naked: the bourgeoisie, owners of capital, confronted the class of propertyless wage-workers upon whose labour capital was daily formed and expanded. Capital's mode of existence, its imperative, is to accumulate and expand. It rapidly created a world market, drawing all nations into relations with the capitalist system of exchange and production. It used its control of state power in the capitalist countries to ensure this expansion. Already in the middle of the nineteenth century, the mighty productive forces called into existence by capitalist industry came periodically into conflict with the restrictive limits imposed by capital's profit system, and this clash resulted in crises of over-production. The wage-labourers necessary to capitalist production were a growing class. As industry expanded and developed and became concentrated in large factories and towns, the organisation of workers to protect themselves against exploitation developed into 'an ever-expanding union', eventually having to engage in 'a national struggle between classes', a political struggle. The class struggle was intensified by the impoverishment inflicted on the workers by capital.

From this Marx and Engels concluded that the competition between workers (selling their labour-power as a commodity, and therefore competing with one another, as must all sellers of commodities) upon which capitalists depend, was undermined by the unity and concentration of workers in bigger and bigger units and their organised 'combination' These conditions as a whole necessitated revolution. 'The proletarians have nothing to lose but their chains. Working men of all countries unite!'

A century and a half after The Communist Manifesto.

Over 150 years later, do the conditions for this unity, for this socialist revolution, still exist? Capital and capitalists rule a small number of earlier industrialised countries: the countries of Western Europe, Japan and, most powerful by far, the US. These – Japan came latest historically – were the centres of a new mode of production that infinitely surpassed in power and efficiency all earlier ones. 'Mode of production' here means not only ways of transforming raw materials into useful products but also the 'mode of exploitation of workers'. Capitalism came into existence as a mode of production based on the exploitation of a propertyless class of wage-workers who must sell their labour-power in order to live. These workers organised themselves, combined against their employers, against exploitation.

Today, in the 21st century, large numbers of workers in these 'advanced' countries have a standard of living far higher than that of their forefathers. This standard of living does not mean that they are no longer wage-slaves, members of the working class. They are better-off wage-slaves in material terms. But the organised power they once had to challenge their exploitation, and even to threaten the overthrow of the rule of capital in each country, has been undermined by corrupted, bought-out, bureaucratic trade-union leaders and political parties (whether they are called Labour, Socialist, Social-Democrat or Communist). For most of the twentieth century – between, after, and even through, the two world wars – the ruling capitalist classes kept the 'social peace' within their base countries, and maintained their power, with the indispensable assistance of, and even at times governing through, these 'labour' and 'socialist' parties of the working class. There were also, of course, bloody intervals of fascist rule.

Above all, the capitalist rulers benefited from the international dominance of Stalinism in the working-class movement. *Without an understanding of this, it is impossible to comprehend the historical career of the capitalist system in the twentieth century.* It remains vitally important to stress this today if we are to grasp the significance of the fact that – with the death of Stalinism and the advance of capitalist 'globalisation' – we find ourselves in an entirely new period. At the core of my argument is the idea that it is the existence of this new period that demands new analysis, new initiatives, and new forms of struggle and of organisation.

The Stalinist bureaucracy in the Soviet Union, basing its practice on the reactionary utopia of 'socialism in a single country', made fatal errors which ensured the defeat of the German and

Chinese revolutions in 1921-3 and 1926-7, then Spain in the 1930s. In the ensuing situation of isolation, the bureaucracy sought – in its own narrow and privileged interests – to establish 'peaceful coexistence' with international capital. To this end it not only carried out bloody purges of the communist movement in the Soviet Union but also the suppression of the revolutionary working-class movement wherever it threatened capitalist power – notably Spain in 1936, and in Italy and France after the second world war. The brutal and bloody crushing of the Hungarian revolution in 1956, following Khrushchev's partial revelations in that year about Stalin's crimes, brought to its nadir the process of disillusionment in communism which the bureaucracy has inflicted on countless thousands of working-class fighters. Only Trotsky and his followers, in their attempt to construct the Fourth International, carried out the continuous struggle, often against brutal repression, to uphold the true heritage of communism as well as to expose and combat Stalinism. For this many of them, including Trotsky, paid with their lives.

Strictly speaking, Stalinism as a ruling, exploiting bureaucracy in the Soviet Union and Eastern Europe and a deadly destructive agency in the working-class movement internationally, no longer exists. But understanding the influence of Stalinist and Social-Democratic parties on working-class consciousness was, in any case, never, by itself, a sufficient basis for understanding capitalism's ability to survive the 'epoch of wars and revolutions' inaugurated by the 1917 Russian Revolution. Marxists have to be self-critical. Most of us failed to turn our attention to the economic, social and political changes – above all an unprecedented rate of expanded reproduction of capital – 'permitted' by each lease of life resulting from the many defeats and betrayals.

To envisage the problems of the re-foundation of the working-class movement today only in terms of the betrayals of Stalinism and 'crisis of working-class revolutionary leadership' would be myopic. The capitalism which has survived into our millennium, has, by reason of its 'globalisation', lost its earlier ability to displace or 'export' its contradictions geographically. But it has new ways of displacing them that have previously unknowable effects on working-class consciousness. These effects must, now that it is possible to do so, be understood and combatted; and new forms of organisation discovered and devised in the course of this process of clarification and struggle. This challenge, moreover, must be confronted in the context of the deadly threats to mankind's very existence, which follow from the overwhelming fact that, with 'globalisation', the capital system has entered its phase of 'destructive self-reproduction'.

The old parties of the working class (certainly, now, not in any sense working-class parties) are responsible in history not only for the erosion of working-class consciousness, but also for the hard times of millions upon millions of older and retired people, unemployed workers, single parents, young women and men deprived of any noble aspirations and often reduced to prostitution and/or drug addiction. And life is infinitely worse for the workers and peasants of the ex-colonial countries. All that is easily understood. But if we look at the work done by Marxists in the last three-quarters of a century on questions of the economy, the condition of the working class, ideology and class-consciousness, does it measure up, in research and analysis, to what Marx and Engels did to follow, and get to the essence of, the development of nineteenth-century capitalism? To ask the question is surely to answer it. New work was, and certainly is now, necessary. Precious beginnings have been made, notably by Mészáros. They must be developed – in practice and theory.

The capitalist powers, to be able to profit as they did from the aforementioned 'services' rendered to them by the old leaderships of the working class, needed the resources plundered from imperialist exploitation of hundreds of millions of people in their colonial possessions and dependencies. This history has shaped today's world of, on the one hand, great concentrations of capital, accumulating to undreamed-of amounts; and, on the other, of billions of people in Asia, Africa and Latin America who are reduced to below-subsistence and barbaric levels of existence, and to social and political breakdowns that kill millions. These men and women – and children – provide a labour force, working for next-to-nothing wages, producing masses of goods for sale in the 'advanced' countries at fabulous profits.

The workers in these 'advanced' countries – fewer and fewer of them engaged in material production – are separated in consciousness and in organisation from the multi-millioned masses exploited by the international companies and banks. And their own exploitation is masked by this separation and distinction. This system goes on, entirely without systemic control, in a way that not only plunders but also destroys natural and human resources, even to the point of threatening the very existence of humanity and of the planet. It goes by the name of 'globalisation'. But it should be added that it is a globalisation of exploitation. As Mészáros writes: 'We had to wait for the occupation and reproductive domination of every corner of the world by the major capitalist powers, leading to the conflagration of two world wars, before the destructive implications of capital's uncontrollability could be fully sized up in their massive materiality.'

The survival of this system has the function *only* of providing further accumulation for capital and preventing the peoples of the world from coming together to control their own labour and their own future. Such is the development of mankind's productive powers today, and such are the dangers of their use for uncontrolled exploitation and profit, that this unity of action and purpose is an elementary necessity.

Without oversimplification, the situation can be stated as follows. Billions of people in Asia, Africa and Latin America provide some millions of people in Western Europe, Japan and North America with millions of tons of goods made with brutally cheap labour. The poverty of these billions is extreme, their expectation of life inhumanly low. Besides these goods, they provide 'services'. These include tourism; and the domestic and other cheap labour of men and women forced to emigrate to Europe and North America. The forefathers of such people, moreover, in the past 'supplied' untold mineral wealth and slave labour without which European and US capital could not have accumulated the basis of its power and wealth of today.

In these poor countries there exists a minority of very rich people who share class membership with the very rich in the 'advanced' countries. In the advanced countries, there are 'receipts' benefiting the population from exploitation of the 'Third World', but in extremely unequal proportions. The rich acquire ever-greater 'super-riches' and power: they become a true plutocracy. The workers and their families have gained materially, in the sense that their bosses have been rich enough, from global super-exploitation, to pay higher wages and benefits – though, today, with the onset of structural crisis, capital requires a clawing back of these past gains. The all-embracing 'market' is sustained by the massive production of waste, the best example of which is arms production, paid for, of course, by taxing incomes.

At the same time, in the 'advanced' countries, the sphere of consumption has a more and more contradictory character. Marx had already noted this contradictory character, and did not share the one-sided criticism of 'consumerism' made by many of today's Marxists. For him, while under capitalism the all-round, social interdependence of individuals took the form of a sphere external to and alienated from workers, nonetheless it was at the same time the basis of a 'personal independence' which could only be fully realised in communism. Then there will be, 'free individuality, based on the universal development of individuals and their subordination of their communal, social productivity as their social wealth.'[16] For this to be possible, the system of exchange and consumption created by the capitalist mode of production are necessary: '... the discovery, creation and satisfaction of new needs arising from society itself; the cultivation of all the qualities of the social human being, production of the same in a form as rich as possible in needs, because rich in qualities and relations – production of this being as the most total and universal social product, for, in order to take gratification in a many-sided way, he must be capable of many pleasures (*genüssfähig*), hence cultured to a high degree – is likewise a condition of production founded on capital.'[17]

Here again it is easy to see how the destructive side of the present phase of the mode of self-reproduction of capital manifests itself and predominates in exchange and consumption. Sophisticated and degrading methods are used to take back from the workers the money they earn. There is an endless round of creation of artificial, transient needs – giving rise to the purchase of goods that are less and less durable, and lack any intrinsic value.[18] An old chestnut has it that the Roman 'mob' was kept harmless with 'bread and circuses'. It was not true of Rome,[19] but, *mutatis mutandis*, it *is* in the 'advanced' capitalist countries today. Capital creates ever-changing 'needs' for feverishly consumed goods and for so-called 'services' – the 'circuses' of degrading media rubbish, the cult of 'celebrity', and so on. And this brings new problems for working-class consciousness, real obstacles to the recognition and assertion by the working class of its revolutionary nature – without which, Marx said, the class is 'nothing'.

Two centuries ago, the Revd. T R Malthus insisted on a working class kept 'on the edge of subsistence'. Whether they know it or not, the good parson's prescriptions are followed today by our 'monetarist' political economists. The millions in Africa and Asia employed at starvation wages by multinationals to ensure the production of luxury goods for consumption in the 'advanced' countries are the sufferers. But Malthus also insisted on the need to maintain high market demand. Today, this means that capital requires a working class that will demand and consume goods produced, in effect, as waste. This, however, should not obscure the impoverishment and degradation of millions, many of them even in the 'advanced' countries. In this present stage of the historical or *structural* crisis of the capital system, its basic contradiction is at a new, intensified level.

> The undisturbed functioning of the genuinely productive constituents becomes ever more dependent on the maintenance and further growth of the *parasitic* sectors – on which increasing numbers of people depend for their livelihood, while others depend on the latter as consumers of their products – thereby paradoxically adding to the contradictions of the overall complex also when offering remedies to its more or less openly acknowledged dysfunctions.
>
> This is where the intrinsic limitations of the capitalist orienting principles of production come to the fore. The deepening crisis of the established system cannot be resolved in terms of simply expanding the 'production of wealth', since within its framework 'wealth' is equated with *surplus-value*, and not with the production of *use-value* by

> means of the creative application of *disposable time.* At the same time the liberating potential of *increased productivity* is dissipated and nullified through the cancerously growing 'false costs' of control in the service of the exploitative dimension.[20]

The workers in the advanced capitalist countries are exploited by their employers – by capital and its 'personifications' – but their exploitation has been and is obscured by the global divisions and benefits from the super-exploitation of the peoples of Asia, Africa and Latin America. This concealment, and the separation between members of the *same class* globally, is what has to be overcome, overcome *practically*, if socialist internationalism is to be re-founded.

What specific combinations of circumstances, particular manifestations of the structural crisis of capital, will favour this overcoming cannot be known in advance. We know only that the structural crisis must produce economic, social and political breakdowns (witness the 2001 situation in Argentina), wars, national crises, and so on. In the struggles forced upon the working class by these events (and by the end of effective reformism in the 'advanced' countries) new relations within the class will be formed, at national and international levels. The great question to be addressed, in practice and in theory, is this. Through our experiences in these struggles, and the forms of organisation we evolve, will we – the working class – learn to do more than resist attack, and to go beyond each particular issue to strengthen ourselves as a class? Will we also be able to discover and carry through the practical means not only to oppose, but also to overcome and replace the rule of capital and its 'destructive self-reproduction'[21] by the necessary control of social production by the producers themselves? Will we be able, that is to say, to make the necessary movement towards communism?

Towards Communism

Communism is the name for that social-metabolic order and culture which must be attained if humanity is to survive the mortal dangers consequent on the continued rule of capital. It will be 'an association', as *The Communist Manifesto* put it, in which 'the free development of each is the condition for the free development of all.' The overcoming of capital's rule, the socialist revolution, let us repeat, does not mean the replacement of one form of exploitation by another, as was the case with all earlier revolutions. Instead, it marks the end of all class society.

In the social order ruled by capital, the mass of humanity is deprived of any independent means of production and compelled to sell itself to the owners of capital. That capital is nothing other than the result of past labour, stored-up labour. Thus, dead labour rules over the living. Capital's rule constitutes an external force, or 'second nature', constraining living humanity. The history of humanity is, on the one hand, that of progress through manual and mental labour towards an understanding of nature, enjoyment of its gifts, and freedom from its hostility and dangers – and the capitalist mode of production led to an unprecedented advance in this respect. The 'second nature' of man's alienation under the rule of capital, on the other hand, cuts off living labour from nature, and bars the way to the potential freedom which human labour has made possible.[22] Only the overcoming of the social-metabolic order of the capital system will create a truly human exchange between human beings and the rest of nature, because it must put an end not only to that system but to exploitation and class society as such. Mészáros summarises the issue as follows. It is a matter of:

> how to reconstitute, at a level fully consonant with the historically achieved productive development of society, the necessary unity of the working subjects with the attainable objective conditions of their meaningful life-activity.[24]

Such 'meaningful life-activity' is not possible for the men and women of today who are inescapably determined in their activity by exchange-value and the command structure of capital. The attainment of self-governed and free activity consonant with the great possibilities – opened up by universal exchange (the exchange of human activities and produced use-values, not the dominance of exchange-value) and highly developed productive forces – will of course be possible only when individuals have free and equal access to the heritage of human culture, enabling them to constantly create and to profit from that 'universal exchange'. The longer the life of the capital system in its period of structural crisis is prolonged, the more such a possibility is endangered. The fight, *here and now*, to defend and advance cultural values against capital's destructiveness is not some liberal-humanist diversion, but part of the one worthwhile struggle, to put an end to the capital system.

Clearly, this historical imperative goes beyond the revolutionary conquest of state power by the working class. And here we face ever more complex and difficult problems. Marx showed that communism was no utopia but a condition prepared and necessitated by capitalism's own inexorable drive for accumulation, which brings with it highly developed productive forces and the world market. Without these productive forces and 'universal intercourse' there could be no communism. In our own 21st century, however, it would be fatal not to take into account the fact that the continued imprisonment of these productive forces by capital has already resulted in their becoming destructive on a massive scale. The self-reproduction of capital, its unending and overriding quest for accumulation, has become a 'destructive self-reproduction' (as Mészáros puts it). Communists have already had to learn – especially after the Soviet experience – the bitter lesson that, as we have already stressed, the overthrow of capitalist state power, plus nationalisation of the means of production, is not enough to bring socialism. And this is not simply a matter of the impossibility of 'socialism in a single country'. Beyond state power and changed property relations, there is the long struggle to transform qualitatively the relationship between labour and capital's hierarchical domination and control, so that 'living labour' truly controls production.[25]

This 'long struggle' means putting to an end the division of labour imposed by the rule of capital. And 'imposed' is the right word, for two reasons. First, because the division of labour under the rule of capital is authoritarian, necessitating a hierarchy of command standing over the producers. And second, because the relation between the producers of the various commodities is materialised only after the fact, and from outside. It stands over them, in the market, where these commodities are exchanged. In place of this alienated 'second nature', this division of labour, which distorts the necessary relation between the social producers and nature and is beyond their control, must be created by a conscious, rational and free (i.e., self-determined) organisation of the work of those producers.[26] As Mészáros writes:

> The social character of labour will manifest itself directly, without the alienating mediation of the division of labour As things stand, however, division of labour makes the conditions and powers of life become independent of man and rule over him.[27]

The same point was made by Harry Braverman, who showed graphically the inhumanity of the detailed division of labour in capitalist manufacture – a division of labour super-added to the overall 'social division of labour' into skills, tasks and branches of production. There is a breaking-down of the skills and tasks themselves in factory production, above all by the introduction of machinery. The inhuman subordination to the machine (itself, of course, stored-up labour) is not difficult to contrast to the future society, in which this division of labour will be overcome by an association of producers, sharing the application and development of science and technique and creating free time for themselves. Braverman quoted to great effect, from John Ruskin's *The Stones of Venice* (1851-3):

> We have much studied and perfected, of late, the great civilised invention of the division of labour; only we give it a false name. It is not, truly speaking, the labour that is divided; but the men: divided into mere segments of men – broken into small fragments and crumbs of life; so that all the little piece of intelligence that is left in a man is not enough to make a pin, or a nail, but exhausts itself in making the point of a pin, or the head of a nail. Now it is a good and desirable thing, truly, to make many pins in a day; but if we could only see with what crystal sands their points were polished – sand of human soul, much to be magnified before it can be discerned for what it is – we should think there might be some loss in it also. And the great cry that rises from all our manufacturing cities, louder than the furnace blast, is all in very deed for this – that we manufacture everything there except men...[28]

Braverman's classic work is concerned above all with the labour process itself, in which human work is degraded. Since its publication, the degradation has developed apace, with short-term contracts, casualisation and insecurity especially marked. In the spheres dependent on the most technologically advanced equipment (Information Technology, IT) such as call-centres, workers are subjected to the most monotonous and soul-destroying routines. But Braverman had already also noted that the *social* division of labour in capitalist society is achieved only through its being 'enforced chaotically and destructively by the markets'.

The whole argument about the division of labour deserves to be re-emphasised. Through this process the workers of the whole world are subjected not only to the iron control of employers and managers over their everyday lives at work, but also to an international division of their labour, which is outside of any human will or control in the proper sense. It is a division imposed by market relations between their products, between things (it is *reified*), not at all by the effort and will of the producers. Together with its uncontrolled consequences, it imposes itself, and is reproduced as the condition of their lives, only 'after the fact' – after the product of their essential human activity, labour, has been completely alienated from them. Sociologists and economists, including many commentators on Marx, have great difficulty in understanding the difference between the social and the technical divisions of labour. They appear to be totally blind to this *particular*, capitalist mode of the social division of labour. They are even more myopic, ideologically blinded, regarding the obvious hierarchical and authoritarian division of labour under capital's rule. This hierarchical division stands in the starkest contrast to the fundamental equality that would have to characterise a socialist self-organisation of labour by free men and women. But it is absolutely essential to capital, because the exploitative, profit-rendering function of labour must at all costs predominate over all consideration of human need.

Thus we are living at an historical stage where productivity has reached previously unimaginable levels, through which it clearly is possible to begin to meet the desperate needs of the billions of impoverished and oppressed people in the world. At the same time, this high productivity is the basis for creating that *free time* which is the precondition of the future all-round development of truly free individuals. This would require a greater and greater concentration (now of course technically entirely possible) on durable and re-usable goods. But the barrier is the existing social-metabolic order. The needs of capital ensure that instead of that free time becoming available for the truly human development of individuals, the enormous increase in productivity can only result in mass unemployment on the one hand and waste-production on a massive scale on the other. There is a greater and greater concentration on quickly consumed and throwaway commodities, with the accompanying sheer waste of human and natural resources in advertising, in 'image-creation' and in satisfying ever-new artificial 'needs'[29]. Inevitably, moreover, along with this goes a corruption of human personality and culture, as people's tastes and perceived needs are more and more distanced from humankind's cultural heritage. The defence and celebration of that heritage, however difficult, is a present and pressing task, and not something that will wait for the socialist future. Those who undertake that task are an indispensable part of the struggle for the social revolution.

Behind this now overweening tendency lies the contradiction noted long ago by Marx: capital is concerned *only* with 'the excess time of the labourers'.

> The absolute spare time gained by society does not concern it. The development of productivity concerns it only insofar as it increases the surplus labour-time of the working class, not because it decreases the labour-time for material production. It moves thus in a contradiction.[30]

This has been very clearly explained by Alain Bihr, who notes Marx's 'prophetic' remarks, to which we have already in part referred, in the *Grundrisse*:

> Capital itself is the moving contradiction, in that it presses to reduce labour time to a minimum, while it posits labour time, on the other hand, as the sole measure and source of wealth. ... On the one side,

> then, it calls to life all the powers of science and of nature, as of social combination and of social intercourse, in order to make the creation of wealth independent (relatively) of the labour time employed on it. On the other side, then, it wants to use labour time as the measuring rod for the giant social forces thereby created, and to confine them within the limits required to maintain the already created value as value.[31]

It follows, comments Bihr, that this moving contradiction makes it more and more evident that true social wealth is

> not value but use value (material abundance), and that the true measure of this wealth is not the labour time socially necessary for its production (as in capitalism) but on the contrary *the reduction of necessary labour time*, the liberation of man with regard to labour, the development of free time: of time liberated from natural necessity and from the social compulsion of labour. Thus, here in outline, very concretely, is at the same time the possibility of the end of labour: of a substantial reduction of working time, which becomes no more than a secondary and auxiliary activity in every person's life; and above all the possibility of organising social production no longer in order to serve the abstract necessity of valorising capital, i.e. actually, to assure the growth of already dead, accumulated labour, but quite simply in order to meet the social needs according to how they are defined by the associated producers themselves once masters of their means of production.[32]

From this analysis a new consideration follows. The *destructive* consequences on the global scale of the perpetuation of capital's rule must surely be confronted even *before* the conquest of power. That is to say, the working-class and socialist movement must take responsibility now for defending and protecting the natural and human conditions and resources of the future positive social metabolic order. Indeed, in today's conditions of globalised capital, with its uncontrolled plunder of natural resources and impoverishment of countless millions in Asia, Africa and Latin America, such defence and protection is an absolute precondition of the necessary unification of all the human forces exploited by and opposed to capital.

A point must be re-emphasised here. The structural crisis the capital system enters with the globalisation of capital is not only 'economic', but seizes the whole of politics, culture and morality.[33] Catastrophes such as the 'ethnic cleansing' in ex-Yugoslavia, the 11 September 2001 attacks on the eastern United States, and their aftermath in the 'war on terror', force us to realise that the socialist revolution will inherit more than the 'economic' consequences of capitalism's destructiveness. And here too it must be the responsibility of the working-class movement to begin to tackle these problems before, and in the course of, the struggle for power; and not only after it. For example, 'globalisation' and its disastrous consequences in the poorer countries have forced the emigration of millions of workers and their families who hold to the Muslim faith. It is surely now clearly necessary, in the working-class movement in every 'advanced' country, to combat every vestige of racism and discrimination, to create the conditions of class solidarity, to put an end to the conditions in which reactionary forces like Islamic fundamentalism flourish.

Here we arrive at the question underlying all others. In a world that has undergone so much change since Marx's day, what can be the concrete meaning of his and Engels' assertion that the workers 'have nothing to lose but their chains, they have a world to win', and of the clarion call: 'Workers of all lands unite!'?

It has been well said that the most explosive contradiction in capitalism is that between its imperative need for an expanding market on the one hand and its need to reduce the condition of living labour on the other. How, then, can a market be assured for the realisation of the invested capital? It is here that the contradiction between capitalist relations of production and the vast increase in productivity of labour manifests itself. From this comes the need for the extraction of absolute surplus value in the 'Third World', for massive military spending and, as pointed out above, for other waste production and the manipulation of consumer demand. All this is now essential to the capital system as it seeks to displace the contradiction between productive forces/ enhanced productivity on the one hand, and, on the other, outmoded social relations of production. Humankind pays the cost in wars, environmental destruction and cultural degradation.

Some conclusions

Always having been essentially dependent on the monopoly of private property enabling it to appropriate the value created by living labour (the dispossessed working class), the capital system in the past went through centuries of bitter class struggles, crises and slumps, inter-imperialist rivalries and world wars, and even revolutions. It faced, many times, massive dysfunctions and the threat of imminent collapse. Yet capital survives, and, in the first years of our new millennium, it relies on certain fundamental processes to maintain and continually reproduce itself.

My first point is that a majority of the world's people, impoverished and oppressed, is super-exploited by the sheer imposition of long and arduous labour at below-subsistence pay (the extraction of absolute surplus value on a massive scale). That this can happen is the legacy of the earlier phases of capitalism: colonial conquest and plunder, and then the 'imperialism' which marked the end of the nineteenth century and most of the twentieth – with its export of capital and division of the world between the great powers. That imperialism made possible a relative stability in the class relations. It calmed the class struggle in the advanced capitalist countries, not only through the capacity for concessions to the working class and a degree of political democracy, but also through the corruption and 'incorporation' of social-democratic, reformist political and trade-union representatives of the working class.

The second point is this. The vast increase in the productivity of labour (especially through IT) and the universality of exchange are precisely what is necessary for (and even *require*) the release of free time for the cultural development of individuals, on which a communist society will rest. Such a society means a social and reproductive process in which the self-determined needs of the 'associated producers' as free and self-governing individuals and communities are the driving force and the *raison d'être*. Historically it is the productive forces developed in the capital system that have opened up that possibility. But capital initiates and controls production *only* for the accumulation of exchange-value (the accumulation and self-expansion of capital itself). This exactly negates the potential of freedom, not only because profit (appropriated new value created by labour and stolen from it) entirely subordinates need and use-value; but also because capital (and its monopoly of private property in the means of production) is *dead labour* – a store of value created in the past by living labour. Dead labour rules over living labour, the living working class and its life-activity.

In this overwhelmingly important sense, the capital system as a mode of production stands in deadly contradiction to the forces of production, which its own imperatives have engendered; and which, by its very nature, it must continue to develop in the sense that science and technique must be harnessed to the pursuit of profit. Capital deals with today's unprecedented increase in the productivity of labour, unimaginable even by its own past standards, in such a way as to benefit from it (to profit from it) *only* by rendering it *destructive*, by actually becoming now a destructive system. It produces destruction (Mészáros writes of the 'destructive self-reproduction of capital'). Instead of the increased productivity of labour being the basis for satisfaction of every kind of need and for creative use of what could be the consequent free time to fashion new material and cultural needs, capital can seek only *profit* from this increase in productivity. The mass of workers by hand and brain, as we have seen, cannot under capital be the inspirers, the controllers, the 'subjects' of their labour: 'They are acknowledged as legitimately existing subjects only as the *manipulated consumers* of commodities.'[34]

Capital finds it possible, and necessary, to pay above-subsistence wages to a select section of the workers in the advanced capitalist countries. They form a market for the commodities produced. This happens notwithstanding the fact that the polarisation of income and living standards, both internationally and within the main capitalist countries, increases. Millions live in poverty and deprivation – one major cause being that essential services, like health, education, public transport and housing, are being savagely cut for all but the well-off because they cannot be made profitable. In 'the market', capital must find new ways of taking back from its workers what they have been paid. It devotes ever-increasing resources to the mad world of 'consumerism'.[35] It goes without saying that the same great trans-national companies are the exploiters of both the impoverished workers in the 'underdeveloped countries' and the manipulated, better-paid worker/consumers of the 'advanced' nations.

My third point is actually part of the second, but is of such importance and has such profound implications that it must have a place of its own. In the nature of capital and its imperatives, goods immediately used and goods used over a period, goods that perpetuate life (medicines, food) and goods that kill (tobacco, addictive drugs), are all the same. They are equal before the market. Their value in exchange predominates completely over their use. They contain value, and are produced, not to be used or to feed or to kill but to render profit, to 'realise' the value put into them by labour, to accumulate capital.

At the extreme – and this not an abstract, logical extreme but a very real and deadly one, standing over our lives – is the fact that so long as goods can render a profit, it is of no account so far as capital is concerned if they are *never used at all*; or if their use is *equivalent to their destruction.* This is in fact the case with that sphere of production that has become absolutely necessary to capital today, namely, arms production and the equipping of armed forces, what an American President christened the 'military-industrial complex'.[36] It takes up a vast proportion of a nation's productive capacity in terms of labour and material resources. It does not even require the existence or creation of a market of millions of individual consumers. Payment is conveniently guaranteed through state budgets and levied on the citizenry, subjected to a political manipulation no less cynical than the commercial manipulation already referred to. The fact that its 'use' is to be scrapped and replaced by something more 'up-to-date', to kill human beings and to reinforce militarily capital's control over recalcitrant peoples is of no account. The threat to humanity of this method of perpetuating the life of the capital system is crystal-clear. The predominance of exchange-value over use-value, production for profit over production for need, finds here its supreme exemplification.

These are the ways in which the capital system is able to prolong its life once it has become redundant, having entered its structural crisis. From the standpoint of capital, the only concern of which is profit, these things are necessary for survival, a veritable blessing. From the standpoint of labour (the working class) of the whole world, from the standpoint of production for need and the freedom potentially inherent in today's productive forces, and, indeed, from the standpoint of humanity and culture, of our future, they are a curse. They are the immediate manifestation of the need, in the name of humanity, for the overthrow of the rule of capital; and for the development of the practical and theoretical instruments through which the working class – our class – can defend the conditions which make possible a new 'truly human' social-metabolic order. Without such a starting-point there can be no contemporary answer to the key question for socialist internationalism, which is: 'Where to begin?'

---

[1] 'It would stand to reason that when the destructive dissipation of natural resources and social wealth becomes the objective condition of capital's expanded reproduction, the continued "rule of wealth over society" can no longer make sense from the standpoint of sustainable societal reproduction.' Mészáros, *Beyond Capital*, p. 810.

[2] Along with others I have written previously of 'reconstruction': see especially my *A New Party for Socialism* (London, 1996). The understanding gained from István Mészáros' work, especially *Beyond Capital*, points unerringly to the need for re-foundation. In this matter, as in all of my present work, readers will see that I, like others, am indebted to Mészáros.

[3] Roman Rosdolsky, *The Making of Marx's Capital* (London, 1973; recently reprinted in a two-volume edition.)

[4] Marx, *Grundrisse*, p.159.

[5] Marx, *Grundrisse*, p. 693.

[6] Marx, *Grundrisse*, p. 706.

[7] 'Finally, in times when the class struggle nears the decisive hour ... a small section of the bourgeoisie goes over to the proletariat, and in particular, a portion of the bourgeois ideologists, who have raised themselves to the level of comprehending theoretically the historical movement as a whole.'

[8] Marx, *Grundrisse*, p. 159.

[9] Marx, *Grundrisse*, p. 161.

[10] Marx, *Grundrisse*, pp. 161-2.

[11] Marx, *Grundrisse*, p. 487.

[12] Mészáros, *Beyond Capital*, p. 811.

[13] Mészáros, *The Power of Ideology* (Hemel Hempstead, 1989), p. 376.

[14] Marx, *Grundrisse*, p. 831.

[15] Mészáros, *Beyond Capital*, p. 620

[16] Marx, *Grundrisse*, p. 158

[17] Marx, *Grundrisse*, p. 409

[18] Mészáros, *Beyond Capital*, chaps. 15 and 16.

[19] Geoffrey de Sainte Croix, *The Class Struggle in the Ancient Greek World: from the Archaic Age to the Arab conquests* (London, 1981), pp. 371-2, shows that very few people were entitled to dispensations of bread and even fewer ever got to see the circus.

[20] Mészáros, *Beyond Capital*, pp. 534-5.

[21] Mészáros, *Beyond Capital*, passim.

[22] 'It is not the unity of living and active humanity with the natural, inorganic conditions of their metabolic exchange with nature, and hence their appropriation of nature, which requires explanation or is the result of a historic process, but rather the separation between these inorganic conditions of human existence and this active existence, a separation which is completely posited only in the relation of wage labour and capital.' Marx, *Grundrisse*, p. 489.

[23] Karl Marx, *Capital*, vol. III, chap. 46.

[24] Mészáros, *Beyond Capital*, p. 349.

[25] '[T]he fact of being tied by a more perfected network of structural determinations to the reproductive and distributive practices of "advanced capitalism" represents a rather dubious asset.' Mészáros, *Beyond Capital*, p. 492.

[26] Here the path-breaking work of Harry Braverman, *Labour and Monopoly Capital* (New York and London, 1974), is indispensable.

[27] Mészáros, *Marx's Theory of Alienation* (London, 1970), pp. 142-3. This point is often, indeed almost always, missed by commentators on Marx's views on division of labour. They cite Marx's remarks about humans in a communist society not being restricted to a particular skill or occupation. ('[I]n communist society, where nobody has one exclusive activity but each can become accomplished in any branch he wishes, society regulates the general production and this makes it possible for me to do one thing today and another tomorrow, to hunt in the morning, fish in the afternoon, rear cattle in the evening, criticise after dinner, just as I have a mind, without ever becoming hunter, fisherman, shepherd or critic.') This freeing of human creativity is a consequence of the availability of free time, and the overcoming of the value relation, made possible by a high degree of development of the productive forces. But to concentrate only on this – of course fundamental – aspect is to ignore the equally fundamental one stressed here: namely, that the overcoming of the value relation and of the imperative of capital accumulation permits a self-organisation of social production instead of a relation of division of social labour imposed after the fact, as a reified relation between things, in the market.

[28] From John Ruskin, *The Stones of Venice* (first published, London, 1851-3), as quoted in Braverman, *Labour and Monopoly Capital*, pp. 78-9.

[29] A typical advertisement in Britain recently has been based on the slogan, 'Are you ashamed of your mobile phone?' – encouraging the disposal of perfectly serviceable devices purely in the name of fashion. Advertising in its early days was different. In Walter Benjamin's Arcades Project, two nice examples are noted. First: 'Handbill of a Parisian textiles dealer from the 1830s: 'Ladies and Gentlemen: I ask you to cast an indulgent eye on the following observations; my desire to contribute to your eternal salvation impels me to address you. Allow me to direct your attention to the Holy Scriptures, as well as to the extremely moderate prices which I have been the first to introduce into the field of hosiery, cotton goods, and related products.' And second, for Fanta Beer in 1866: 'Yes, long live the beer of Vienna! Is it native to this land that produces it? In truth, I do not know. But of one thing, there can be no doubt: it is a refined and comforting brew. It is not like the beer of Strasbourg or Bavaria... It is divine beer, clear as the thought of a poet, light as a swallow in flight, robust and alcohol-charged as the pen of a German philosopher. It is digested like the purest water; and it refreshes like ambrosia.'

[30] Marx, *Capital*, vol. III, pp. 257-8

[31] Marx, *Grundrisse*, p. 706.

[32] Alain Bihr, 'Actualiser le communisme', in *Carré Rouge*, no. 18 (summer 2001). My translation.

[33] See Chap. 5.

[34] Mészáros, *Beyond Capital*, p. 527.

[35] This can of course have its comic side. A recent newspaper report revealed that a 'Dutch judge found that the razors of Wilkinson and Gillette are equally the best, and both may claim in their advertisements to be the sharpest available. In the latest skirmish between the duelling blademakers, Gillette had asked a Utrecht court to halt Wilkinson's Dutch advertising campaign for one of its razors. Gillette said Wilkinson's ads falsely implied that the product was better than Gillette's competing one. Wilkinson countersued. The judge ruled that the commercials by both companies were within the boundaries of poetic licence (*sic*) granted to advertisers, and that most listeners would not believe them anyway.' *International Herald Tribune*, 23 April 2004.

[36] 'The great innovation of the military-industrial complex for capitalistic developments is to obliterate in a practically effective way the literally vital distinction between consumption and destruction.' Mészáros, *Beyond Capital*, p. 590.

5

THE PROLETARIAT UNDER GLOBALISED CAPITAL

The 'advanced' countries

This chapter addresses a central question: that of the proletariat as a class, now that capital is 'globalised'. It is a question that can only be understood by approaching it from a worldwide perspective. But, first, it is useful to note the changing picture as it appears in the 'advanced' capitalist countries. The much-vaunted, so-called 'British Marxist historian', Eric Hobsbawm is amongst those who have pictured the last few decades as a 'golden age', and a whole school of post-1950s sociology saw the period as one of working-class 'embourgeoisement'. To answer such uncritical critics, I cannot do better than quote John Lea's *Crime and Modernity*:

> [We can note] a number of features of capitalism in its phase of destructive reproduction. Socialisation and homogenisation are replaced by social polarisation and fragmentation. The welfare state and political compromise between social classes as stabilising mechanisms are replaced by the direct power of private property and market mechanisms. The state becomes both more authoritarian in its substitution of social policy for security and risk management, and weakened by the global power of private capital and the crippling of the political process. An important consequence of the latter becomes the weakening of the social or the public sphere of politics as a form of negotiation and compromise between social classes and other groups and as the terrain of policy formation and implementation. Public communication becomes increasingly a form of cynicism, obfuscation and contentless babble.[1]

And earlier in the same book:

> Capital is increasingly relinquishing a dependence on the traditional mass working class composed of 'Fordist' blue collar workers in high-wage stable jobs and a vast white collar salariat of 'organisation men'. The driving force for this change is the drive to retain the profitability of an increasing mass of capital. However, not only can profitability decreasingly afford a strong, stable, well-paid working class with which it has to compromise socially and politically but, more importantly, it decreasingly needs it. As a consequence it is losing interest in the modernist institutions of political compromise with these strata and with high levels of welfare and citizenship rights designed to secure their reproduction and to ameliorate class conflict.
>
> With redesigned labour processes emphasising cheap unskilled labour, capital is able to substitute global mobility in search of new sources of labour for investment in the socialisation and integration of the working class characteristic of the Keynesian period. Increased mobility of operations means that the most powerful corporations are able, on threat of moving elsewhere, to secure significant reductions in taxes destined for the welfare rights and education of such a workforce. The costs of socialisation and reproduction can be shifted back on to the working class itself in a process which increasingly equalises labour conditions in the Third World and advanced capitalist countries.
>
> The fastest growing sections of working-class jobs are now in low-wage, part-time and temporary employment, especially in services. ... At the very bottom of the social structure increasing numbers of people are virtually outside the legal labour market and concentrated in ghettos, inner cities and decaying older industrial areas, they function as labour supply for a growing informal and shadow economy of untaxed and criminalised activities. The share of total income (after housing costs) of the poorest tenth of the population fell from 4% in 1979 to 2% in 1991/2 while that of the richest tenth rose from 20.9 to 27% over the same period. In the US, percentage share of the poorest fifth in total aggregate household income fell from 4.3% to 1.2% over the same period (US Census Bureau 2000).[2]

It is interesting to compare Mike Davis's characterisation of the 1970s in the United States:

> The postwar virtuous circle of good jobs, rising incomes, cheap land and quality public services was beginning its slow disintegration into

> the present vicious circle of social polarisation, expensive land and declining public sector. [By 1970] the percentage of Southern Californian households with incomes at the minimum mortgage threshold fell from over half to barely a quarter.[3]

Earlier, in his *Prisoners of the American Dream*, Davis advanced as his 'central hypothesis' that 'the historical era defined by the equation of 'Americanism' with democratic capitalism – that is, by the expansion of bourgeois democracy and mass consumption under the aegis of the United States – is approaching its terminus'. Yes, and even the threadbare mask of a fight against communism in Vietnam had disappeared when the US government decided to export 'democracy' to Afghanistan and Iraq.

John Lea shows clearly how the conditions of expanded reproduction of capital in the decades following the second world war are undermined as the structural crisis gathers. Certainly capital has been able to profit both economically and politically from those conditions, and is still profiting. John Lea and István Mészáros have pointed unerringly to the structural obstacles to capital's being able to continue in the same way, and we have seen the massive proletarianisation consequent on 'globalisation'. But there are important 'other sides' to the apparent basis for the confidence of capital's spokesmen that they need no longer fear the working class being the 'gravediggers' of capital, as Marx called it.

These 'other sides' (see above, Chapters 1 and 4) are inevitable consequences – negative ones from capital's standpoint – of the socialisation of production brought about by capital's own imperative of accumulation. The totally unprecedented development of means of communication and social intercourse made possible by computerisation and the internet certainly facilitate exploitation of labour and manipulation of markets worldwide. But these are means of communication, means of access to information, increasingly available to ordinary working people and to intellectuals. Computers are sold in millions. In our age, when the threat of cultural and natural destruction posed by capital's uncontrollable mode of production and reproduction becomes more evident every day, protest, criticism, forms of resistance and methods of organisation are immediately exchangeable, nationally and internationally, between millions upon millions of individuals and groups. There are many and varied movements and manifestations of resistance to particular threats and dangers, expressions of outrage against abuse of human rights, ventures to find forms of self-organisation of communities.

How will all these, with their promise of a truly popular movement, be brought into a working relation with a renewed 'real movement', as Marx called it, of the proletariat? The answer will have to be learned in experience and in theoretical as well as practical struggles. What is certain is that the new means of communication will greatly facilitate this process. Only with the social revolution can humanity place itself in free, common and conscious control of the forces of production and communication developed under capitalism. But, here and now, the working class and those intellectuals who join it – of whom there will be more and more as they react to capital's threats – can, and will, align themselves with those forces, turning them against the inhuman social relations in which they are all imprisoned.

'This little corner'

Marx, in his time, posed the question: if there is a socialist revolution in Europe, with capital still ascendant in the rest of the world, 'will we not be crushed in this little corner?' Capital has continued in the 'ascendant': it is now truly global. Mészáros has shown how this 'globalisation' brings to their limit the means for displacement of contradictions by the capital system, thus creating at last the conditions for structural, as opposed to conjunctural, crisis. That is to say that, whereas previous, conjunctural crises were crises of the functioning of the capital system, from which – however serious their effects – readjustment and recovery were possible, it now becomes a question of the historical limits of the system as a whole. Its very structure is unable to cope with the accumulated contradictions.

Just as Marx always eschewed any speculation about the society and culture that would result from the social revolution, so he did not speculate about the forms that might be taken by the class struggle on the anticipated, but then not yet existing, global scale. Now is the time to engage with that problem. In what ways does the labouring class necessary to 'globalised' capital confront it and struggle against it as its structural antagonist?

There is a most difficult problem here, both theoretically and practically. Before the globalisation of the recent past and the present, the political and ideological forms of the class struggle between the capitalist class and the proletariat were concentrated in the nation state. That relative correspondence between the economic and the political structures is in the process of being undermined. That is to say: there is no political structure of control, or representation, which corresponds to the globalisation of capital. A vitally important consequence is that the space for reformist compromise, and the basis it provided for the forms of capitalist rule in the advanced capitalist countries throughout the last century, has disappeared. But there is more: where now is the arena in which the working class can conduct its struggle against the class enemy, as the scope for social advances, the gaining of democratic rights, and even class compromise, is ever narrower?

Capital is, yes, still located in nation states as well as operating and being constituted at the international level. Particular capitals and the capitalist class in each nation have at their service the state apparatus of that nation. And the working class can still *to a certain extent* seek expression and representation as a class in the framework of its nation-state. However, capital now has very different requirements, in the 'management' of the labour force from those it had in the past. In major capitalist countries like Britain, the ruling capitalist class throughout most of the twentieth century found it necessary and convenient to, as Trotsky put it, 'rule through' reformist, labour parties and trade union bureaucracies. We now have a very different, more and more fragmented working class, its trade unions emasculated by reactionary legislation and representing a decreasing proportion of workers – in Britain in 2005, only some 12 per cent. Capital finds that institutions of negotiation and reform are less necessary. Trade union officials concern themselves less with organising for defence and struggle against employers, and more with 'services' to their individual members. Zygmunt Bauman is harsh, but surely just, in his characterisation of the moral character of the ruling class in this breakdown of the old norms. There is, he says, a

> disconnection of power from obligations: duties towards employees, but also towards the younger and weaker, towards yet unborn generations and towards the self-reproduction of the living conditions of all; in short, freedom from the duty to contribute to daily life and the perpetuation of the community.[4]

There is thus a profound change in the approach of the capitalist class to its forms of rule. Along with the privatisation of publicly owned industries in Britain, for example, has gone the virtual replacement of a 'welfare state' with privatisation of services and attacks on universal rights and entitlements. All this is, clearly, part of the overall situation which we have already characterised as one in which a refounded working-class movement must at all costs take responsibility here and now for the defence – indeed the very preservation – of the elementary conditions of any human future.

One of the consequences of the rapid erosion of the existing institutions of class compromise is that when the capitalist state is confronted with opposition and insecurity, it must – and will necessarily – resort to more authoritarian forms of control. The preoccupation of politicians with 'law and order', policing, identity cards and 'national security' – not to mention the hysterical fear of what is called an 'underclass' – is the preparation and growth of this authoritarianism.

In considering the causes and consequences of the rolling back of state welfare provision and democratic rights, it is of prime importance to remember that the establishment of those rights was the product of generations of workers' organisation and struggle, forcing compromises on the employing class. The constriction of the political and legal sphere in which those struggles were conducted is even more significant — from the standpoint of understanding our present and future tasks — than the losses themselves. Capital and its 'personifications' now operate in the global economy that is simply not compatible with the political and legal 'space' in which the interests of the working class, or of the ordinary people at large, can be or need to be taken into account. Instead, the so-called 'neo-liberalism' of the last two or three decades – supposedly leaving the economy to the 'natural instinct of men to trade and barter' – actually requires only legal-administrative mechanisms set in motion and applied by appointed managers in offices, with any kind of representation of human interests totally excluded. The attempt to impose the so-called European Constitution provides a prime example.

All this is to say that the 'legitimacy' of the old forms of rule was supported by a degree of representation and the weight of popular consent, established through real – albeit limited – democratic and judicial channels. There is no necessity for such legitimation under military rule, or in a dictatorship or other form of authoritarian or despotic state. In the aftermath of 9/11 particularly there have already been definite tendencies in this direction in national/domestic political relations, as well as in the unilateral actions in the wider world of the US regime and its subservient allies in office in the UK. Neither, of course, are there any such processes of legitimation for the operations of global big business and the administrative/regulatory regimes being developed on its behalf (such as the 'European Constitution'), any more than there are for the World Bank and the International Monetary Fund (IMF). These processes need not, and do not, refer to any other constituency. And what is the philosophy, or rather the unreasoned and unreasoning ideology, on which this regime rests? It is the assumption ('there is no alternative', after all) that the market in all commodities, including labour-power, is a naturally functioning system of working parts, *things* – including the monstrously named 'human resources' – that are merely to be managed and administered by experts. They are not to be debated, negotiated and fought over by humans with human interests, needs and aspirations.

All these considerations lead to the conclusion that, in these new historical circumstances, working-class internationalism will be refounded only through struggles of a changing character; and through forms of organisation yet to be discovered in practice.

What is the proletariat?

The *Concise Oxford Dictionary* says of 'proletariat': '(Rom. Hist., often derog.) lowest class of community; (Pol. Econ.) indigent wage-earners, labouring classes.' And it defines 'proletarian' as: 'member of the proletariat (from Latin *proletarius*, one who served the state not with property but with offspring).'

As becomes apparent when we consider the widespread use of child labour by transnational companies in Africa and Asia, the above Latin definition is interesting. First, however, it is important to note fundamental aspects of wage-labour which today have more relevance than ever before. In his book *Karl Marx*, Korsch noted that

> between the value of the new commodities produced by the use of labour-power in the workshop, and the prices paid for this labour to its sellers, there is, according to Marx, no economic or other rationally determinable relation whatever.

But this is not strictly true. The relation between the value of labour power (to which its price approximates) and the value added to the product by the labour that labour-power becomes when used by the employer, is the vital one for capital, because it is through that relationship that surplus value is created. And, more to the point, for present purposes (i.e., in considering the proletarianisation of hundreds of millions of workers in Asia, Africa and Latin America) is the question brought to our attention especially by the French Marxist anthropologist Claude Meillassoux, on whose work what follows is largely based.

Meillassoux notes that Marx, for strictly theoretical reasons, assumed that the price of labour-power was equal to the subsistence and reproduction needs of the wage-labourer. But the fact is that for whole periods, and over large areas, this correspondence does not exist. In the capital system, labour-power is a commodity, bought and sold on the market. Its value is determined, as in any other commodity, by the necessary labour-time involved in its production, and will thus tend to approximate to the value of the labouring family's subsistence. Its price is affected by supply and demand. It is not difficult to see that today, in the poorer countries, wages are in fact lower than the cost of the subsistence of the labourer and his family. Meillassoux comments:

> Because of the absence of any rational relation between the wages and the vital needs of the workers, capitalist profit is very often accompanied in the dependent countries – and more and more in others also – by a super-exploitation of labour, that is, by taking away from the worker his living substance, when, lacking an adequate wage, his health is weakened (by illnesses caused by work), his physical integrity is broken (by accidents at work), and his life-expectancy, already less than that of those in better-off classes and occupations, is diminished.

He gives a compelling example:

> This excrescence of profit through the mutilation of life falls outside the wage calculations of the enterprises. When there is super-exploitation, the relationship of forces between the classes opens the door for even more. In Amazonia, certain big owners recruit workers from distant areas, give them seasonal work, then when it comes to paying them have hired killers to kill them. Superabundant 'labour-supply' and the prevailing relationship of forces permit this horrifying practice which reduces manpower costs to the bare necessities for employing the activity of workers for the season before sacrificing them.

And he concludes:

> It is not a matter, here, of assuming what the logic of supply and demand of labour can give rise to, but of grasping that such a logic is at work when conditions favour it and that there is nothing in the free functioning of capitalist profit opposing this mass assassination.[5]

In Chapter 4, we noted that, notwithstanding the dreams of many sociologists, the proletariat has not disappeared. On the contrary, the globalisation of capital in the last few decades has brought with it proletarianisation on a massive scale. To the wage-slaves of the older capitalist countries, whose forefathers in the nineteenth century Marx saw as the force for socialist revolution, are now added hundreds of millions of men, women and children in Asia, Africa and Latin America. The number of wage-workers in the so-called developing world was 1.9 billion in 1980, 2.3 billion in 1999, and 3 billion (one-half of all humanity) in 1995. The urban population in the 'Third World' multiplied six-fold between 1975 and 1995.[6]

Many examples could be given of the relation between workers in the older capitalist countries and these 'new' proletarians. Only one or two can be instanced here. First, the city of Leeds. It was for years the centre of the British clothing industry – one factory alone employed 10,000 workers. Today the work-force in the industry in Leeds consists of only a few hundreds. In Bangladesh there are some 1,800,000 garment workers, most of them women. A second concerns the relocation of the last Majorette toy-manufacturing company in Europe, reported in the journal *Capital* on 24 February 2002. Samuel Holder writes:

> One thousand French workers were sacked. Did they for all that cease to be members of the working class? Did they completely forget that they once worked in that factory? Obviously not. While they were at it, Majorette created a factory in Thailand and took on 1,000 workers (earning ten times less than their French equivalents). Yes but, we will think, with the navel-gazing of French revolutionary militants who have the Paris Commune of 1871, June 1936, May 1968 and December 1995 behind us, these super-exploited Thai workers are unorganised and have no class-consciousness. No way; reports were to show that on the Sunday morning, a number of them went to the union meeting, discussed their problems, learned fighting songs and how to act in case of a demonstration against their employer, etc. The boss of this factory made no mystery of the fact that if these Thai workers did not prove sufficiently productive, then he would re-locate to China (where wages are even lower).[7]

It is obvious, surely, that these Thai workers have 'nothing to lose but their chains'. But do they have the same 'structurally antagonistic' relation to capital as do the workers of Europe, North America and Japan? That is to say, can they, together with those latter workers, respond as it were to Marx's call: 'Workers of the world, unite!'?

The other side of the proletarianisation of new millions with globalisation is of course the advantage gained by capital because of the 'competition' between the workers of the older capitalist countries and those of Asia, Africa and Latin America. This has many ramifications economically – and potentially politically – as Meillassoux in particular has pointed out:

> For the native workers of the European countries, it took centuries of struggle to put in place first workers' mutual aid schemes, then social insurance (which the employers never ceased to challenge once they were obliged to contribute). The globalisation of the economy today endangers these gains everywhere they exist, favouring what is called 'competition' between millions of workers far apart and dispersed, without any common regulation. Putting workers into competition with each other on the global scale in fact involves different degrees of poverty of scattered populations who do not know each other, faced with a management controlling the market everywhere thanks to ultra-sophisticated means of transmission and transport. It has been patiently sustained for two decades by the great international financial institutions through the systematic application of policies of structural adjustment, first in the weakest dependent states and now in Europe.[8]

The great transnational companies in Asia, Africa and Latin America have derived enormous benefits from this global proletarianisation. Not only do they pay notoriously low wages. They are for example not taxed in the way they are in their 'home' countries, where past struggles have established minimum standards of living, sustained by state-administered 'welfare' provisions.[9] They have, therefore, not even a minimum responsibility for the education and health-care of the workers, nor for their survival after the end of their working lives. These capitalist companies have been able in the second half of the twentieth century to amass untold wealth through this global expansion of the workforce. At the same time, this massive accumulation of value means an overproduction of capital, with the certain consequence of global economic crises.

In the industrialised capitalist countries, the production and reproduction of the commodity labour-power – that is, of the (alas) indispensable labouring class – must be assured through the money-income of the workers (their wages and benefits), used to maintain their families. But in the 'underdeveloped' countries the cost of production and reproduction of labour-power no longer presents itself as a problem of paying adequate wages! It is assured – at the minimum level required – by quite different means. In these countries millions of families are still involved, as Meillassoux shows, in the traditional 'domestic mode of production', where subsistence agriculture sustains pregnant women, babies, children, adult men and women, and the old. Added to this 'benefit' to the capitalist employers is another – the gigantic growth in agricultural productivity in Europe and North America, making possible the import of very cheap foodstuffs to be sold to the millions of new proletarians in the cities and towns of the 'underdeveloped countries'. Not only is the cost to the capitalists of labour-power vastly reduced, but also labour-power is reproduced for capital in the countries to which workers migrate as well as in their 'home' countries – and at a tiny fraction of the cost of such reproduction in the older capitalist countries.

And there is an additional benefit to capital. The economically forced emigration of workers to Europe and North America means that the employers in the industrialised countries have to hand a supply (which their governments turn on and off) of what Meillassoux calls 'ready-made' workers. That is to say, the capitalists have had no responsibility, financial or any other, for the costs of rearing and maintaining these workers before they appear on the labour market. 'These exoduses renewed, profitably and on a massive scale, in the form of a class of wage-labourers displaced and with no security *('précarisés')*, often at the expense of the emigrants themselves, the plunder exercised by the slave trade of past centuries.'[10]

Today's capitalists have other bonuses, compared with the exploiters of the past. They escape the responsibility of the traditional slave-owner to husband, house, feed and ensure the survival of the slave and his family.[11] And they employ the emigrant and migrant workers in an age in which they can take advantage of advances in productivity. In this connection, it will be recalled that Marx noted long ago that the 'primitive accumulation' of capital in Britain was based to a considerable extent on the movement of 'ready-made' workers from country to town. The notorious 'Highland Clearances' in nineteenth-century Scotland were one of his major examples.[12] Another example today is the system of peonage in Latin America. In recent decades, capital in South Africa and other countries profited greatly from the prevalence of migrant labour, since when no work was available the migrant workers must return to be maintained in their original homes.[13]

Workers and their families in the dependent countries of course suffer in more respects than that of inhumanly low wages. The functioning of the capitalist economy as a whole, globally, imposes on them conditions, in all aspects of their living standards, which still separate them widely from the workers in metropolitan countries. The problems they face are difficult for any citizen of the 'developed countries' to conceive, yet the crucial question is that these conditions are, again, consequences of the inherent logic of capital:

> To make the provision of food dependent on market conditions (purchasing power, ability of the consumer to pay) is to substitute a speculative, countable, material, deadly 'value' for a process of renewal of life. When stocks of foodstuffs build up while starving populations perish; when pharmaceutical products are not distributed to needy sick people because they cannot pay, we have gone from an economy of life to an economy of death. These examples are everyday ones and show that the logical conditions of profit are not necessarily those of life. The insistence on effective demand is at the source of unemployment as it is of all the crises affecting individuals through illness and death. But these crises are inherent to the formation of capitalist profit.[14]

This is not the place to waste space by taking up the cynical arguments of politicians, like Baroness Thatcher, on the virtues of 'the market'. What is worth noting, however, is the way in which the vulgar economics of such pundits manage to co-exist with a neo-Malthusian prejudice about the dangers of population growth – a prejudice entirely, and quite unjustifiably, separated in this way of thinking from its 'economics'. This sort of contemporary thought is the acme of a (capitalist) ideology in which human beings and their needs are considered only as 'things' at the service of capital accumulation. Any thinking and any practice capable of tackling humanity's real problems today will need to make a radical break with that ideology:

> Until now, the growth of human beings has not been treated as inherent to the economy: generally, demography has been treated as governed by its own laws. In reality, there are continuous interactions between, on the one hand, human beings, from whom emanates energy-work, and on the other hand, the labour-power extracted from this energy as a means of production, and finally the production of subsistence goods as means of production of the human producers.
>
> There is a field of political economy which needs rethinking, based on this continuous transformation of subsistence into labour-power and into producers of subsistence: a political economy capable of extending the analysis of exploitation to the explanation of phenomena considered natural, accidental or abnormal, such as famine, death, sickness, forced labour, concentration camps, and able to give back to human beings their central place as subjects of the economy and not that of 'human resources', as today's capitalist economy, with its dehumanised, brutal and revealing vocabulary, would wish.[15]

Marx on the proletariat

For Marx, the proletariat was 'nothing if it [were] not revolutionary.' Can this assertion be understood in the same way today as when it was made in a period of revolutionary struggles in Europe? The answer is, 'Yes and no'. But at this point I must first summarise my argument so far, before introducing an additional consideration.

First, the working class confronts capital as its only structural antagonist (see Chapter 4). This truth has today acquired much greater urgency. Capital's continued rule cannot but threaten humanity with destruction, and the working class is the only force that comes into conflict with it as a class – capable of overthrowing it and replacing it with the humanly necessary system of social control, that is to say, collective self-control, over production. The labour performed in society, so long as capital rules, is 'productive' only insofar as it creates surplus value – that is, reproduces capital itself. It is only the labouring class that creates capital, creates all the wealth in society. It is this class that, *in its nature*, is the bearer of the future society of free producers

Second, many people besides Marx recognised that the working class was an exploited and oppressed class. But they did not understand that its necessary opposite, capital, was the motor of a social system, the contradictions of which would stimulate crises and breakdowns; and that, in the course of these, the struggles of the working class would prepare it for social revolution. Today the social system ruled by capital, after many conjunctural crises, partial and temporary political defeats and setbacks, and massive world wars, has reached an entirely different kind of critical stage – that of its structural, historical crisis. The absolute necessity of replacing capital's governing mechanism of destructive self-reproduction stares humanity in the face.

Third, 'nothing if not revolutionary' has too often been understood in a narrowly political sense. Its true meaning becomes clear only when we remember that Marx saw the proletarian revolution as above all a social revolution, distinct from all earlier revolutions. It follows that the class-consciousness (not only theoretical, but also, to use Marx's term, practical consciousness), which the working class needs to develop, is much more than a political consciousness – consciousness, that is to say, of the need to overthrow the state power of the bourgeoisie. This is something that Marxists writing about class-consciousness and revolutionary politics have signally failed to recognise. My own earlier writings on this question typify the wrong understanding to which I am drawing attention.[16] The work of Mészáros is the signal exception to the general trend.

Fourth, given that the destructive side of the social-productive system subordinated to capital and its needs now predominates, this social essence — that is, the not solely *political* character — of the proletariat's revolutionary nature and role takes on the greatest possible importance practically and theoretically. Despite its destructive aspects and its degrading of human life through exploitation and oppression, the imperative of capital accumulation/reproduction did, for a whole epoch, at the same time advance the productive powers of society. In this way it prepared the necessary material conditions (high productivity of labour and international intercourse) for a future social order in which the freely associated producers would decide and control the priorities of life – socialism.

The wanton plunder and destruction of nature resulting from the uncontrolled rule of globalised capital has become common knowledge, thanks to the tireless work of many extremely capable writers and fearless, committed protesters. One, perhaps the most important, aspect of this is the constant threat of degradation and destruction of the men, women and children of the working class. Recalling that the capitalist mode of production brought with it an unprecedented development of mankind's productive forces, we must not now fail to recognise a decisive change once capital enters its stage of destructive self-reproduction. The change is this. The alienation capitalism always meant for the workers not only continues, but is intensified to the extent that the most important productive force of all – labouring humanity – is no longer developed. On the contrary, it is threatened by capital with degradation and destruction.

Fifth, the entry of the capital system into its phase of 'destructive self-reproduction' has of course had the most obvious and drastic consequences for the super-exploited working classes of the dependent countries – examples of which I cited in Chapter 2 particularly. But the dangers are by no means confined to them. In this destructiveness and degradation humanity is confronted by a tendency inherent in the capital system from the beginning, one which can be ended only by ending that system and not by partial remedies. Building on Marx's *Capital*, Harry Braverman, author of the classic *Labour and Monopoly Capitalism* (1974), explained very well how work itself is degraded as the worker is reduced to a unit of energy in production. Workers are cut off from all conscious conception, planning and control of the labour process (not to mention the fact that they are deprived of the slightest trace of ownership of the product or control of its destiny). Marx had said in *Capital*:

> We presuppose labour in a form that stamps it as exclusively human. A spider conducts operations that resemble those of a weaver, and a bee puts to shame many an architect in the construction of her cells. But what distinguishes the worst architect from the best of bees is this, that the architect raises his structure in imagination before he erects it in reality.[17]

In contrast to this fundamental human characteristic of labour, we have the work of the wage-labourer employed by capital, who has become merely the bearer of a commodity, labour-power. Only when bought, then owned and used by a personification of capital does labour-power actually become labour. The prior conception, governance and outcome of the productive process are contained not in the labourer's head but in the whole socially available technique and science – which, in society as presently constituted, is in practice available only to a sufficient volume of capital in the particular field. So far as capital and its personifications are concerned, the worker is nothing but the envelope of that labour-power which has been bought by part of his (the capitalist's) capital (the 'variable' part):

> It is only under capitalist conditions that the masters take over the entire process, repeatedly reshape and reorganise it to suit their own needs, and parcel it out as tasks to workers for whom the process as a whole is now lost.[18]

Sixth, with the development of machinery, then of mass production methods, then of automation, the operative's activity was often virtually reduced to simple repetitive motions, or even to just watching over a tiny part of the total process. Today, the technical innovations yielding new materials and especially Information Technology have not only accentuated this development of alienation but have made possible the disappearance of large categories of industry. The capital system cannot cope in any human fashion with the consequent vast increase in productivity of labour – that is to say, it cannot deliver the now entirely possible creation of a large measure of free time for all. Instead the main result is large-scale structural unemployment – unemployment that is not merely the regular appearance of a 'reserve army of labour', but involves the permanent removal of whole sections of workers from employment. For the workers in the older capitalist countries, this is already a qualitative change in their lives and expectations. But they must also expect henceforth – because of capital's structural crisis – a persistent attack on the defences (social security, welfare benefits, etc.) which their past struggles had yielded in earlier, expansionary periods of the capital system's existence. It is this attack that is already well underway.

Seventh, it is surely true that, until now, the immediate conditions and interests of these workers in the older capitalist countries – and by no means only those of the 'labour aristocracy' – have not coincided with those of workers in the dependent countries. But the structural crisis makes it inevitable that this divergence of immediate interests will give way to the objective, at the moment only latent, common interest vis-à-vis capital.[19] In Western Europe, the benefits of the 'welfare state' are constantly being eroded. In the United States, there is an ever-increasing polarisation of wage-levels. In the last quarter of the twentieth century, the minimum wage (allowing for inflation) went down by a huge 40 per cent; and business lobbyists were campaigning for a law permitting the employment of youths of sixteen and seventeen at 20 per cent below the minimum.

Eighth, we have here, in reality, a development which is the direct opposite of what was confidently assumed by 'experts' who could not go beyond the ideology of capitalism. For a good part of the latter half of the twentieth century, 'social scientists' blithely repeated the revealed truth that workers in the 'Third World' were living in 'developing countries'. The implication of this was that these countries were on their way to being like the 'developed' ones, and that the conditions of workers there would become like those of the workers in Europe and America. Today, we may say that 'everyone knows' that the gap between rich and poor countries is ever-widening – and this is evidenced by the mass protests generated by Sir Bob Geldof and others at the time of the meeting of the G8 countries' leaders at Gleneagles in Scotland in July 2005. Millions of children are condemned to lives of unpaid labour and even slavery. The AIDS virus has its hold on over one-third of the population in several African countries. Famine and war ravage one country after another in Africa and Asia. And even all this understates the case. In the words of Mészáros:

> Keeping millions in destitution and starvation when the wasted millions (e.g., on arms, 'defence') could feed them fifty times over puts the enormity of this system of domination in perspective.[20]

Indeed, the impoverishment of the masses in Africa, Asia and Latin America, far from signifying their 'backwardness', has to be understood as integral to the global capital system, and as capable of being changed only at the global level. The millions of people compelled to work for the multinationals are victims not only of the super-exploitation of their labour. They suffer the consequences of the break-up of their previously existing systems of solidarity (e.g., norms of support for the older generation, mutual aid, etc.). These have given way to the subjection of isolated cultivators to a 'market' in agriculture totally dominated by the interests of multinational companies – a 'market' that has wrecked the lives of millions. Among the results are mass emigration from country to town, where social and cultural breakdown is everywhere manifest; and forced emigration to Europe and the United States, with the well-known social, economic and political consequences. We now have many documented accounts of children, forced into labour from infancy, who are then dispensed with in their early teens as their cheap labour-power is replaced by that of their younger brothers and sisters. They are then left with nowhere but the street, the hazards of which need no description here.[21] And we should add that such stories make clear how fertile grounds are being created for recruitment to fundamentalist movements.

In summary, then, my argument is that we have arrived at a qualitatively new historical situation. Contrary to the sociologists' myth about the disappearance of the proletariat there is internationally a proletarianisation of massive proportions. Contrary to the myth of the 'development' economists and sociologists, we have mass impoverishment and starvation. Contrary to the myth that 'globalisation' is some benign process of bringing universal progress by way of 'the market', we have an unprecedented and galloping polarisation and unevenness of development. Billions suffer severe malnutrition and often starvation; 90 per cent of US citizens, according to the 2001 US Census, own a car, and 20 per cent own three. Undoubtedly, some of the millions of working people in the US and Western Europe who have been characterised by sociologists as 'bourgeoisified' may even themselves have believed it to be true. But they can expect a rude awakening when the insurance companies and pension funds upon which they depend for their retirement renege on their commitments, as, in the early years of the 21st century, confronted by stock-market collapses, they have already begun to do. Can we expect a new school of sociology that will invent a new explanatory category – re-proletarianisation?

The prospects for the 'new' proletariat

The 'new' proletarians of Africa, Asia and Latin America cannot in any way hope that they and their descendants will emulate the historical experience of the working classes of Europe and America. The latter were citizens of states in which an expanding capitalist system could eventually 'afford' parliamentary democracy, civil rights and the granting of reform concessions and benefits in response to workers' struggles. Nor will the workers of the ex-Soviet Union, Eastern Europe and China see their hopes of such advances fulfilled. The restoration of capitalism, as the Stalinist regimes have collapsed, generates such aspirations only catastrophically to deny them. All these workers, as a class, find themselves involved in a system no longer in its earlier, objectively progressive, phases. Rather they have joined in one that has reached the end of its global expansion, which is now in structural crisis and forced to turn in upon itself. And this essentially means that it turns against the working class, in search of ways to deal with its internal conflicts and contradictions. Here lies the crucial question. What are the implications of this new historical situation for the class struggle, for the struggle for a new, socialist order of society?

In the most general terms, the answer is this. 'Globalised' capital can no longer displace or defer its contradictions by expansion geographically, can no longer, as it were, 'export' them. The basic conflict, deriving from the capitalist mode of exploitation, is now concentrated into one between the two classes on the only scale on which the proletariat can actually be 'revolutionary' and (remembering Marx's aphorism) not 'nothing' – that is, on the global scale. The processes involved in this final 'internalisation' of capital's contradictions, with its resultant unfolding class conflicts, constitute the essential reality which must assert itself against and through the inherited divisions and conflicts of immediate interests in the world working class.

This is not meant to be some bland picture of a now 'favourable situation'. There is indeed a qualitative change in the parameters of the class struggle. Marx's insistence on the necessity, for the social revolution, of a 'communist mass consciousness', remained an aspiration so long as the objective conditions necessary for it to develop did not exist. The difference today is this:

> When the objective conditions implicit in such an aim [producing 'mass communist consciousness'] are in the process of unfolding *on a global scale*, only then may one realistically envisage the practical articulation of the required organs of socialist offensive.[22] [Emphasis added]

This 'practical articulation' will have to be achieved through experiences and struggles in a historical period where Rosa Luxemburg's warning 'socialism or barbarism' has a chilling ring of reality. As Mészáros says, capital's

> normal way of dealing with contradictions is to intensify them, to transfer them to a higher level, to displace them to a different plane, to suppress them as long as it is possible to do so, and when they cannot be suppressed any longer, to export them to a different sphere or a different country. This is why the increasing blockage in displacing and exporting capital's inner contradictions is so dangerous and potentially explosive.[23]

This structural crisis is not only 'economic'. It runs through the whole of society and culture. Politically and socially, just as is clear when we focus on the 'economy', the crisis is one of the system of domination as a whole. The state machine and all political and legal institutions – the family, education, the systems of values and morality – all are in open crisis because they are called on to regulate and control a society faced with new and insoluble problems, with whole areas in a condition of breakdown or near-breakdown. Politics is riddled with corruption and crime. In 'democratic' countries, politicians – right and 'left' – put 'law and order' and 'control of crime' at the top of their electoral agendas, attempting to respond to the insecurity felt by the citizens.

These political developments are not merely ideological. Long established laws, rights and institutions are being changed. The creeping reactionary development is gruesomely illustrated when, in the name of responding to the growth of racism, exemplified for instance by the vote for Le Pen in France's presidential election of 2002, racist immigration controls are reinforced by 'socialist' as well as conservative governments. And – in the name of defending 'democracy' in the 'war against terrorism' – the Bush administration imposes imprisonment without trial, complimenting itself on the result of a poll showing that four-fifths of US citizens put strengthening of their 'security' before preservation of basic democratic rights. This in the 'land of the free, home of the brave'. Bush and his associates are no doubt oblivious to the lessons of history, and do not anticipate the potential ferocious reaction of the American masses once they sense that after all their rulers cannot protect them. The fall of the great Roman Empire and of the feudal states in Europe should be remembered.[24]

The recent examples given above are not isolated ones. Once the impact of the onset of the capital system's structural crisis in the older capitalist countries makes impossible the established methods of rule through class-compromise and reform concessions, then social control must be achieved by other means. Law and the repressive forces of the state machine must more and more be strengthened against all possible threats to the functioning of capital's social-economic system. 'Globalisation' unfailingly implies that the global contradictions are manifested and concentrated in specific ways within each country, and not only extensively. The state's policies against internal threats will match the foreign and defence policies of the US Government, so nakedly revealed in the 'war against terror' following the attacks in New York, Washington DC, and Pennsylvania on 9/11.[25]

It would be complacent in the extreme to think that the single-minded ruthlessness shown by capital's representatives in the 'war against terror' – prefigured by their actions in Indonesia, Chile and elsewhere – will not be manifested in dealing with the working class. The anti-trade-union laws introduced in more than one country in the last few decades are but a mild anticipation. When capitalist states strengthen their political and military means of repression (on the global arena and domestically) it is in order to respond to any resistance to the necessary intensification of exploitation and also to counter any challenge to their power. The immediately perceived challenge is from 'rogue states' and terrorist organisations with big financial resources and highly developed weaponry. Al-Qaida and the like do not of course threaten the overthrow of capitalism. Far from it. Men like Osama Bin Laden are in their own way very much men of globalised capital. But they are certainly a prime example of the capital system's problem of keeping some degree of control over the effects of its own fundamental uncontrollability. They do indeed threaten capital's ability to keep order – that is, order within which exploitation can continue unhindered. The defences built against them are indispensable, especially given US capital's need to assert its control universally, globally. These same defences will of course be there to suppress any and every challenge by a refounded working-class movement in the coming years.

The build-up of nuclear missiles and other weapons of mass destruction is itself a significant part of the gigantic waste and destructiveness made necessary by capital's need to deal with its own contradictions and conflicts. It is clear that the unfolding of the structural crisis has unleashed new and dangerous forces – wealthy and heavily armed criminal organisations, terrorist and fundamentalist organisations with their capacity to appeal to oppressed youth, etc. They are at the same time the product of 'globalisation' and a constant threat to the defences of global capital itself. However, it is vitally important to recognise that these same forces constitute an entirely new set of problems, which will have to be faced and overcome by the social revolution. This set of problems is part of the whole global threat of destruction posed by the continued survival of the social-metabolic system ordered by capital's unquenchable thirst for surplus value and self-reproduction on an ever-expanding scale. Here we approach what is perhaps the most fundamental issue that must be tackled in the struggle to re-found the international 'class movement' of the working class.

The totality of the crisis

It would be a great mistake to see the political sphere, and in particular the state, as somehow merely secondary to or a 'reflection' of the economy and its contradictions in the era of structural crisis. It is a fundamental and distinctive characteristic of capitalism that its mode of exploitation is directly economic and not exercised through political power or status. However, the state has always been necessary to the capital system, not only to control in one form or another capital's antagonist, the working class, but also to set and implement the rules necessary to stop the consequences of competition between capitals from getting out of hand. As the structural crisis unfolds, there are important changes in both aspects.[26] As the contradictions of the system intensify, with the necessity to take back the past gains of the workforce, and to ditch the old reformist methods of rule, the strengthening of the repressive functions of the state against the working class becomes necessary. To this must be added the crucial fact that the state and government become, not subsidiary to, but an essential part of, the very functioning of today's great capitalist enterprises. Not only are major policy decisions (domestic and foreign) taken to facilitate their operations, and massive government contracts (especially in armaments) handed out, but enormous funds are made available for 'research and development' and subsidies granted for investment in designated areas.

There are those who claim that the intimate relations between capital and the state mean that the system has acquired the means permanently to overcome its contradictions. In reality, these relations – crucial as they are to the system today – are perhaps the most powerful confirmation of Marx's definition of the most basic contradiction of capitalism. That is, the contradiction between the ever-increasing socialisation of production on the one hand, and private appropriation of the product on the other.

---

[1] Lea, *Crime and Modernity*, pp. 132-3.

[2] Lea, *Crime and Modernity*, pp. 107-9.

[3] Mike Davis, *City of Quartz: excavating the future in Los Angeles* (London, 1998, first published, 1990, p. 174.

[4] Zygmunt Bauman, *Globalisation: the human consequences* (Cambridge, 1998), p. 9.

[5] Meillassoux, *L'Économie de la Vie*, pp.13-14.

[6] My authorities here are J. Petras and D. Veltmeyer, in their book, *Globalisation Unmasked*.

[7] *Carré Rouge*, no. 21, pp. 13-14.

[8] Meillassoux, *L'Économie de la Vie*, pp. 16-17.

[9] 'Historically, in the industrialised countries, the workers and their political allies arrived , little by little and at the price of often bloody struggles, to establish the mode of fixing wages starting from evaluation of human and family needs. To the hourly wage, which remains fundamentally determined by a relationship of force, are added, due to the law and due to collective agreements, payments based on the needs of reconstitution, maintenance and reproduction of life: minimum wage, unemployment, sickness and accident benefits, pensions, family allowances, etc.' See Meillassoux, *L'Économie de la Vie*.

[10] See Meillassoux, *L'Économie de la Vie*.

[11] Auguste Blanqui wrote, as long ago as 1834 in *Le Liberateur*: 'Approximately, as plantation owners put slaves to work, with the difference that the worker is not capital to be husbanded like the slave.' Cited in Walter Benjamin, *The Arcades Project* (Cambridge, Mass. and London, 1999), p. 734.

[12] Marx, *Capital*, vol. I, chap. 27. Even today Tory historians think it worth devoting ink to denying the reality of the 'Highland Clearances': see Michael Fry, *Wild Scots: ... highland history* (London, 2005).

[13] Meillassoux, *L'Économie de la Vie*, pp.78-9

[14] Meillassoux, *L'Économie de la Vie*, p. 15.

[15] Meillassoux, *L'Économie de la Vie*, pp. 68 and 81.

[16] For example, my *Marxism and the Class Struggle* and *Labour Review* article 'What is Revolutionary Leadership?', published in the 1960s and early 1970s.

[17] Marx, Capital, vol. 1.

[18] Braverman, *Labour and Monopoly Capitalism*, Appendix 2, p. 317.

[19] Mészáros, *Beyond Capital*, p. 685.

[20] I have left to the final chapter (on the prospects of refounding the working-class movement) the crucial question of the effects of 'deregulation' and neo-liberalism' on the casualisation and fragmentation of labour, de-industrialisation, etc., and the effects on working-class organisation and consciousness. This is perhaps the most important of the new problems posed by 'globalisation'.

[21] See especially Schlemmer, *The Exploited Child.*

[22] Mészáros, *Beyond Capital*, p. 675.

[23] Mészáros, *Beyond Capital*, p. 684.

[24] I should perhaps apologise for the plethora of quotation marks in these paragraphs, but the loss of meaning in many of the expressions used is itself part of the crisis we are discussing.

[25] According to '*The Global Intelligence Report* of 25 February 2002'. Under the emerging Bush doctrine, if a nation supports or hosts a group that intends to attack the United States, or if it deliberately fails to act against such a group, then that nation is in a de facto state of war with the United States. The act of supporting or hosting such groups is a threshold that renders all other aspects of a bilateral relationship of no consequence. At a time and place of its choosing, the United States will act against both the group and the state.

In order to prevent the emergence of follow-on al-Qaidas, the central feature must be to deny them sanctuary. Ideally, as some have suggested, the United States could work to abolish the poverty and misunderstanding that have given rise to al-Qaida. Unfortunately, even if this were possible, there is no time. The threat, in the eyes of the Bush administration, is a matter of months and the abolition of poverty is a matter of generations. Therefore, if the carrot is impossible, then the stick will be used.

[26] See Mészáros, *Beyond Capital*, p. 253: As an attempt is made to gain control over the system's uncontrollability, we are subjected to a trend of increasingly political determinations in 20th century economic developments. This means a reversal of the long period of capital's historical ascendancy in which economic determinations were dominant in the social metabolic process of reproduction.

6

TOWARDS REFOUNDATION 1: REALISTIC OPTIMISM

During the Spanish Civil War of the late 1930s, an interviewer said to the anarchist leader, Buenaventura Durruti: 'You will be sitting on top of a pile of ruins if you are victorious.' Durruti replied:

> We have always lived in slums and holes in the wall. We will know how to accommodate ourselves for a while. For, you must not forget, we can also build. It is we who built these palaces and cities, here in Spain and in America and everywhere. We, the workers, we can build others to take their place. And better ones. We are not in the least afraid of ruins. We are going to inherit the earth. There is not the slightest doubt about that. The bourgeoisie might blast and ruin its own world before it leaves the stage of history. We carry a new world, here, in our hearts. That world is growing this minute.

It will no doubt surprise many to read that the solid grounds for Durruti's prognosis are greater today than they were then. What lies at the roots of a realistic optimism? First is the understanding that capitalism, far from being triumphant, as its advocates claim, is a system which has entered its period of decline or structural-historical crisis.[1] Second, the collapse of Stalinism in 1989-90, far from marking a victory for capitalism, removed the greatest obstacle to a refounded working-class socialist movement, depriving the capital system of by far its most important support in the class struggle. Third is the fact that, with 'globalisation', a massive and universal proletarianisation has come about, and despite the ideological offensive about disappearance or 'embourgeoisement' of the working class, this vastly increases the potential force of capital's only structural antagonist. The enormous changes in the character of labour, in particular the increased proportion of 'white-collar' workers and the growing dominance of Information Technology, do not – as is often claimed – refute Marx's concept of the proletariat. Rather are they a remarkable confirmation of his insight concerning the impact on the labour process and the working class of the inescapable growth of machine production and socialisation of production.

'Refoundation' and the social revolution

The capital system's more and more destructive consequences surely give greater urgency to Marx's assertion that 'the proletariat is nothing if it is not revolutionary'. 'Revolutionary' must be understood in Marx's sense of *social*-revolutionary. Clearly there cannot be any revolutionary restructuring of society – the transformation of its production, reproduction and progress – except by the producers themselves. Yet we are faced today by a 'destructive self-reproduction' of capital, involving not only destruction of nature but also a constant danger to the producers themselves and to the whole of mankind's cultural heritage. Every threat of degradation (physical and moral), reduction, disintegration, dehumanisation of the class of producers is a threat to the future of mankind that must be resisted. To resist that dehumanisation by every means is to defend the essential potential foundations of the future social order that must be achieved when the rule of capital is ended. This is a responsibility no less urgent than the defence and protection of the environment, and of the natural resources that are every day ruthlessly and uncontrollably plundered by capital. As Mészáros writes:

> Potentially overreaching itself is the hallmark of capital's relationship to the elementary conditions of social metabolic reproduction, in the absolutely inescapable interchange of humankind with nature.[2]

My argument here is that this responsibility to resist is central to the refoundation of the international movement of the working class – the only force capable of putting an end to the rule of capital. But, clearly, this generalisation by itself is abstract and ineffectual. Thc question is; can we find ways to develop a practice in which the recognition of this responsibility forms part of and advances that 'elaboration of specific strategies and "mediations", arising from the particular determinations of changing needs and circumstances, which represent the greatest challenge to contemporary Marxist theory'?[3]

In answering positively, the most important consideration is surely once again Marx's insistence that the revolutionary ending of capital's rule will be a *social* revolution, achievable only when the producers as a class, collectively, become practically engaged in the necessary social transformation. The now global scale of the capital system's operations and interconnected spheres of exploitation of unevenly and unequally developed nations and communities certainly makes this task look more difficult than ever before. Yet this difficulty is but the inevitable corollary of the fact that only now, precisely because of capital's having reached its global limits, do the objective conditions for the socialist revolution actually exist. And so, recognising that the socialist enterprise is structurally unrealisable without its full articulation in the manifold autonomous ('self-managing'), and thus irrepressibly pluralist projects of the ongoing social revolution, the forbidding but essential task is 'to devise a viable alternative to an immensely complex global system which has on its side the "curse of interdependence" in resisting change'. Such an 'alternative' will come into being only as 'all particular groups (inevitably reflecting a multiplicity of given interests and divisions) ... define their position in the form of interconnected, and if conditions permit also coordinated, but definitely not identical specific objectives and strategies'.[4]

In conditions of 'globalisation', what Mészáros calls this 'inherent pluralism' of a refounded movement towards socialism must be firmly grasped. To do so is critical if a necessary emphasis on Marx's insistence that the achievement of the social revolution requires a 'communist mass consciousness' is not to be reduced to an abstract ideal. And this abstraction is indeed what it has become in the outpourings of the numerous self-styled 'Marxist' parties and groups. What is decisive is that only a truly mass movement of people can effect the social revolution – that is to say, a revolution in which people take control of their own lives.

Here we return to the fundamental consideration that the proletarian revolution, unlike all earlier revolutions, does not substitute one form of class exploitation with another of its own. It ends class society. In earlier revolutions, one exploiting class established its own mode of exploitation as the central controlling force of the social metabolism, determining its form and relationship with nature. This ruling class found the political and ideological means to ensure its monopoly of the means of production. Only for the members of this class was there the chance of participation in the heritage of human culture. The mass, the direct producers, were exploited and deprived. The socialist revolution places all humanity in a relation with nature and the need to produce that is no longer mediated by class division. It opens up the prospect of relations between individuals which are not so mediated. It begins the abolition of privileged access to culture, opening it up to all.

For these reasons Marx called the social revolution the human revolution. That revolution, said Marx, comes about – as did earlier ones – when the old production relations become a barrier to the development of the productive forces which have been developed within them. In the case of the revolution against capital, Marx saw, the productive forces and the 'universal intercourse' foreshadowed by the world market will have provided the basis for human liberation. Not only is the revolution the work of the exploited majority rather than of a new exploiting minority class; private property is also abolished. The creation and reproduction of the resulting social order is the work of all, the association of free and equal individuals. It is not mediated by the necessities of a mode of exploitation of human being by human being, as it is within capitalism. My argument here is that, at the beginning of the 21st century, it has become possible to make more concrete

Marx's general insight into the necessity of social revolution to end the rule of a capitalist system in irreconcilable conflict with humanity's needs and potential.

In the first place, the history of the twentieth century shows unmistakably that the very future of humanity, even of the planet itself, requires the ending of the rule of capital, with its imperative of accumulation and uncontrollability. But there is more. As Mészáros, especially in *Beyond Capital*, has insisted, only the development since Marx's time of the capital system to world domination and ascendancy could produce the necessary conditions for its structural crisis, as opposed to its merely conjunctural crises. It was in the last three decades of the twentieth century that it became possible to see the fundamental contradiction between productive forces and the social relations of capital's rule in its full and comprehensive development.

It is this contradiction that now confronts humanity on the global, that is to say, potentially truly universal, scale. What Marx saw as the material basis of communism – 'universal intercourse' and highly developed productive forces – takes shape before our eyes. Today's technological wonders, above all in electronics and Information Technology, where means of production and means of communication are more and more the same thing, expose the redundancy of capital's rule. The people of every corner of the world, even the previously most isolated, are, as we know, drawn into capital's net. The 'electronic revolution' means that virtually instantaneous and free contact can be available between humans anywhere on the planet.

The individual's potential freedom, however, goes beyond this new and totally unprecedented extension of the conditions of universality of intercourse. The impact of Information Technology in all its aspects is intensive as well as extensive. That is to say: at the same time as the 'opening up' of the world to its farthest extent, there is an 'opening up' of the innermost riches of culture and relations between individuals through the internet and electronic communication. Even while the rule of capital persists, the reality of this enrichment can be perceived, for example in educational techniques, in the ability of individual users to gain access to information, literature, music, and entertainment; and, indeed, to organise against capital! Here are new 'material conditions' for what Marx and Engels foresaw as 'an association, in which the free development of each is the condition for the free development of all'. More than ever, Marx's and Engels' injunction makes a directly relevant appeal: 'The proletarians have nothing to lose but their chains. They have a world to win'.

Towards unity

Only a few years ago, in the major capitalist countries, the satisfaction of basic needs – for health services, education, defence against loss of employment, provision for the unemployed, adequate housing, provision for retirement, the ability to organise – through rights won long ago tended to be taken for granted. But there is now a systematic attack on all such established rights, raising life-and-death questions. It will inevitably become more and more apparent that capital will not return to a stage at which it can stave off opposition by granting reforms; that, on the contrary, it is more and more compelled to take back what the working class has gained in past struggles. The resistance to this clawing back cannot avoid sooner or later coming up against the reality that, not only will there be no restoration of the 'welfare state' as a whole, but that – within the present system – not a single one of these basic defences can be restored.

No matter, then, how much better off in material terms the workers in the advanced countries are, compared with those in Asia, Africa and Latin America. They too face the catastrophic consequences of capital's 'destructive self-reproduction'. Opposition to these consequences should not be seen as merely a dogged determination to return to an earlier status quo. Its positive content must be brought to the fore: it is a fight for the future, a fight to defend, against capital's destructiveness and degradation of the producers, the most vital forces of a reconstructed, socialist society. The workers in these countries inevitably see their struggles initially in purely defensive terms, and fight within the old forms. But major struggles have already forced them to begin to test out new ways of fighting; and to develop a consciousness that they are now involved in a quite new period which forces them to find ways to change their organisational forms and methods. Then will come into focus the unity of their own interests and struggles with those of others on a worldwide scale. They will see their fight as one with the struggles of the opponents of environmental destruction; of the oppressed and impoverished ex-colonial peoples; of people taking their stand against the debasement of culture; of those who fight to end such abominations as 'ethnic cleansing' and the wars that ravage Africa. To repeat: it is a common struggle against the degradation now being inflicted on nature and on humanity by capital in the period of its global, structural crisis. And this is a *positive* struggle, the *only* positive life-work today. It is the work to protect and defend the natural and human foundations of the society of free men and women that must replace the rule of capital.

'The muck of ages'

Early on, Marx and Engels began to clarify the necessity of this fight against degradation. In the mid-1840s in *The German Ideology*, they wrote that the proletariat is

> a class which forms the majority of all members of a society, and from which emanates the consciousness of the necessity of a fundamental revolution, the communist consciousness which may, of course, arise among the other classes too through the contemplation of the situation of this class. The communist revolution is directed against the hitherto existing mode of activity, does away with labour, and abolishes the rule of all classes with the classes themselves, because it is carried through by the class which no longer counts as a class in society, which is not recognised as a class, and is in itself the expression of the dissolution of all classes, nationalities, etc., within present society.
>
> Both for the production on a mass scale of this communist consciousness, and for the success of the cause itself, the alteration of men on a mass scale is necessary, an alteration which can only take place in a practical movement, a revolution; the revolution is necessary, therefore, not only because the ruling class cannot be

> overthrown in any other way, but also because the class overthrowing it can only in a revolution succeed in ridding itself of all the muck of ages and become fitted to found society anew.

The last sentence here is vital for our concerns. The many-sided fight – against the degradation of culture and nature by the continuing rule of capital – is the preparation and beginning of the revolution, 'necessary ... [for the working class to] succeed in ridding itself of all the muck of ages and become fitted to found society anew'. From the Industrial Revolution onwards, the working people in the capitalist countries have sacrificed and fought to build up their defences against the 'muck' heaped upon them by their exploiters. The peoples of the colonial countries have sacrificed millions of their own to achieve independence from their oppressors. Now is the time for a new stage of struggle. In its present predominantly destructive phase, the capital system piles upon labouring humanity an unrelenting torrent of that 'muck' of which it must rid itself. That is not a task that can wait for some revolutionary apocalypse in the distant future. The dangers are too great. The many self-styled socialist revolutionaries will remain relatively tiny and ineffectual groups so long as they fail to recognise that the getting rid of 'the muck of ages' is something that has to begin now, if the necessary – and necessarily social – revolution is to be achieved. This is what I mean when I write of taking the responsibility to defend and protect the elementary foundations of the future society.

A most instructive example of this necessary defence can be found at a much earlier stage of capitalist development, a development which even then had destructive implications. Marx drafted, for the International Working Men's Association of the 1860s – the First International – a resolution on education and the responsibility of the working-class movement to defend the rights of children. It contains the following:

> We deal here only with the most indispensable antidotes against the tendencies of a social system which degrades the working man into a mere instrument for the accumulation of capital, and transforms parents by their necessities into slave-holders, sellers of their own

> children. The right of children and juvenile persons must be vindicated. They are unable to act for themselves. It is, therefore, the duty of society to act on their behalf. If the middle and higher classes neglect their duties toward their offspring, it is their own fault. Sharing the privileges of these classes, the child is condemned to suffer from their prejudices. The case of the working class stands quite different. The working man is no free agent. In too many cases, he is even too ignorant to understand the true interest of his child, or the normal conditions of human development. However, the more enlightened part of the working class fully understands that the future of its class, and, therefore, of mankind, altogether depends upon the formation of the rising working generation. They know that, before everything else, the children and juvenile workers must be saved from the crushing effects of the present system.

Already here, in 1866, 'the future of mankind' must be protected by the working class against the destructiveness of capital.

Marx's resolution also provides a priceless lesson in how to fight for reforms not as a reformist but from the standpoint of the social revolution. Opposing himself to the anarchists, he shows how the working class must work within, and even through, the state which it must eventually overthrow:

> This can only be effected by converting social reason into social force, and, under given circumstances, there exists no other method of doing so, than through general laws, enforced by the power of the state. In enforcing such laws, the working class do not fortify governmental power. On the contrary, they transform that power, now used against them, into their own agency. They effect by a general act what they would vainly attempt by a multitude of isolated individual efforts.

This defence and protection of the elementary foundations of a future truly human society is the task of the working class itself, and not of any self-appointed 'leadership'. This is in no way in contradiction to *The Communist Manifesto*'s affirmation that communists seek to be the most far-sighted elements in the struggles of the working class. It re-emphasises the accompanying sentence: that the communists have no interests separate and apart from those of the working class. Only from such a standpoint can we envisage the way in which the coming together of many partial (plural) and different struggles can take place, and work to realise it. What forms will these struggles take? How can they become truly international? How can they establish bases for beginning to assert truly human relations against the inhumanity of the rule of capital? These are the questions that must, and now can, be confronted in practice, and theoretically addressed in a serious way. Only in this way can human reason be applied – in the interests of men, women and children throughout the world – to nature in the conditions of today's (and tomorrow's) highly developed means of production.

Internationalism

Alain Bihr has made very well the point that whatever the obvious difficulty of the task, a socialist re-orientation of the working-class movement requires that capital and its mode of exploitation be confronted at the level where it actually takes place – that is at the global level – economically and politically:

> Given the transnationalisation of capital, given the growing international centralisation of industrial capital and even more of finance capital, given the transnational organisation of the ruling class (within the networks and cartels of multinational companies, of transnational organisations like the World Trade Organisation, the IMF and the World Bank, etc.), it is the transnational organisation of the proletariat that today becomes a vital necessity for the conduct of the class struggle.[5]

Here we are back with the main problem. Given the enormous changes wrought by 'globalisation' – in particular, the sharpening of the divisions within the working class which must be overcome if the necessary unity is to be achieved – will the proletariat fulfil what Marx saw as its destiny? Its destiny, that is to say, as the force that can end the rule of capital, a rule now more dangerous than ever. To repeat a passage from Mészáros:

> ... the positive outcome depends not on the recognition by intellectuals that the historical justification of the capital system is over, but on the material force of a conscious social agency capable of eradicating

> capital from the social metabolic process, superseding thereby the rule of 'alien wealth' over society. If that agency proves to be unequal to the task, there can be no hope for the socialist project. But then, there can be no hope for humanity either.[6]

We have already noted – but it bears repeating – that it is not possible to predict when, or in what form, the socio-economic and political effects of capital's structural crisis will provide the conditions favourable to a refoundation of working-class internationalism. We cannot know in advance exactly what new forms of organisation and expressions of class-consciousness will prove necessary to confront global capital. What is at the same time true, however, is that the transnational companies' ever-growing need to coordinate widely separated operations, and to ensure uninterrupted production on a global scale, makes them vulnerable to industrial action and solidarity by their workers. This must be a central positive element in the refoundation of the working-class movement, as it takes up the basic questions of unemployment and closures, wages, erosion of working conditions, defence of democratic rights, and so on.

A spectacular example is the longshoremen's dispute on the US west coast in the summer and autumn of 2002. The employers began their attack with a lockout, and in the subsequent long-running struggle the Bush Administration invoked the infamous Taft-Hartley laws to enforce normal working. Despite all this, the workers won the dispute. The principal reason was that their resolute action (supported by solidarity from other workers in the US and internationally) tied up billions of dollars' worth of parts and raw materials. These were essential for the internationally coordinated operations through which the auto and other industries now operate; and these internationally coordinated operations have been forced on the companies so that they can take advantage of differential wage-rates and levels of union organisation.

This strike action – and the earlier, mid-1990s, action in Britain by the Liverpool dockers (for which, see the indispensable 'labournet' website) – also demonstrates another, and crucial, element in the new, emergent forms of class struggle. That is the use of electronic communication for mobilisation of solidarity by the workers, as in this strike. And here a new factor needs to be considered. At the centre of the 'destructive self-reproduction' of capital is the transformation of the means of production entailed in the 'information revolution'.

More and more, the means of production become identical with the means of communication. This suggests a new form of the contradictions of the capital system in its globalised phase, in that the technological developments it finds necessary can be used against it. If it was true in the eighteenth century that 'all economy is economy of time' it is infinitely more true today and for the future. The potential for a development of mankind's productive forces contained in this revolution is incalculable. Undoubtedly, electronic communication and use of the internet, with instant contact and response, will be at the disposal of all those who take up the struggle, and immensely facilitate the necessary internationalisation. Can we not say that in this way, at every point where it resists the destructive drive of globalised capital, the working class, as itself the principal productive force, will be taking into its hands and putting to truly productive use the very means of production developed by capital?

In a very real sense, this will be a social-revolutionary act, the beginning of the release of productive forces from the deadly grip of capital, an anticipation of the positive content of what Marx saw as the essential 'universal intercourse'. Like the protection of the natural environment and of the physical and mental health of the producers themselves, this use of the modern means of communication/production against capital is part of the necessary taking of responsibility for the elementary bases of the future society. Even more important, it will be a vital contributor to turning defensive into offensive struggles, something that is absolutely essential.

At the more fundamental level, this, in an important sense, is a preparation for – even a beginning of – that 'alteration of men on a mass scale' necessary for the social revolution. In the course of taking power from capital and its representatives and effecting the transition to socialism, the working class will transform itself into 'the associated producers'. The producers themselves will organise not only production in the individual units and sectors, but will find ways to take responsibility for the regulation and advancement of the production of use-values in the economy as a whole, in a rational, truly human use of natural resources. There will be created a unity of productive work with decision-making, overcoming the old division of labour, especially the division between mental and manual labour. A refounded internationalism confronting global capital is vitally necessary. The practical mastery of the revolution in the means of communication is essential to such a process of refoundation. And, at the same time, acquiring that mastery will be a powerful and necessary foundation for the producers to build the future socialist society on the basis of those advanced productive forces and 'universal intercourse' without which it would be impossible. Indeed, electronic communication and the internet surely go much further than anything Marx could have imagined in facilitating 'universal intercourse'.

Of crucial importance in the long term is that the objective development of globalised capital, now that it has entered the period of its structural crisis, brings what Mészáros has termed the 'downward equalisation of the differential rate of exploitation'. This provides the conditions for overcoming the division between workers in the dominant capitalist countries and those in the 'superexploited' world, a division that has been so very favourable for capital.

A striking example of the differential rate of exploitation was given in an essay by major Filipino historian and political thinker, Renato Constantino. He wrote: 'Ford Philippines, Inc., established only in 1967, is now (four years later) 37th in the roster of 1,000 biggest corporations in the Philippines. In 1971 it reported a return on equity of 121.32 per cent, whereas its overall return on equity in 133 countries in the same year was only 11.8 per cent. Aside from the incentives extracted from the government, Ford's high profits were mainly due to cheap labour. While the US hourly rate for skilled labour in 1971 was almost $7.50, the rate for similar work in the Philippines was only $0.30.' The relative privileges enjoyed in the capitalistically advanced countries have started to erode in the last

> three decades, as a result of capital's narrowing margins and of its ongoing transnational globalisation. This downward equalisation of the differential rate of exploitation is a most significant trend of development in our time, and it is bound to assert itself with increasing severity in the coming decades.[7]

It almost goes without saying that to organise more and more on the now necessary global scale, workers will need to create new forms of what were first called their 'combinations', and later 'trade unions'. This will mean either turning upside down their existing bureaucratised unions and driving out their pro-capitalist leaderships; or – as some French workers have already begun to do – building new types of unions; or both. Once a truly internationalist turn is made by the workers' movement, it will find that transnational operations have by no means given unqualified advantages to the employers. Transnational companies must have coordinated, continuous and uninterrupted lines of supply and interchange, with precise sequences and transfers of materials, parts and information. They are involved in monopoly competition on a massive scale, with constant threat of heavy losses if the smooth flow of their operations is disturbed. In other words, they are therefore inescapably vulnerable to internationally organised working-class action. Furthermore, the very real threat of destruction posed by capital's continued rule means that workers in their organisations will find willing allies, adept at using modern methods of communication, among those opposing capital in other ways. This is the most essential significance of the 'anti-globalisation' protesters (already experienced in the new means of communication) and the movements to defend the environment and endangered communities.

The 'other side' is well aware of all this. It sees the 'danger' of the internet. A public relations expert called in to advise multinationals on how to deal with protestors against globalisation is said to have told his clients that the 'greatest threat to the corporate world's reputation comes from the internet, the pressure groups' newest weapon. The agile use of global tools such as the internet reduces the advantage that corporate budgets once provided.' What a nice expression: 'global tools'! And the US professor of economics, Harry Cleaver, has written that 'the most serious challenge to the basic institutional structures of modern society flows from the emergence of computer-linked global social movements'.

Marx wrote about intellectuals who would 'join' the proletariat. Among today's scientists there are many who understand the gross distortions of research and technique, who can put at the disposal of the working class the theoretical work their education facilitates. Besides this, they can offer their particular expertise – in the field of information technology and in projects that can bring together workers in the advanced and in the ex-colonial countries – and begin to make inroads into capital's monopolistic control of production.[8] This makes more real the prospect indicated by Marxist historian Ellen Meiksins Wood, when she wrote that after the collapse of reformism based on Keynesian theory

> ... political action cannot just take the form of *intervening* in the capitalist economy but must increasingly take the form of *detaching* material life from the logic of capitalism. *That* is the kind of thing the left should be thinking about, instead of allowing itself to be paralysed by the bogeyman of globalisation.[9]

David Hookes, at a conference in Moscow, indicated the possibilities for projects of sustainable development out of the grip of capital:

> It is possible, now, not after a future seizure of state power, to set up a worldwide alliance of producers that can consciously connect their productive activities together, that can access a web of problem-solving scientific and technical expertise. For instance in Russia there is a vast army of unemployed or semi-employed scientists and engineers created by the Stalinist state, *inter alia*, to create the means to protect itself. They can be connected together in a web of expertise accessible to a network of cooperative producers anywhere on the planet.[10]

(A striking example of the contemporary relevance of *The Communist Manifesto*'s 'intellectuals who go over to the side of the proletariat'!)

Cooperatives of producers have in the past always come up against ruthless restrictive measures by banks and capitalist competitors in the total system, and such problems will certainly confront any future ventures. However, such ventures, given the new possibilities just indicated, will be a vital component of that combination of the many struggles and movements arising from resistance to globalised capital. In *Beyond Capital*, Mészáros emphasises that the transformation of – at first inevitably defensive – struggles, into the necessary socialist offensive, requires the combination, or coordination, of multifold movements concerned with many different issues. These movements are not in themselves necessarily socialist in content. It is in their combination, and the impossibility of realising their goals under the reign of capital that their social-revolutionary character inheres. (And see my booklet *A New Party for Socialism.*) I have dwelt here on the uses of electronic communication by the opponents of capital, not least because this is highly relevant to addressing this vital question of combination and coordination.

In this context, it is perhaps even more important that in the past, those who made attempts at cooperative production could not but be limited by their national or local character. Now they will be able to begin to reach out to the future genuinely 'universal intercourse' and the 'mass communist consciousness' that must accompany it. This will mean a highly significant positive change in the content and scope of what Marxists have understood as the class consciousness necessary for the socialist revolution. That is to say, it will clarify in practice the complex and hitherto unanswered question of the relation between the fight for conquest of state power on the one hand and projects of independent cooperative production on the other. It cannot be said too often that 'class consciousness' is not, as Marxists have so often thought, only a consciousness of the way of pursuing the class struggle in such a way as to overthrow the state power of the bourgeoisie (a consciousness thought to be imparted to the working class by a self-appointed 'revolutionary leadership'). On the contrary, it must be a 'practical consciousness' (Marx) acquired by the working class through its experiences and enriched by theory. It will mature as something much richer and more vital as the class, in its struggles, summons up the feelings and the spirit of the sacrifices and the courage of its ancestors – the spirit they acquired in their fight against oppression and exploitation. In this way it will learn to make more vivid and realistic its hopes for the truly human future.

The 'material grounds' today

A refounded working-class internationalism for the 21st century will draw a great deal from a noble past of struggle, but however important the lessons of former achievements and setbacks, these are not the central questions. The workers' 'class movement' as a socialist internationalist force cannot be a 'reconstruction' of former organisations and programmes. It will need to be founded on confrontation with, and comprehension of, the actual 21st century form and power of its antagonist, capital. The first big question, therefore, concerns the realism of the following:

> The material ground of the workers' solidarity – on the basis of which the structural parameters of capital can be challenged – is being objectively reconstituted by the global integrative processes themselves. For, without the latter, capital cannot fulfil its controlling functions at the present juncture of history.[11]

Undoubtedly, until only a few years ago, it could seem utopian to say:

> For a long time, the forces of socialist emancipation were greatly handicapped by capital's ability to assume a conflict-attenuating transnational mode of functioning while denying its equivalent to its labour force trapped within the confines of various particularistic determinations and divisions. The necessity to overcome such determinations and divisions through the reconstitution of materially anchored international solidarity represents the greatest challenge to labour for the foreseeable future.[12]

Central to the problem of grasping the new foundations upon which working-class internationalism must now be built, and going beyond what Marx knew to be essential in his own day, is the articulation, since the third quarter of the twentieth century, of the capital system's structural crisis. Here begins a period in which the objectively essential self-reproduction of capital becomes predominantly destructive:

> In sharp contrast to the predominantly productive social articulation of capital in Marx's lifetime, contemporary capitalism has reached the stage where the radical disjunction of genuine production and capital's self-reproduction is no longer some remote possibility but a cruel reality, with the most devastating implications for the future. For the barriers to capitalist production today are overcome by capital itself in the form of securing its own reproduction – to an already large and constantly growing extent – inescapably as destructive self-reproduction, in antagonistic opposition to genuine production.
>
> In this sense, capital's limits can no longer be conceptualised as merely the material obstacles to a greater increase in productivity and social wealth, and thus as a brake on development, but as the direct challenge to the very survival of mankind.[13]

Recognition of this threat is already a powerful force in stimulating opposition to the workings of global capital, but when and how can such opposition find itself in the conditions for an effective challenge to the system?

> The limits of capital can turn against it as the overpowering controller of the social metabolism not when its interests collide with the general social interest of increasing the powers of genuine production – the first impact of such collision could be felt, in fact, a long time ago – but only when capital is no longer able to secure, by whatever means, the conditions of its destructive self-reproduction and thereby causes the breakdown of the overall social metabolism.[14]

Unless the specifically developed forms taken by the contradictions of capital in its present stage of development are confronted, practically and theoretically, then there will be no effective refounding of the proletarian class movement in preparation for that 'breakdown'. The transition to 'imperialism', in which monopoly and finance capital predominate, with massive export of capital, division of the world between the great powers and world wars for its redivision, was already well under way as the twentieth century began. And it already demanded changes in analysis, strategy and tactics that Marx could not have known. Now the 'globalisation' of capital as its structural crisis unfolds means new contradictions, new problems for capital in combating or postponing these contradictions, and thus new challenges, practical and theoretical, to the working class in its struggle against capital. An indispensable contribution of the work of Mészáros lies in the way he has consistently over several decades drawn attention to the significance of Marx's insight, in a letter to Engels, that has been almost totally neglected by most Marxists:

> The historic task of bourgeois society is the establishment of the world market, at least in outline, and of the production based on that market. Since the world is round, the colonisation of California and Australia and the opening up of China and Japan would seem to have completed this process. For us, the difficult question is this: on the Continent revolution is imminent and will, moreover, assume a socialist character. Will it not necessarily be crushed in this little corner of the earth, since the movement of bourgeois society is still in the ascendant over a far greater area?[15]

It is not at all difficult to draw conclusions. Capital has continued 'in the ascendant' on the world scale until our own day – not only in terms of geographical expansion but in the form of a new totality. And it has proved to have the capacity to exploit the productivity of labour on a massive scale and to displace its internal contradictions in new ways. Contained in this 'movement of bourgeois society' to the present global level, however, was a momentous consequence – namely, that it is only now that the conditions for a historical/structural crisis of the whole system (as against local and conjunctural crises restricted in space or in time) could come about. The outward signs of this critical inability of the capital system to nourish human life with the productive powers which have matured during its 'ascendancy' are now everywhere glaringly apparent. Not only are poverty, starvation and disease rampant in the world; the crisis now reaches into every sphere of human life – political, cultural, moral. Never before has it been so self-evident that a socialist perspective and strategy must be internationalist. Stalin's 'socialism in a single country' was rightly challenged in its own period from an internationalist standpoint, but the issue remained disputed. In our times that dispute has been resolved by the resounding verdict of history. It is no longer enough, however, only to learn the indispensable lessons of the 'soviet experiment' and the historical period of which it formed such an important part. The crucial point is this. By the time of the collapse of Stalinism at the end of the 1980s, world capital – far from being able to gain a new lease of life from what its apologists and political time-servers called the failure of communism – was already entering the stage of its structural crisis. In its period of 'destructive self-reproduction' it was in no position to resolve the problems of the former Soviet bloc and to make possible a new phase of progressive development by doing so.

In this new phase, the very structure of the capital system has basic and inherent contradictions that are in essence beyond its ability to eliminate or control. It is in the struggles to respond to and comprehend these contradictions of 'globalised' capital and their consequences that the working class and those who join it will re-found the necessary internationalism. Mészáros summarises these contradictions, inseparably interconnected and impossible to confront one by one, as follows:

> (1) the contradiction between monopoly and competition;
>
> (2) the contradiction 'between the increasing socialisation of production and the discriminatory appropriation of its products';
>
> (3) the contradiction 'between the growing international division of labour and the drive of the strongest national powers for hegemonic domination of the global system';
>
> (4) the structural antagonism between transnationally expanding capital and national states.[16]

Here we arrive at the most vital consideration of all. It is this. The social processes which reproduce, are involved in, and are consequent on, these contradictions are mutually interconnected and interacting to form a totality, which is not only global, as 'everyone' knows, but is by its nature out of control. 'By its nature', because every particular capital entity can survive and continue to be reproduced as the social relation of domination and exploitation which it is, only through the drive to accumulate, in competition with others. The system as a whole is uncontrolled and uncontrollable. It is this imperative[17] of accumulation that lies at the root of all the massive destructive consequences of 'globalisation'. And, as I have stressed, these amount to the totality of the crises which the anti-capitalist movement is, in its own way, addressing. First, the plunder and exhaustion of natural resources, the pollution of the atmosphere and disruption of the food chain, global warming, and the threat of the destruction of the planet. Second, mass structural unemployment, the ravages of poverty and disease in Asia and Africa. And, third, the virtually uninterrupted series of wars and the existence of weapons of mass destruction, 'ethnic cleansing', and social breakdown of all kinds in every country.

In the earlier periods of its ascendancy, capital found the means economically to attenuate its contradictions for a time, usually by 'exporting' them through territorial expansion and conquest. That option no longer exists; and the most important consequence of this is that the resulting social problems, as well as the many movements of protest, are met by increasing erosion of people's rights and use of old and new forces of state repression. These, together with the intervention of the state machine to subsidise, protect and at times rescue capitalist enterprises at national and regional level, make nonsense of the 'neo-liberal' chatter about curbing the role of the state. In the years between and after the two world wars, state interventionist – for example, Keynesian and 'New Deal' – policies could be used, not only to stimulate economic revival, but also to administer social palliatives in the form of welfare benefits. It could even be correctly said that, as Trotsky put it, social-democratic reformism was needed to serve as 'a form of rule' by the capitalist class in some countries. But in this period of structural crisis, of the 'articulation of capital's limits', state/political intervention in the economy goes along with the attack on past reform gains and on people's rights. The use of the law to cripple trade-union organisation is a particular, and central, example of this. And this necessity for capital is the entirely sufficient explanation for the craven servility of the European 'socialist', 'social-democratic' and 'Labour' parties in abandoning not only their never-serious socialist rhetoric but also even the reformist form of their long-standing service to capital. They now become enthusiastic 'parties of government' to carry out the necessary attack on past working-class gains. Examples could be taken from Britain or any Western European country. A recent one from Germany may suffice:

> As Gerhard Schröder tries to cut £60 billion from Germany's health and welfare budget, a series of rolling strikes has compounded the struggling Chancellor's woes. So short of money is Schröder that he has little room for manoeuvre with the striking public services union, Verdi, whose leaders are infuriated by the budget cuts, defying calls for a pay freeze by demanding a 3% rise. 'Slashing welfare affects the needy – it's grossly unfair to make them suffer,' a union spokesman said. In the northeast of the country last week, the authorities in Mecklenburg-Vorpommern, one of the poorest states, were forced to close a hospital they could no longer afford to run. 'We have not been able to go on. There is no more money in the kitty,' said Gunter Gotal, the administrator of the University Clinic hospital in the town of Greifswald. Nearly all the patients from the 88-bed hospital have been moved out and most of the 470 doctors have been told to stay at home or take a holiday. 'There was nothing else to do. Only the cancer patients and those in intensive care remain,' Gotal said.
>
> Under pressure from local politicians who had hoped to avert the shutdown, many doctors and nurses agreed initially to work unpaid overtime. But the hospital was still unable to balance the books. 'They are not dramatising the situation – it is serious,' said Andreas Crusius, the vice-president of the national doctors' association. He predicted more hospital closures throughout the country as the chancellor's money runs out. Opponents of the Social Democratic chancellor said his austerity measures would ensure that unemployment reached 4.4m next year and investors would be driven from Germany.[18]

This definitive end of social-democratic reformist parties as organs of the working class comes together with the collapse of the Stalinist regimes in the Soviet Union, Eastern Europe and China, and the seamless transformation of the Stalinist bureaucracy into an apprentice capitalist class. Communist parties everywhere are completely 'denatured'. And all this is one of the most important of those consequences of the structural crisis that has to be recognised and acted upon in the struggle to refound the socialist internationalism of the working-class. Essentially, the means of political control over the working class through social-democratic and Stalinist parties has gone, a loss which will have untold consequences once there is a major revival of the class struggle in the advanced capitalist countries. Given the structural crisis of capital and the necessity of clawing back the past gains of the working-class movement, it is only a matter of time before the working class is compelled to confront the necessity of finding its own political forms of struggle adequate to the new situation. Trade unions cannot avoid being more and more in conflict with governments (including 'socialist' or 'Labour' ones) as well as particular employers. My earlier booklet, *A New Party for Socialism* tried to deal with this.[19]

By the year 2003, this process was already under way. In France, the response of the Raffarin government to the erosion of pension funds (a 'global' phenomenon) was to impose on public sector workers an extension of several years to their working lives. Trade unions found themselves having to organise rolling strikes and even short general strikes. The magnitude of such a problem leaves no room for compromise in the long and medium term, and a major confrontation at the political level, i.e. a political mobilisation in the class struggle, is unavoidable. The same year, in Britain, after years of Blair's New Labour regime, the strike of firefighters for a living wage provoked the government to threaten the imposition of a compulsory return to work enforced by law. Thc threat came from the party founded a century earlier to defend trade unions from the law. By June 2003 the *Times* reported the stirrings of a significant political development in the country's largest trade union, Unison:

> Activists will vote next week on whether to coordinate pay claims across such areas as the NHS and local government, with coordinated industrial action planned across the board if those claims are unsuccessful. In a move which would shake the Labour Party to its

> core, it is also preparing to create a new political fund which could be used to support other parties, including the far-left Socialist Alliance. Any move to back non-Labour candidates in elections is feared by some Union leaders as creating *de facto* disaffiliation from the party. … [The motion in question] speaks of dismay 'at the actions of the Government over the Fire Brigades Union strike where calls for modernisation and changes to service provisions were provocatively used as a device to undermine the union's claim for a pay rise.' Unison is raising the heat on industrial relations by proposing to make contributions to its strike fund regular and permanent rather than the ad hoc arrangements it presently employs. It will vote on making annual payments of £11 million to the strike fund, which currently stands at £127 million. Additionally, the move by the left within the union to create a political fund which would back candidates such as the Socialist Workers Party in elections, could cause the biggest upset yet in the unions' relations with the Labour Party.
>
> Unison leaders are seeking to head off the move but senior sources concede that confidence in Labour within the union has been rocked by the Iraq war, plans for foundation hospitals and the continued use of the private sector in public services. …

As for some of the inspirers of these proposals who hope that money would flow into their own 'left' organisations instead of the Labour Party, they need urgently to learn that a truly working-class party will be a party *of* the working class. It will not be one supplied to it by those who know best. And, as for the question of 'vanguard' parties in general, a party for socialism – for the social revolution – will be formed from those workers who take the lead in the struggles to come. They will emerge as men and women genuinely in the vanguard of coordinating and strengthening those struggles. Together with socialists (I don't like the word 'intellectuals' that is often used in this context) who join them, they will prove themselves the most far-seeing in these struggles. They will have learned from the longstanding mistakes and misconceptions of 'vanguardism' and applied themselves to the new theoretical tasks posed by the rule of capital as its structural crisis deepens.

Forced more and more into these essentially political conflicts, trade unionists will have to find ways to confront and succeed in another, internal, conflict. For many decades their unions have been controlled by entrenched bureaucracies, composed in the main of careerist office-holders. These bureaucracies not only limit the role of trade unions to negotiations with employers; they see capitalism as the only possible form of society, and in the course of the last hundred years they have become more and more integrated with the capitalist state and its organs. An example from France may be cited. When the trade-union federation, the CGT – traditionally led by Communist Party members – found itself at the head of a mass mobilisation against the government's pension reform, it was even forced to propose a general strike. Yet its secretary in charge of pension matters, Jean Christophe Le Duigou, answered questions from *Le Monde* in a typically conservative way:

> Q: Is the CGT sufficiently clear in its intentions? Some people are criticising you for not really going for a confrontation.
>
> A: We are in a logic of demands. We don't have any political objective, either to defeat the government or to show that it is right-wing, which everyone knows. Our wish is to build a movement based on the public and private sectors that can win a trade union fight. It cannot be based on a political alternative. Building a movement on our demands is exacting enough. There is no slogan that could take us beyond the totality of the problems. To suspect us of not wanting a confrontation with the government on the pretext of not radicalising the action is a false accusation. The real debate is about the demands we are pursuing.

And particularly interesting was Le Duigou's response to the next question. He and his colleagues sensed that trade unions face a new situation, but he very deliberately distanced himself from the looming conclusions:

> Q: In your opinion, what is the relationship between the trade unions' demands and the political sphere?
>
> A: The role of the trade unions is more extensive, broader than the role they traditionally developed. But (!) the trade union movement cannot substitute itself for politics at some given moment. Today we suffer from a lack of democracy. The trade union movement cannot

> entirely fill this gap, but it can contribute towards it. We in the CGT are elaborating an approach through demands that are no longer subordinated to a political alternative.

The words of Rosa Luxemburg, Leon Trotsky and many others, over a full century ago, are forgotten: a general strike poses the question of power! François Chesnais's commentary on the strikes in France on the pension reforms was thus appropriately entitled 'The workers now directly confront the trade union apparatuses'.[20] This is of course directly related to our theme of 'refoundation'. Chesnais writes:

> The movement of strikes and demonstrations is the expression at the level of the class struggle of the election results of 21 April. If polls had been taken, they would almost certainly have shown a close correspondence between the 3 million electors who voted 'far left' in the first round of the presidential elections (many of them belonging to the Communist Party and even the Socialist Party) and the workers who participated in the strikes and demonstrations starting on 1 May 2003. Considered in relation to the long historical development of the class struggle in France, the two events (electoral on 21 April 2002 and 'social' in May-June 2003) mark a real turning-point in the political history of France. This time we truly are in the presence of that 'recomposition of the working class and its placing on a new axis', except that the new axis is not that of a party, as Trotsky hoped. Still less is it that of a trade union leadership. Neither is it, for the time being, that of a programme. ... Workers are entering into a process which combines action with becoming conscious of what is at stake. From this process there can develop, although it is in no way guaranteed, a programme and new forms of political organisation, perhaps including a new anti-capitalist workers' party.

The importance of our earlier emphasis on pluralism is that battles like these will join with many other forms of struggle against the consequences of capital's rule in its period of 'destructive self-reproduction'. But ... (and it is an important 'but'), in approaching the tasks of refoundation, it is essential at this point to confront what is perhaps the most difficult question of all. The deregulation/ 'neo-liberal' policies, 'technological revolution', etc., characteristic of the period of structural crisis/'globalisation', present new problems to the working-class movement, affecting directly the content and forms of the class struggle in the advanced capitalist countries.

In this book, I have stressed the essentially identical nature of the working class whatever the period or the circumstances. But it is now absolutely necessary to see that in the last few decades the labour process itself and the immediate relations between workers and their employers within the advanced capitalist countries have been greatly changed. I cannot do better here than reproduce a contribution by Claude Luchetta. One does not have to agree with everything he says to recognise his sharp characterisation of these changes, and some of their implications:

> The working class has not disappeared. But its image is blurred because its status has been much modified and fragmented within production itself. This modification must be studied if we want revolutionary Marxist activity to retain its meaning.

The modifications in the wage-labouring class and their causes:

> First it is necessary to get rid of a received idea. The working class, defined as all those men (and women) who sell their labour-power, still exists. Let us recall that for Marx, the wage-labourer is one who is 'free' to sell his labour-power 'for a determinate time' to the owner of the means of production. And the labour-power of the wage-labouring class does not have a natural origin but is a historical given according to a given form of civilisation. In other words, the working class is constantly in evolution. Its contours are not defined once and for all. There exists no abstract and timeless essence of the working class. ... More than 7 million workers represent 28 per cent of the active population of France. Workers constitute 24.5 per cent of the population in the United States, 33 per cent in Japan, 30.6 per cent in Brazil. In France, 40 per cent of children are brought up in a working-class family. While at the beginning of 1980s industrial workers were the great majority of workers, today they are a minority. One worker in two works either in transport and distribution or directly in production. The decline in occupations linked to production has also

favoured a diversification of occupations: sorting, packaging, delivery, gardeners, fitting/assembly, insulation. This diversification goes along with chronic under-employment. In 2001, 30 per cent of unqualified workers were employed part-time. In 1982, 40 per cent of unqualified jobs were held by 'CDD's (people on fixed-term contracts, three years maximum, possibly renewable), those in temporary jobs replacing someone, or employed by an agency handling such replacements, and those in an 'interim' (training period, often unpaid); today the figure is 17 per cent. The de-qualification is considerable: 31 per cent of workers taken on for jobs officially requiring no qualification hold a CAP (*certificat d'aptitude professionelle*) or a BEP (*brevet d'enseignement professionnel* – technical trade diplomas which used to carry a quasi-virtual guarantee of employment at a wage level negotiated between employers and recognised unions).

At the beginning of the 1980s, the number of industrial workers was 50 per cent greater than other employees. Today, other employees, paid at close to the minimum wage in difficult jobs, liable to insecurity, 'flexibility' and the risk of unemployment, exceed numbers of industrial workers by 15 per cent. Workers' jobs total 12 to 13 million in France. The job with the most spectacular growth in recent decades has been ... maternal assistance. By contrast, the number of secretaries and typists has fallen by more than 30 per cent (at least 200,000 jobs). These changes in the working class are partly due to the way that the sizes of enterprises have evolved. Between 1975 and 1996, the percentage of establishments in the industrial sector with more than 200 workers declined from 54.4 per cent to 39.7 per cent, a tendency determined by the big industrial and financial groups to which the small units are subordinated. For example, automobile manufacturers directly carry out only a quarter of the construction of a vehicle. The rest is done by small enterprises, which they control. The number of such enterprises grew by almost five times between 1980 and 1995 (from 9,200 to 44,700). Big mergers are the source of the systematic turn to sub-contracting.

These phenomena (reduction in the size of firms, systematic sub-contracting) greatly aggravate working conditions: intensification of productivity, flexible working hours, periods of lay-off for temporary workers, individualisation, harassment. At the same time, the culture of skill is lost and qualification is replaced by 'competence'. It should not be forgotten that the working class first organised itself in craft unions. But I shall return to that. Smaller, fragmented units of production do not favour trade union organisation and make the task of inspection of work difficult. In short, contrary to the environmentalist ideology which values small production structures as bearers of a different 'quality' of life, small and medium-sized enterprises serve to increase the number of insecure jobs which need no qualifications. They are also the most destructive of crafts, and of older workers.

Changes in the labour market have had devastating effects on social relations and workers' organisational forms. Since the 1970s renewal of the working class has posed a problem. At Peugeot (Sochaux-Montbeliard) in the course of the 1980s production was reorganised by management, breaking up work-teams and relocating certain units to avoid or divert workers' resistance. In 1990, the replacement of non-qualified labour was done through hiring temporary workers – unqualified but adaptable – on a massive scale. A dichotomy between 'young' and 'old' was created, helping to deepen the crisis of militancy. The 'collective worker' tended to disappear. Stagnation in wages and a system of bonuses reinforce a negative prejudice already held by young people against factory work. 'Working-class culture' is something negative in the eyes of the new generations. ...

The value of labour-power is also the result of ability. It is no longer work that is valued, but management relations in the firm. The relation between worker and boss is based on 'confidence': a contractual relation without guarantees and without any recourse. The group identity of workers is weakened; capitalist rationality imposes a fluid and programmed web of individual competences.

Moving from a valuation of human labour based on qualifications and national diplomas to an evaluation based on 'competence' is not a natural transition or an economic inevitability. A political-economic choice is made (in the face of increased international competition) for optimum exploitation of labour-power. Qualifications meant: standard time for apprenticeship; social recognition of different trades; collective agreements; national diplomas guaranteed by the state. 'Competence' implies another way to value (or exploit) labour. Not only 'labour-power' (measured in physical capacities, technical or professional training, etc.) is at the employer's service, but the whole person. 'Competence' is concerned with manner of life. At the limit, labour-power is no longer sold for 'a determinate time' as Marx showed, but for the whole of one's existence ('lifelong training'!). The individual becomes entirely a prisoner of the labour market. Self-exploitation totally internalised by the workers is in place.

Luchetta continues with a description of what, he queries, might be called 'a broken-up workers' movement':

> The question then is to reconstitute the fabric of collective working-class resistance. Trade union organisation means resistance and identity. But only 9.1 per cent of wage-workers in France are in trade unions, one of the smallest percentages of union membership in the world. The number has not stopped falling since 1995. Life was stamped out of the CGT by Stalinism and it has never recovered; subordination to the politics of the '*gauche plurielle*' (Socialist Party/Communist Party alliance) and the historical enfeeblement of the Communist Party contribute to paralysing any initiatives. Militant groups have difficulty renewing their numbers. Regional union bodies are often in rampant crisis. The most combative militants were expelled from the CFDT in the 1980s: the CFDT section at Usinor-Dunkerque, for example, was beheaded to 'modernise' French iron and steel production, with mergers and tens of thousands of sackings. The remaining opposition to the union apparatus gave way at the last congress.
>
> SUD (alternative, more militant unions in some trades) feeds on the deficiencies of the CGT and CFDT but has not yet made real inroads into the main body of the working class, and seems locked in a 'minority' identity.
>
> Turning in on itself and atomisation of the working class are the result of management relying more and more on contractualisation. The firm 'speaking' directly to its workers must dispense with trade union counter-power, which becomes an obstacle: there is no longer any need for collective representation of the workers. During the last election campaign leaders of the German CDU even envisaged collective agreements signed contractually at enterprise, not national, level and without trade union representation. In France, proposed state reforms aim to reduce the state apparatus to its purely regulatory and repressive (defence, justice and police) functions, to contractualise and make fixed-term appointments for all public servants. The Region will become the most appropriate political space for the operations of finance capital.[21]

These tendencies were clear decades ago in the United States. In a passage entitled 'Deregulation and all that. What happened to the anti-trust laws?', George Winslow wrote:

> Nearly 100,000 unionised jobs were eliminated as a result of mergers in the 1980s. Workers who survived those cutbacks faced an increasingly insecure future – a state of affairs that made it harder for unions to demand better wages and working conditions. At the same time, deregulation had an enormous impact on several heavily unionised industries. After deregulation of the phone and telecommunications sectors, which began with the breakup of the old AT&T monopoly in 1984, local phone companies eliminated more than 300,000 jobs – most of them unionised. As a result of the corporate restructuring, deregulation, and a tougher attitude toward labour, unionised workers dropped from 29 per cent of the work force in 1975 to 18 per cent in 1985 and less than 14 per cent today [that is, 1999].[22]

Ricardo Antunes has summarised well some of the implications of such changes:

> There has been a reduction of the traditional industrial labour class. In parallel, on the other hand there is a significant underproletarianisation of labour occurring in the diverse forms of partial, precarious, casual, subcontracted labour attached to the manufacturing industries, to the informal sector and to the private sector. Therefore, one can see a significant heterogeneity, complexity and fragmentation of labour.
>
> The whole large group of salaried workers that makes up the service sector, plus the subcontracted and informal workers, the domestic workers, the unemployed and the sub-employed, added to the workers directly producing and acting as a class, will constitute the social segment with the greatest potential to oppose capital. Obviously, this possibility depends on the socio-economic particularities of each country, on its insertion in the international division of labour, as well as on the subjectivity of social beings living from labour and their political, ideological and cultural values.[23]

---

[1] See Mészáros, especially his *Beyond Capital*, François Chesnais, *Le Mondialisation du Capital* (Paris, 1999), and Hillel Ticktin's articles in the journal *Critique* (1973), passim.

[2] Mészáros, *Beyond Capital*, p. 171.

[3] Mészáros, *Beyond Capital*, p. 699.

[4] Mészáros, *Beyond Capital*, p. 699.

[5] Alain Bihr, 'Actualiser le communisme', *Carre Rouge*, no. 18 (summer 2001), p. 37.

[6] Mészáros, *Beyond Capital*, p. 811.

[7] See Mészáros's article, '*Implications of Ongoing Developments: the coming century of "Socialism or Barbarism"*', p. 8.

[8] A good example is the initiative of the Liverpool dockers who, after losing their jobs following the great strike of 1995, combined with physicist David Hookes.

[9] Robert W. McChesney, Ellen Meiksins Wood and John Bellamy Foster (eds.), *Capitalism and the Information Age* (New York, c.1998), p. 47.

[10] David Hookes, '*The Quantum Theory of Political Economy*', accessible on David Hookes's website.

[11] Mészáros, *The Power of Ideology*, p. 376.

[12] Mészáros, *The Power of Ideology*, p. 380.

[13] Mészáros, *Beyond Capital*, p. 599.

[14] Mészáros, *Beyond Capital*, p. 599.

[15] Marx to Engels, 8 October 1858, in *Marx and Engels, Collected Works*, vol. 40, p. 347.

[16] Mészáros, *Beyond Capital*, p. 161.

[17] It is this 'imperative' that constitutes the only objective content of Margaret Thatcher's famous TINA – 'there is no alternative' That is to say, from the standpoint of capital, there is no alternative. From the standpoint of humanity and its future, the very opposite is true: not only is 'another world' possible, the alternative to capitalist globalisation must be found.

[18] See report by Michael Woodhead, the *Sunday Times*, 8 December 2002)

[19] Cliff Slaughter, *A New Party for Socialism* (London, 1998).

[20] François Chesnais, 'The workers now directly confront the trade union apparatuses', *Carré Rouge*, no. 26 (June 2003).

[21] This long quotation is from Claude Luchetta, 'Les transformations de la classe ouvriere', *Carré Rouge*, no. 24 (December 2002). My translation.

[22] George Winslow, *Capital Crimes*, pp. 265-6.

[23] See *Critique* nos. 34-35.

7

TOWARDS REFOUNDATION 2: NEW FORMS OF THE STRUGGLE?

It must again be stressed that we cannot know clearly in advance what organisational forms will be taken by the plurality of struggles tending towards a refoundation of the international working-class movement – and necessarily including those in protection of the natural and human/cultural conditions of the future socialist society. But we do know – and I have emphasised this in Chapter 6 – that the massive proletarianisation continuing to take place poses entirely new problems for making the relationship between local and regional struggles and the overall conflict between capital and labour. This process of proletarianisation has many aspects, ranging from the entry of masses of women into the labour force to the penetration of the 'labour market' in hitherto isolated areas, and includes the worldwide effects of de-industrialisation and the casualisation and 'precarisation' of employment.

A few examples, however, can be given of the forms taken in the recent past by acts of resistance that already promise the necessary response to the threat posed by globalised capital. They speak for themselves, except to say that, in this context, the point is to consider them in the light of one or more of the following considerations:

(1) resistance and solidarity has to become transnational, internationalist;

(2) it must take responsibility for the elementary conditions of the future society;

(3) what are required are coordination and combination, not control from above;

(4) ways have to be found of combining working-class organisation and action with the interests and initiatives of others who oppose the threats from globalised capital.

In presenting these examples of the new and essentially pluralistic forms of struggle of the necessary, emergent movement of masses, there is one other thing I need again to make clear. I most decidedly do not imply a rejection of Marx'sand Engels' project of bringing together in one party the most far-seeing members of the working-class movement, the real communists. Insistence on the necessary pluralism of a mass movement for socialism does not imply any dilution of the rigour of Marxist theoretical work. On the contrary, it is an insistence that is inescapable from the standpoint of Marxist theory and the necessary struggle to develop it in accordance with changing conditions. What certainly must be rejected, however, is the all-too-common conception that 'leadership' means building a party already in possession of the necessary revolutionary consciousness which it will supply to the working class from without.

7.1.1 Example 1: Workers' Aid to Bosnia – by Bob Myers, an organiser of Workers' Aid to Bosnia and Kosova (1998)

Its very hard now, probably impossible, to capture in a few words the events of the autumn and winter of 1992-3. In a few months hundreds of thousands of people had loved ones killed. Not just that, the survivors were driven from their homes. Two million of them. Families became refugees, split up for months or years, the lucky ones making it into 'fortress Europe', the rest into refugee camps in one place or another. All this took place less than a day's car drive from Brussels. Here is not the place to give a history of the break-up of Yugoslavia. All I want to do is give a glimpse of people in ex-Yugoslavia who tried to fight, morally and militarily, against ethnic cleansing and ethnic oppression and a glimpse of the activities of people outside the region who tried to support them.

Throughout 1992, the world's media brought increasing news from towns and villages being ethnically cleansed. Vukovar, the antinationalist industrial town in Croatia, was shelled flat by Se nationalists. The Croatian nationalist leader Tudjman publ denounced the aggression against 'his' people but privately smiled a a centre of opposition to his rule was destroyed. In Bosnia, Sarajevo was surrounded. The Muslim side of Mostar was reduced to rubble, attacked first by Serbian nationalists and then by their Croatian counterparts from the other side of the river. The centuries-old bridge across the Neretva finally collapsed under artillery bombardment. Refugees who could escape poured out of Bosnia. Others sought refuge in towns held by Bosnian soldiers only to find that these soon were besieged, shelled, and left without heating, light, food, medicine and weapons.

From the start the United Nations imposed an arms embargo on the area, supposedly to try to halt the killing. It had no effect on the ethnic cleansers, who controlled most of the old Yugoslav army with some of the biggest stockpiles of military hardware in Europe. The embargo only hit their victims, mostly those of Muslim ancestry, who had only limited weapons – hunting rifles and then what they could slowly capture.

Across Europe and beyond, people with any sense of feeling for their fellow human beings watched the news in growing anguish. How could this be happening? Why could no one stop it? In the spring of 1993 came the news of concentration camps. So much for the 'never again after 1945' talk on the lips of the world's great statesmen. The only response to all this misery was from aid organisations who attempted to take food to the refugees, but even this soon became impossible as the nationalist forces strengthened their stranglehold over the remaining Bosnian communities holding out against their advance.

Apparently responding to public pressure, the UN finally made a move. It sent troops to assist the aid convoys in getting through. All this was done alongside a description of the war by the UN, western governments and media as an 'ethnic' or 'civil' war. Apparently Bosnia's Muslim, Croat and Serb populations had all woken up one morning determined to kill each other. From the start the 'humanitarian' organisations, the UN and all the other great organisations – like the European Parliament – talked about 'warring factions' and treated them as equally to blame. The world was reminded of 'primitive Balkan tribesmen' with their murderous characteristics that had been seen many times in the past. If people wanted to kill each other what could the world do but try to help the innocent civilians whose terrified faces could be seen on every news broadcast? The perspective of the Great Powers and UN became one of separating the 'warring factions' – in effect to divide Bosnia, the same plan as the ethnic-cleansers.

If this had been all I could see then like many others I would probably have turned off the TV and put aside the papers. For me, the future is a world without borders between people, but now a bloody slaughter was taking place designed to drive people apart. Events seemed so monstrous that, if there was nothing that could be done, then it became hard to even watch the news on TV. However, this was not the whole picture. Hidden from just about everyone's view were the people determined to resist this barbaric ethnic division. For some time I had been reading articles from a Serbian socialist, an oppositionist and follower of Trotsky [Radislav D], who, like many real socialists, had been living in exile, driven out by the autocratic Tito regime. Within socialist circles he had been fighting an almost lone battle in the late 1980s to show that the destruction of Yugoslavia was being organised not by some outside force – like German capital or NATO – as many on the left thought, but primarily by the Serbian regime itself.

The Yugoslavia established in the second world war by the partisans had been whittled away by the years of Tito's bureaucratic rule and was finally being destroyed by Milosevic. The real death of Yugoslavia came in 1989-90 when Milosevic began the total suppression of the Kosova Albanians. While the institutions of something called 'Yugoslavia' might still have existed, any idea of a federation of the region's peoples was finished. Open, extreme discrimination and oppression were now the name of the game. Milosevic, previously a businessman and bureaucrat in the energy sector, had become leader of the Serbian Communist Party on the back of an anti-Albanian hate campaign. Radislav D's articles showed that the Serbian leaders' so-called 'defence of Yugoslavia' against 'breakaway republics' was a fraud. Moves towards independence by Slovenia and Croatia were only a reaction against the growing arrogance, brutality and chauvinism of the Serbian regime as it tried to convert the eight self-governing regions of Federal Yugoslavia into its fiefdom – a 'Greater Serbia'.

Another revealing picture of events came from Bosnian refugees. At a meeting in London in June 1994, where some 60 people came together to discuss how to respond to the war, I listened to a woman from the Bosnian mining town of Tuzla. She explained how her town contained all ethnic groups fighting side by side in the trenches and organising the town's defences. For her the description of 'civil war' was a fraud put about by Milosevic and parroted by the UN. This lie helped put an equals sign between all sides in the war. It hid the true picture of a long-planned and organised assault on a unified Bosnia by the Serbian and Croatian leaders. She denounced the racist press coverage of 'Balkan tribesmen' and pointed out that all the past wars on Balkan soil were in fact clashes between the shifting great empires – Turkish, Austrian, Russian, British, French, etc. She recounted Tuzla's militant history as a part of the Balkan people's efforts to free themselves from control of the empires and their local servants. Tuzla's traditions of solidarity and militancy had shown themselves more recently too. Tuzla miners, themselves very poor, had collected money for the British miners on strike in 1984-5. Many people in the town had watched and hoped the miners would defeat Margaret Thatcher.

This focus on Tuzla was reinforced by [a letter from] my Serbian socialist contact. The Tuzla miners, he wrote, were defending a simple principle of the right of everyone to live and work together. The ethnic cleansers were besieging the town, using starvation to defeat the resistance. Couldn't British miners and trade unionists return the solidarity of 1984-5? Couldn't they try to get food to the town? Our little meeting united on trying to initiate this proposal. We would appeal to the trade unions and people at large in the UK and Europe to get food through to Tuzla. But knowing the existing trade union structures were mostly uncritically supporting their own government's 'non-intervention' stance, we decided that rather than simply appeal for them to take action we would start a convoy ourselves. The plight of the communities resisting ethnic cleansing could not be resolved by our handful of people – it needed a popular uprising – but we hoped that our example would help develop such a movement.

We started from zero. None of us had ever done anything like this. We needed money, food, lorries, drivers and so on. We had nothing. In a few cities we started putting up collecting stalls in the streets, we held public meetings, we lobbied trade union conferences. Money started to come in and we found the public keen to help. Some gave to us just as they would give to the 'humanitarian aid' collectors but many people were enthusiastic that our appeal was not simply to feed hungry people but to clearly support those resisting ethnic cleansing. We were showing a side of the war few people knew about. We got better organised. Such was the mood in the country at large that we managed to get permission to collect food inside big supermarkets. On a good day a small group of volunteers could get a ton of food and maybe £500 by asking every shopper to buy an extra item. We bought our first lorry and refugees painted our logo and telephone number on it. People saw the lorry on the streets and rang in volunteering to join the team.

Two lorries set off from the strike-bound [Dundee] Timex factory in Scotland, stopping in towns along the way, raising money, spreading awareness, gaining more active supporters. Six weeks later ten lorries assembled at Dover ready to head off across Western Europe. Five more lorries joined, from France, Hungary and Sweden. We were given official receptions at town halls and factories. A delegation from the convoy got a standing ovation from the European Parliament – but no practical support.

The convoy finally reached Zagreb in Croatia, only a couple of hundred kilometres from Tuzla. But from here the main route, down the Zagreb-Belgrade highway, was blocked. By whom? Well, to start with, by the nationalist ethnic cleansers who controlled all roads into Tuzla. But as we went from office to office in Zagreb we found something else. Zagreb housed the headquarters of the UN military forces charged with getting aid through. We were sent backwards and forwards, from military HQ to the UN High Commission for Refugees, to the Croatian government, everyone refusing to help. The real picture of UN activity began to emerge. No one wanted to help us because we were taking food to people resisting ethnic cleansing. Food could sometimes be got to refugees, people already driven from their homes, but not a finger was being lifted to help the besieged communities who were fighting to prevent the fall of their towns. No airlifts were organised, no convoys were being escorted in. Tuzla had a large airport. UN helicopters shuttled backwards and forwards but the only food landed was for UN personnel in the town. All the time the Western governments and the UN were replying to popular feelings at home by telling their citizens – 'leave it to us, we are getting help to the victims'. It was a fraud, just like their arms embargo, which only hit the resistance. The 'humanitarian aid effort' was a cover-up for the real UN/NATO/UK/US plan to divide Bosnia – exactly as the ethnic cleansers proposed. Lord Owen from the UK would shuttle backwards and forwards with various maps and proposed 'peace settlements', and they all carved up Bosnia in different ways, sometimes with borders passing right through single towns. Of course, to the outside world this made sense if it was true that all the communities hated each other. But they didn't. They were being driven apart by force. The delivery or non-delivery of food was being used as a weapon, both by the ethnic cleansers and by the great power governments. The so-called NGOs – non-governmental organisations – revealed themselves for the most part to be governmental-NGOs, in that with their uncritical stance towards the UN and Western governments they helped camouflage the filthy diplomatic/political/military intrigue going on behind the slaughter.

We took our lorries and blocked the UN military headquarters for several hours, holding up placards reading: 'Why are you letting Tuzla starve? Open the aid routes.' Local Croats joined us, venting their own anger over the way the great 'international community' had stood by as Vukovar was destroyed.

But we were still just a small campaign. Yes, we had raised more money, food, lorries, volunteers, etc., and spoken at more meetings than we had at first thought possible, but the movement we had behind us was still too small to make any impact on the UN. Almost no political parties or European trade unions or civil rights movements said anything or did anything to support the opponents of ethnic cleansing in Bosnia. Some of them followed the line of 'we must support the UN's peace effort', others looked more radical by saying 'we are for unity and so we support the maintenance of Yugoslavia'. Both lines of argument lent strength to Milosevic.

The main road to Tuzla remained blocked by the hidden alliance of armed ethnic cleansers and UN military. There were disagreements amongst the convoy team about what to do. They were people from many different countries and different backgrounds only just starting to work together. Three lorries set off to try to find a way to Tuzla through the mountains. The other people returned to their own countries. By letting people know about the UN's role and demanding that the UN open all aid routes, they pushed forward a campaign for the main road to Tuzla and central Bosnia to be opened. Several weeks later the three lorries reached Tuzla – the first outsiders for over a year, apart from UN personnel 'observing' the war.

The lorries' arrival, though bringing only the tiniest amount of food, was a great boost to the miners and townsfolk. They thought the world had abandoned them. Now friends had made it through. But there were many problems. The desperate miners' hopes were raised. They thought the lorries were the advance guard of the whole European trade union movement. Twenty thousand miners and their families needed food. We had to explain that we were in our own battle against the prevailing outlook of all our institutions and especially against our so-called 'Labour' leaders. In March 1994 an uneasy truce was brokered between the Croat nationalists and the forces of multi-ethnic Bosnia. The onslaught from the Serbian nationalist forces continued unabated but the truce opened up a route into Tuzla – not along main roads, they all remained blocked – but via a crazy route over mountains, forest dirt tracks, farm land and bits of road not under enemy control.

From the UK it would take a couple of days to reach Zagreb with all the hold-ups for customs checks at borders. From Zagreb, the pre-war route to Tuzla was a five-hour drive. Now it was taking sometimes a couple of days, if we were lucky – but usually four, five or even eight days as we slowly crawled along the mountain tracks and passed through the endless checkpoints of different armies, queuing in lines of lorries, sometimes stretching for several kilometres, and arguing and quarrelling with various nationalist/local gangster/political figures along the way. The Croatian nationalists wanted a share of our load to pass through 'their' enclave. We refused to give them so much as a tin of beans. Some 'aid' organisations handed over a third of their loads to get through. For us our food was for the community fighting against ethnic cleansing and no one else. Sometimes these local gangsters arrested our drivers or held us up for days hoping we would hand over aid, but all we did was kick up the biggest fuss we could, in the media, through politicians and so on, and we always got through – eventually.

When we planned our first convoy we had not thought where the initiative would go after that. All the time our approach was to find ways to turn the general concern of people into an organised movement of solidarity, not just taking food (by itself that could not defeat the ethnic cleansers) [but] a political movement that would organise solidarity in every possible way – a movement that would oppose the Western governments' support for the division of Bosnia and its multi-ethnic communities, and that would fight alongside them to defeat such a barbaric plan. Everywhere we got a good response from people, but they all looked to us to organise things – and we couldn't. Our tiny handful of people could barely keep the convoys going. Debts running into tens of thousands of pounds loomed over us continually. Breakdowns in our fleet of clapped-out lorries threatened disaster. We had no office, no paid organisers, and no funding but what we collected on the streets. It needed millions of people to organise themselves, or make their existing organisations take action. But none of this happened. People supported us, cheered us along, helped us, but this support never rippled outwards, never lit up a wider 'bush fire' because our little efforts were dwarfed by the 'damping down' influences of all the existing social organisations supporting the UN's 'peace initiative'.

Most of our volunteers were unemployed, young people by and large, people who hated the idea of ethnic cleansing. They didn't have jobs, they didn't have influential positions, they were not in trade unions, but one way they could express their feelings was through organising the convoys, so they kept them going. As soon as one got back we started collecting for the next one. All through 1994 and into 1995 the convoys went back and forth; dust and heat in summer, snow, frozen brakes, dirt tracks turning to vast mud quagmires in winter. Altogether, from the campaign in the UK and sister organisations in Spain and France, we took over a hundred lorries.

From the moment we first arrived in Bosnia we began to make friends and find eager collaborators amongst trade unionists, especially the miners and teachers, whose unions were really the only surviving mass organisations apart from the army. Industry had come to a halt as roads were blocked and men and women had gone to the front lines. But the teachers kept the schools going unpaid, defending multi-ethnic education and a vision of a society completely in contradiction with the plans of the ethnic cleansers. And the miners kept working to supply Tuzla's electricity generating station with fuel.

We also met up with the student union at the university. We visited health workers at the hospitals and staff at the orphanages and other institutions. We sat and talked with committees and individuals. For the most part we met with men and women who told us that before the war they never cared who was Croat or Muslim or Serb. They hated the nationalist politicians of all ethnic groups who wanted separate societies. The miners told us about the days in 1992, before the war started. The parliament in Sarajevo had become dominated by the three Bosnian nationalist parties, supposedly representing the three ethnic groups. The squabbling between them paralysed parliament. The 'Yugoslav' army, increasingly composed only of Serbian and Montenegrin troops and under officers now subordinated to Serbian fascist paramilitary groups, had attacked Croatia and seized a third of its territory. Across Bosnia there were barracks of these 'Yugoslav' troops, and their tanks lined Bosnia's borders to 'protect' Yugoslavia.

In the summer of 1992 huge demonstrations were held outside the Bosnian parliament in Sarajevo. The crowds, led by large numbers of

Tuzla miners, shouted their opposition to all the nationalist parties. Some shouted out that if parliament could not settle anything they would disband it and take control. Then sniper shots rang out. The demonstrators dived for cover. Miners edged their way up to the hotel from which the shots came. They seized the gunmen – Serbian nationalists – and handed them over to the police. Days later the gunmen were released and barricades organised by Milosevic supporters began to appear in Sarajevo. They were put up to prevent people voting in a referendum about whether Bosnia should break from the Milosevic-controlled 'Yugoslav' Federation. The people who were able to vote overwhelmingly chose an independent, multi-ethnic Bosnia with equal rights for all citizens. But events had gone beyond votes. Milosevic replied with war.

All across Eastern Europe people had brought down the old tyrannical regimes. The question was what to replace them with? People had the opportunity to begin thinking collectively about this only with the first days of freedom. In Yugoslavia any such discussion was drowned in a deafening artillery bombardment. Across the country gangs went from village to village driving out the ethnic 'undesirables' and all those who refused to support their actions. When we drove to Tuzla we would pass through mile upon mile of villages deserted and empty, every house burnt out. Milosevic's troops, with their control over all heavy weaponry, commanded the mountaintops and began a bombardment of every town that held out. Tuzla fared better than most. Its people with their militant history fighting fascism during the second world war, and with a spirit of ethnic unity, were better prepared than some. Miners' battalions dug trenches and fortifications well outside the city, and throughout the war the Tuzla region remained the biggest 'free territory' – free to all people.

We learned all this and much more in formal meetings with people like the Mayor and City Council, the local army commanders, in visits to mines, factories and schools or in people's homes where we stayed and shared people's lives during our brief visits: electricity for a couple of hours a day on alternate days; water for half an hour before sunrise. With no fuel the streets were reclaimed by pedestrians and horses, and of course the huge fleet of brand new, white 4x4 Landcruisers of the UN and NGO 'humanitarian business circus' that can now be seen in every political conflict around the world. These people stayed in Tuzla's hotels or they rented houses. We all found beds with local citizens, ordinary folk, soldiers, students, nurses or in the student halls. During our stays we would talk and learn about the history of Yugoslavia, about people's hopes and their personal tragedies – too many tragedies.

Right from the first visit we felt this spirit of resistance to nationalism, barbarism and ethnic division and realised we had to help this spirit make its voice heard in the outside world, which knew only about 'Yugoslav ethnic hatred'. So we began to arrange for delegations to get out from Tuzla and come to the UK or France or Spain to meet with people so that others could hear what we had heard. These delegations of miners, teachers and students came and told their stories. They asked for help. Bill Speirs, the President of the Scottish Trade Union Congress, was persuaded to visit Tuzla. The telecommunications workers' unions in the UK and France joined one convoy with lorries of supplies for their fellow communications workers in Bosnia.

On the convoy going out, during meal breaks and overnight stops, the French and British telecommunications men chatted with other people who had been before. They could not agree with our idea that the UN should drop its arms embargo and let the victims of ethnic cleansing defend themselves. The telecommunications men said: 'Surely more guns will only lead to more killing?' When we reached Tuzla the telecommunications men went off with their fellow workers from Bosnia, visited their homes and workplaces and handed over the food they had brought. Two days later we all met back to give a press conference for the Bosnian media. One of the British telecommunications men spoke on behalf of his UK and French co-workers. He thanked his new Bosnian friends for their hospitality and went on to say that in the time they had been there they had been able to find out how things stood. As a result they were now returning to their trade unions in France and Britain to campaign for the lifting of the arms embargo. Direct person-to-person contact had helped them see what no amount of lectures, resolutions or pamphlets could have done. It proved the worth of our trying to do everything we could to break down the barrier that existed between the embattled multi-ethnic communities and the world outside – a barrier put there, not only by the ethnic cleansers, but also by all the world's great 'democratic statesmen' who were going along with the plan to carve up this unity.

In Europe, public hatred of ethnic cleansing was widespread but unfocused, and held only by individuals as individuals. There was no social movement, no coming together to protest, to organise, to act as an external wing of the resistance movement. However, even without this much-needed support the balance of forces inside Bosnia began to change. In the first few months of war a highly prepared force, whipped up by a frenzy of anti-Muslim propaganda, had swept through Bosnia, in most places meeting little organised resistance. A few enclaves like Tuzla and Sarajevo held out, but elsewhere the towns and villages were 'cleansed'. The front lines then settled down and for the next two years remained fairly static. The longer this went on the worse things got for the ethnic cleansers. Their victims began to acquire arms, mostly through capture. The ethnic cleansers' morale deteriorated. Against unarmed civilians they had swaggered but against people armed and fighting for their lives the bravado evaporated. When the front lines advanced there was looting. People got rich by taking everything of value from the homes of the fleeing refugees – money, washing machines, fridges, electric cables, door frames, everything. But when front lines got bogged down there was no more loot.

In Tuzla in early 1995 we found spirits were high. The Tuzla defenders were starting to push back the front lines. Behind the scenes the US moved in to take the diplomatic initiative. Tudjman and Milosevic were told to accept the fact that they could not wipe out the 'Muslim' resistance and carve up Bosnia between Croatia and Serbia as they had planned. As the war continued the odds increased of the resistance breaking out and turning the tide. This was a threat not just to the nationalist forces, but also to the West's desire for a docile, manageable atmosphere for the global free movement of capital. A triumphant resistance could well create the space to attempt the social changes the majority of people wanted. A subservient welcome for McDonald's and the World was by no means certain in a land which had just been liberated.

Meetings were held in private rooms, but before any of the ex-Yugoslav politicians could put their names to a deal there remained a small problem. No matter how the maps were drawn there were people in the 'wrong' places. The nationalist politicians could not be seen to be selling out 'their' people, so these 'impediments' had to be moved before a deal could be signed publicly. The result was the massacre at Srebrenica. The UN had declared it a safe haven. For three years 30,000 hungry, terrified Muslims had sheltered in the besieged town with the UN flag waving over them. In July 1995 the Serbian nationalists advanced into the town without resistance. The UN simply handed it over without a shot. The Dutch UN and Serbian commanders drank champagne together before the Dutch drove off, leaving the Muslims at the mercy of the ethnic cleansers. Women and children were bussed to the front line of the Tuzla free territory and pushed into no-man's land. Eight thousand men between the ages of sixteen and 60 were murdered. One woman who escaped to Tuzla climbed into a tree and, surrounded by other traumatised refugees, hanged herself. Her photo appeared across the world and again the public was shocked. The West's complicity behind her tragedy, however, was masked from view.

Srebrenica was followed by a Serbian army withdrawal from occupied Croatia and the expulsion of the indigenous Serbian population by Croatian troops. On all sides miserable refugees trudged to a future with no home and no hope – Muslim, Serb and Croat alike, all used as propaganda and military fodder by 'their' politicians and then dumped, betrayed. In November 1995 Bosnian Muslim, Serbian and Croatian political leaders were flown to the Dayton air base in the USA and a deal was done to divide Bosnia. UN/NATO troops poured in and became the new masters over an exhausted, war-weary population. Today, seven years later, 30,000 Western administrators control Bosnia. It remains divided even if the front lines have vanished. There is no fighting, but nothing is settled.

Our work continued. Bosnian friends asked us to help them try to reach out from their 'ethnic ghettos'. We helped the Tuzla teachers meet up with leaders of education unions from Croatia, Serbia, Vojvodina, Serbia and Kosova at a meeting in Hungary. These contacts were the beginning of a long road. This first meeting between Kosovar Albanian and Serbian teachers' representatives did not lead to Serbian teachers speaking up against the Serbian brutality in Kosova, but the meeting certainly did lift the spirits of the Bosnians. They developed their union work across Bosnia, into the Serbian-held sector as well as in the new 'Muslim' State. They were determined to oppose the people who wanted ethnically-divided curricula in all schools. Only Tuzla still sent all its children to common schools.

In 1998 we helped the Bosnian miners' union organise an international workers conference to discuss government proposals to privatise the mines. The conference, attended by people from thirteen countries, bringing all their own bitter experiences of privatisation, helped the Bosnian miners to decide to fight the government plans. From their visits to miners in the UK, though, they knew they could not do it alone, and they appealed for international support. Once again the forces supporting resistance to the 'new order' were too weak and the Bosnian government slowly advanced its privatisation programme. As in the rest of ex-Yugoslavia more and more parts of the previously 'socially owned' property slipped into the hands of politicians, war profiteers and foreign capital. When Bosnian miners spoke of their opposition to the reintroduction of capitalism – 'a system that would eat us alive' – it became possible to see a shadow of the forces that had necessitated Belgrade's violence against the Yugoslav people.

Throughout the war we had known of the dark cloud hanging over Kosova but never had the resources to open up contacts there. After the Dayton agreement we began to wind down the convoys and were now able to make contacts there. During the NATO bombing of Kosova in 1999 many people leapt up to denounce 'imperialist aggression' without saying a word about the 'imperialist aggression' that had been going on since 1990 when Milosevic's troops had occupied Kosova, disbanded its parliament and begun a wholesale persecution of the 2 million Albanians living there.

Two of us reached Kosova in 1996 and over the next three years made more visits. While all kinds of 'left' organisations have recently written their various explanations of how western capital encouraged the Albanians to break away from Yugoslavia, people who went to Kosova found the opposite to be true. On our first visit we were guests of the Kosova miners' union at the famous Trepca mineral mines. From them we learned how in 1989-90 the miners, alongside the teachers' trade union, had led the protests against Milosevic. The miners had staged underground hunger strikes and marches to Prishtina. One of their slogans had been 'Defend Yugoslavia'. This was aimed against Milosevic's moves to change the Yugoslav constitution, removing Kosova's equal status with the other republics. It was only after their efforts to defend the Yugoslav constitution failed and Serbia seized control of Kosova that the miners and others turned towards the call for independence. They were left with no other road to follow.

When Milosevic used force to end Kosova's autonomy, mass protests broke out and Belgrade retaliated with arrests, shootings and the sacking of all state employees in Kosova: miners, teachers, health workers, etc. – 180,000 people. When we arrived in 1996 the Albanians had already spent six years under a state of total and arbitrary police/military rule accompanied by unemployment, hunger and fear. Over the next three years all our delegations reported a deteriorating situation. At Dayton the Western leaders had elevated Milosevic into a 'great peacemaker'. While the UN trumpeted the Dayton agreement as bringing 'peace' to Bosnia they kept quiet about the clauses supporting Milosevic's control over Kosova. This policy remains intact today. Despite the bombing, despite the switch to backing a new horse in the Serbian presidential elections – the Western policy makers remain opposed to Kosova breaking from Serbian control – and oppression. Their reasons were the same for refusing to lift a finger to help the resistance in Bosnia – the fear of a self-organised popular uprising, out of control by any 'reliable' regime.

On our first visit to Kosova we met various people, told them about what we had done in Bosnia and listened to their opinions. Despite their poverty they felt our best help would be in getting their delegations to the UK and elsewhere to let the world know what was going on. However, by 1998 the activities of the Serbian paramilitaries in Kosova – burning villages, surrounding the towns – led to an appeal to us to try to get food through to the mining town of Mitrovica. Before it had been possible for us to reach there by car. Serbian friends in Belgrade had helped us get Yugoslav visas to visit them and we had then just driven over the mountains to Kosova. But this backdoor method was not possible for lorries. They needed proper papers to enter Serbia. For several months we tried to get visas from the Yugoslav embassy in London but without success. Then due to a temporary shift in international diplomacy we suddenly got visas. We transported food collected by Bosnian miners down to Kosova. Already the town resembled many of the besieged Bosnian towns during the war. Villages alongside the main roads were being ethnically cleansed and burned down. The community in Mitrovica feared the worst.

All this time the US government and British government, now New Labour with an 'ethical foreign policy', were shamelessly lying to the Albanians. They told them to stick to their peaceful protests and that eventually they would be free. At the same time they were telling Belgrade that they would not countenance Kosova independence. Then the volcano erupted. Milosevic had ridden to power on an uncontrollable force of ethnic hatred. His only way to escape the growing discontent from poverty in Serbia itself was by continually racking up flag-waving nationalist fervour. Paramilitary groups increased their attacks on the 'hated' Albanians. In turn the Albanians' patience with their ten-year-long passive resistance finally wore out. It had got them nothing but empty promises from the west. Now they turned to armed resistance against their tormentors. But the limited supply of arms they could lay their hands on was even more meagre than it had been for their fellow-victims in Bosnia.

The western politicians were caught in a dilemma. They wanted a stable Balkans and had backed Serbian control over Kosova in the hope that this would keep the lid on Albanian discontent. Any such discontent could ignite fellow-Albanians scattered by previous Western diplomatic intrigues in 1919 across Macedonia, Montenegro, Greece and Albania itself. However, Milosevic's form of control was now threatening to create the very explosion the West hoped he would contain. On the other hand the West feared taking any action that would support the Albanian movement. Politicians in the West and in the UN were further worried that public criticism at home was again mounting. Hadn't all these politicians promised 'no more Bosnias', and yet it was happening again?

As refugees poured out of Kosova and into Prishtina from other towns NATO decided to act – not in support of the Albanians or out of concern for their tragedy but simply to find a way to put the lid back on things. No troops were to be sent in, because that would automatically act as armed assistance to the Kosovar Albanians. [In 1999] bombing raids started – a tactic that could do nothing to stop the mass ethnic cleansing but was instead designed to force Belgrade to become more pliable.

NATO troops finally went in after a deal was done with Milosevic, but they went into a country which had been depopulated. As in Bosnia, NATO became the new masters. The Albanian refugees returned to find a new occupation force. Understandably, at first this was welcomed unquestioningly. The European left could easily denounce the 'imperialist invaders' but failed to recognise that as far as the Albanians were concerned the new occupiers were treating them better than their previous colonisers.

During the bombing it was easy for all kinds of people to shout slogans and argue for or against the bombings. But all their slogans were half-truths at best. The 'anti-imperialists' wanted to fight only one side of imperialism – NATO – and not Milosevic. Supporters of the bombing ignored the fact that it was NATO itself that was half-responsible for the tragedy and assumed that this was some kind of benign intervention. They said nothing about the killing and destruction in Serbia. For us, with close friends in Belgrade and in Kosova, working in daily contact with Albanian refugees who had lost all contact with families driven into the mountains or into neighbouring countries, we could find no slogans adequate to deal with the problem. All we could do was describe the whole picture we saw. The Kosovars faced death. They needed help from people who had no hidden agenda. They needed allies amongst the Serbian people. But where was there any such a movement of internationalism and solidarity? They didn't exist. Not surprisingly then, the Kosovars looked to NATO to save them from the immediate threat. All we could do was point to this gap between the help the Kosovars needed and what actually existed – and try to close that gap. We took food to refugees in Albania and re-made contact with miners from Mitrovica, with whom all contact had been lost when the town was ethnically cleansed. Then through the education union we made contact with resistance groups in the mountains inside Kosova who desperately needed food. We made plans to take food to the Albanian Kosova border from where they would walk it across the mountains. Before this could happen the 'peace' deal was done. So instead we took a large convoy of food directly to Mitrovica.

There we found excitement, happiness, sadness and fears for the future, all intermingled. The Albanians celebrated the removal of the hated Serbian police and paramilitaries. Young people danced and sang in the streets every evening. In their lifetimes the streets after dark had always been unsafe territory. Amidst the happiness many people mourned lost relatives and contemplated life with destroyed homes and villages. The situation for the miners was even more serious. For ten years they had been locked out from their mines – which legally they jointly owned – by Serbian guns. From the mountains and exile they had rushed back to save the mines from flooding as the Serbs withdrew, only to find they were once more locked out – this time by UN guns. French troops occupied the mines and refused to let the Albanians in. As the miners started to organise protest marches against the NATO theft of their property we began work outside the region to publicise their plight.

Today Kosova, like Bosnia, is under NATO/UN control. Western politicians place their hopes on political changes in Belgrade making it possible for them to stitch together some deal whereby Kosova remains under Belgrade control but which allows a partial withdrawal of UN troops. The future of the mines remains undecided. The Serbian state claims them. Western businessmen claim parts of them. The Albanian miners claim them, the Albanian politicians claim them. But the UN will decide. One thing is for sure – the people of Kosova will not end up in control. For a start they lack the money necessary to re-open production. So, as in Bosnia, everything that used to belong to 'the people' will end up in private hands. For many this makes little difference. In previous times the 'people's property' was actually controlled and used by the bureaucrats for their own benefit. But for the miners in Kosova and Bosnia the privatisation process will bring closures and unemployment.

Whatever the frustrations with the UN presence, the Kosovars would continue to accept it as long as the threat to their existence from Belgrade remained. While the politicians of the West began their intrigues to replace Milosevic with a more acceptable figure – a Milosevic Mark II – we tried to help the development of contacts between the Kosova Albanians and Serbs who would speak up for the Albanians' right of self-determination. We organised a visit to the UK and France for a representative of the Kosovar miners and a journalist from Belgrade, one of the few outspoken critics of Serb nationalism. Together they spoke at meetings, calling for support for the Kosovar miners' efforts to regain control of their mines.

Given the current situation, what did we achieve, what did our friends in ex-Yugoslavia achieve? Jeffrey Sachs, a Harvard economist advising the Polish government after the collapse of the Soviet empire, wrote as follows:

'The complications of privatisation begin with the fact that the ownership of the state enterprises in ... Eastern Europe is already politically contested. In many cases workers wonder what all the fuss is about, because, of course, they already own the firms. Privatization should begin by establishing that central government owns enterprises and has exclusive power to engage in privatisation. ... The government should reject workers' claims to full ownership.'

Sachs goes on to recommend 'shock therapy' in order to minimise resistance to this plan, i.e., act fast and catch the workers off their guard before they make alternative plans. Looking back it is now possible to see that this proposal was carried through across Eastern Europe. The only slight change from the vision of the Western advisors was the extent to which the old Communist Party bosses formed alliances with various criminal gangs and took control of property themselves rather than, as the Western advisors hoped, simply helping to transfer assets to the control of international banks.

In Yugoslavia Milosevic and the other former 'socialists'-turned-capitalists hoped to pursue the same policy, but unlike elsewhere they were not able to catch the masses totally off their guard. As the Party bureaucrats tried to begin to implement economic policies suited to the new capitalist environment they ran into opposition – not a clear opposition calling for 'down with capitalism' or 'stop privatisation' or anything like that. All such ideas had been far too discredited by the bureaucratic tyranny that had existed in the name of 'socialism'. No, most Yugoslavs had no hard opposition to the idea of capitalism or privatisation. All they wanted was a better life. But far from that happening, things were getting worse. All across the Yugoslav Federation people were protesting against unemployment, against non-payment of wages, against corrupt politicians. The political elite found that their dream of converting the 'people's property' into their personal property could not be achieved simply through political decree. The protests had to be broken up. But how? Milosevic hit on the key with his support for the ultra-right's campaign against Albanians. From there on his party and state machine, state-controlled media, etc. worked overtime to whip up hatred against non-Serbs. People were turned against each other. Popular frustration, anger and discontent were channelled by the political elite away from themselves and against other ethnic groups.

In some areas this was not so hard to do, but in other places – like Tuzla – the partisan struggle against fascism in the second world war had left a legacy of integrated, intermarried and tolerant communities. This legacy could only be undone with the utmost violence. The world's great democratic statesmen, the institutions of 'democracy' like the EU and the UN, faced with a choice between this violence and the possibility that a spark of opposition to the smooth introduction of capital to Eastern Europe could kindle wider protests, all came down on the side of the violence. While they talked of a united Europe they let Bosnia be torn apart.

Did the violence succeed or not? Writing at this point it is not possible to say. Yes, the people of Yugoslavia were beaten and battered sufficiently by Milosevic and the other former 'communists' for privatisation to be carried through in Serbia and elsewhere, and for a great deal of the assets of the people to be destroyed or transferred to private control. This process is going on right now. But the resistance to ethnic division and ethnic oppression was not completely destroyed. Across the region people still carry a vision opposite to the ethnic cleansers and are working for the kind of society they want. These forces are small but they take their place today alongside the many other voices opposed to the existing state of the world. As this global, multi-faceted movement for a different kind of human society grows, these ex-Yugoslavs, with their long hard fight against the division of people, will strengthen it with their experiences.

If our actions helped even in the smallest amount to keep alive that spirit of resistance in Bosnia, Serbia or Kosova then our work was worthwhile. In 1998 we had a book launch in Tuzla of our book – *Taking Sides: against ethnic cleansing* – a scrapbook of all our collective efforts. From the audience that came to the launch we had many people who got up to say in their own way: 'Thank you for the food you brought, but thank you even more for coming when the world turned its back on us.' Practical international solidarity is a must in a world in which capital, commodities and the search for profit are free to roam the world while people are forced to remain in one place. Over the last year we have been contacted by an anti-fascist group in Moscow who had been demonstrating against the war in Chechnya. After reading about our convoys they expanded their protest campaign to include collecting food and clothes for the Chechens – calling upon Russians to repudiate the violence of their political leaders by helping the victims. From southern Africa we received calls from young people developing a movement against the wars in Congo and Angola. They too wanted to go beyond resolutions and protest demonstrations and were trying to find the ways to link up with people across the region in an effort to unite against the continuing plunder of the continent's resources.

7.1.2 Workers' Aid (continued). Rough additional notes by Bob Myers, written at the beginning of the 1999 NATO bombing of Serbia

What follows ('rough notes, etc.) I put down on Saturday. Now – Sunday – it's looking out of date and it's clear to everyone that the NATO countries' policy is bankrupt, and that at this moment they think their only way out is an intensification of the bombing that might force Milosevic's hand; a forlorn hope surely. Every single thing they've said (Blair, Short, Cook etc.) has proved false. I haven't thought out at this point what we should do and say about this crisis for them – to 'expose' them in words which few but us would read is not difficult, of course, but how to make an advance that's meaningful?

They talk – now! – about providing emergency accommodation for tens of thousands of refugees in NATO countries including Britain, and keeping hundreds of thousands in a 'tent city' in Macedonia. Meanwhile thousands are dying in the open.

1. Why don't we take advantage of this crisis and weakness in the enemy camp to fight to make the unions call upon thousands of families to take in those who are now stranded. The Labour government would be in a difficult position to refuse assistance for those who agree to do such a thing, given their present admission that they 'did not foresee' the present catastrophe. I can't see that such a demand would be an 'acceptance of the fact' of the ethnic cleansing. It would be an elementary act of solidarity and a necessary holding operation to enable the Kosovan working class together with us to mobilise the fight to get back their homes and their country and to win independence.

2. If we decided on this call, we would not wait for the union bureaucracies to respond, but should begin to try and actually do it at all levels of the movement where we can (Trades Councils, branches, regions, student unions, etc). And we (Workers Aid, Movement For Socialism) would ask of all our supporters and those who respond to the Kosovan appeal to take up the same thing.

3. We would also have to say that there must be no restrictions to entry on the grounds that these are not political refugees.

No doubt we will be denounced (again) as humanitarians not socialists if we make such a call. I think it's very clear that such elementary defence measures are essential to enable the class to prepare the necessary offensive; and that to be able to move in and take advantage of the ruling class's undoubted crisis at this point is one of the points at which we can begin the necessary reorientation of the trade union movement towards the necessary (a necessity as yet of course entirely unperceived) political offensive against capital and its destructiveness.

7.1.3 'Rough notes/some difficult questions', 3 April, 1999, by Bob Myers

Milosevic no doubt sees 'the fight for sacred Kosova' as his main card in retaining power in Serbia. He will not stop this fight because of NATO bombing. The bombings will in fact strengthen his hold as 'leader of his people' against the invader. And it strengthens him in another way, i.e., by compelling Russian politicians to solidify Russian support for him.

The Kosovars should not support the bombing, because it will help Milosevic drive the Serbian population into his hands, and it will lead to more, not less, ethnic cleansing, and it is directed at the people of Serbia, not at Milosevic and his power. NATO ground forces? What NATO will do on the ground or in the air will not be determined by the Kosovars' needs but by the NATO powers' interests and strategies. These most definitely do not include the independence of Kosova. On the contrary, such strategy as they have is directed at ensuring the power of a more compliant Milosevic as the boss who will ensure 'order' in the region. The crime of Blair, Clinton and their regimes is that they have landed the Kosovars in this death-trap, where they can see no way to avoid destruction other than to turn to NATO. This will be the case even among the many who understand the lessons of Bosnia, that the 'Great Powers' (UN, NATO) move in only to put the seal on successful ethnic cleansing, not to stop it. The Milosevic regime will certainly eventually lead to profound social crisis, revolutionary struggles and counter-revolutionary repression. And as this comes about will not the question of workers' aid to the Serbian people arise?

Those who criticise or oppose the Kosovars' demand for NATO intervention must address the question: Am I supposing that it is better for them to be killed by Serbian forces than by NATO forces? We don't have any choice but to say to the Kosovars: 'We can't oppose your calling on NATO; you look around the world, including the working-class movement, and you see no alternative. We see our job as working (and working with you) for the development of such an alternative.'

There is no doubt that ground engagements between Serb and NATO troops would make national heroes of the Serb soldiers and security forces and of Milosevic himself.

... A general consideration we should hold on to (I tried to make this emphasis in the earlier rough draft on Kosova, and it follows what I was groping for in the notes on 'trade unions and socialism' in the MFS bulletin. I don't think it's far-fetched, but an attempt to make sense of these entirely new experiences in terms of our view of the structural crisis, qualitative change in class relations, and the political consequences thereof summed up in our 'new party' orientation and Meszaros' conclusions about the bankruptcy of the old reform and defensive strategies and necessity of the 'socialist offensive') ...

The support/interest from Spanish unions, STUC, Camden Unison, dockers(?), Durham NUM(?), Canadian Auto workers, Australia, at least raises the question of what the unions can and must do (what role they can have) in the face of the qualitatively changed situation, a situation now agonisingly concentrated in the sharpest possible form: what to do about the destruction of a people in the interests of establishing a 'new (inevitably counter-revolutionary) world order' after the collapse of Stalinism and social-democracy. Can we see here a glimpse of (even encourage work which might make a beginning towards the realisation of) the way the workers' organisations can and must take a political lead in defending and mobilising humanity against a capital system which in its structural crisis is destroying the foundations of the future society? That (i.e., everything!) is what is really involved in the tired-sounding question: don't the unions have to make political demands? We should be able to write now something much more positive and meaningful than Trotsky could in his notes on 'trade unions in the epoch of imperialist decay'.

(It occurs to me that we should think about the way the Liverpool dockers, once they embarked on their international work, found themselves taking up issues like the dictatorship in Turkey.)

7.2 Example 2: Argentina

The economic collapse and the mass reaction to it by masses of people in Argentina in 2001 provide a glimpse of the undoubted explosive consequences of globalised contradictions and of the type of change in forms of organisation and struggle. The following account is from the journal *Carré Rouge*.

7.2.1 Claudio Katz, 'The significance of the *argentinazo*[1]', *Carré Rouge*, no. 20 (winter 2001-2)

The massive size of the uprising, the crushing victory over the forces of repression, the success in driving out a government which was impoverishing the people, make the revolutionary days of the *argentinazo* a turning-point in the history of popular rebellions in our country. The days crowned a decade of intense preparatory struggles and opened up a new stage of more radical and massive movements, already seen in the *cacerolazo* [a form of struggle consisting of going on to the streets and banging pans to make the loudest noise possible] which forced the new government of Rodriguez Saa to get rid of the most corrupt members of his cabinet. ... The fall of a 'progressive' civil government in the service of the IMF as a result of direct action and popular mobilisation has few precedents worldwide. The success of the uprising was because struggles of all sectors of the population hit by 'structural adjustment' (economic measures dictated by the IMF) converged: in 48 hours workers, unemployed, the middle class and youth demolished the Cavallo-De la Rua regime and its state of siege.

The actors in the struggle

The eruption of the *argentinazo* was preceded by a long sequence of revolts, starting with the *santiagazo* [popular uprising in the town of Santiago del Estero] of 1993 and followed by uprisings in the localities of Cutral-Co and General Mosconi. What predominated in the two main days of the rebellion was the mobilisation of unemployed and casual workers of the Buenos suburbs and provinces, demanding food. Millions of workers plunged into absolute poverty assembled in their neighbourhoods, blocked the roads, and showed the way to all sectors. Even if the actions of this *piquetero* movement had little effect on this occasion, the forms of struggle which it introduced served as the model for all the popular upsurges.

The *argentinazo* involved a succession of strikes and demonstrations by workers in the telephone services, aero and ceramics industries, railway workers, council workers and teachers, which had an important impact both before and after the mass strike of 13 December 2001 called by the three trade union federations. As has traditionally been the case in Argentina, these movements formed the backdrop to the general revolt. For the umpteenth time, they proved that strikes 'have some use' and that socially very hard-hit workers play a decisive role in big confrontations. But in the key two days the organised intervention of the working class did not have the power of 17 October [1945, when workers' action halted a US-inspired coup], of the *cordobazo* or of the general strike of 1975, because leaders of both CGT and CTA [trade union federations] hid far from the epicentre of the struggle for fear of its overflowing.

The middle class were at the head of the spontaneous explosion of Wednesday 19, when the Plaza del Mayo [the square containing the Casa Rosada, seat of the President of the Republic, and traditional place for mass demonstrations] was occupied. Financial measures, including the confiscation of bank deposits, were the last straw in a week of protests outside the banks and several years of resistance to pauperisation. The electors of the Alliance which had initiated the *cacerolazos* on the invitation of Chaco Alvarez produced a deafening uproar under the windows of his associate, Cavallo. They had been on the streets in earlier protests (e.g., against the floods). This time no one stayed at home. The *cacerolazo* introduced the explicit demand to finish with De la Rua and Cavallo with a demonstration directed at the centre of power, shattering government hopes of dividing the population between 'pillagers in the urban neighbourhoods' and property owners in the centre. The 'pillage psychosis' whipped up by the secret services and media to terrorise the middle class into opposing the 'vandals' was abandoned. The government fell precisely because its state of siege was rejected . In contrast to 1955, the middle class was not pulled behind a 'guerillism' [refers to the military regime following the US-supported coup which overthrew the Peron government in 1955] hostile to the working class and did not provide a social base for military coups d'etat. It was now more impoverished, more secular, and more radicalised.

The youth were in the front ranks. They defied police beatings, stood up to teargas, in the face of the police horses they regained every inch of lost ground a hundred times over, ensuring victory in the battle of Thursday 20. This was the definitive baptism of fire for a whole generation which had not lived under military dictatorship, but had suffered the social genocide and the police brutality of the last 20 years. The students, employees and *motoqueros* [highly exploited youth who earn their living by working as couriers on motorcycles and scooters] resisted at the side of the Mothers of the Plaza del Mayo, recreating the heroism of the1970s. The children of the fighters of the *cordobazo* already have to their credit the success of an *argentinazo* and constitute the moving force of the battles which will unfold from that victory. The only political current present at the heart of the rebellion was the extreme left. No elected MPs, publicly responsible persons or public representatives from any other political tendency put themselves on the streets during the repression. These people know how to make speeches, but avoid participation at the side of the people on the barricades, which might have risked their skins. While the right [in Argentina this term refers to a small hard-line right tendency] called for more repression, and the Peronists prepared the new government behind closed doors, the old centre-left members of the Alliance disappeared. By participating, the majority of the left parties showed brave and revolutionary conduct.

But the extreme left today faces a challenge of another kind: to find the road to a political fusion with the masses which will permit the opening of a path towards socialism.

7.2.2 François Chesnais and Jean-Philippe Dives, 'A profound process of self-organisation', from their *Que se vayan todos!, qu'ils s'en aillent tous* (Nautilus 2002)

The forms of organisation were diverse. The 'oldest' (going back to 1993-4) is the one known under the name of the *piqueteros* movement (from the word for 'picket').... Workers thrown on to the streets adopted this name to refer to the forms of action they had to take once away from the factory, following a brutal de-industrialisation which took over 15 years. Bringing trade union experiences and struggles in the factories together with the struggles of impoverished youth, they were marked by proletarian forms of struggle (building barricades, assertion in the face of police and motor traffic, controlling the degree of confrontation). Actions consisted of cutting off roads (*le corte de ruta*) and burning tyres, but also organising 'people's soup-kitchens' around the pickets and developing a whole series of activities connected with day-to-day survival. In the main towns, every time civil servants and other wage-earners were not paid because the provincial governments' funds were empty (which happened many times) they joined the actions, contributing to maintaining the link between the *piqueteros* and the workers still in jobs. Other forms of self-organisation were inspired by the *piqueteros*' example. In the poorest areas, they went from collective canteens to organised mutual exchange, to help in schooling children, with collective libraries and accommodation for the sick. Closed factories were re-occupied by their workers and became centres for a decentralised cooperative system and common use of resources for social needs. Savers – a large number of whom (nearly 50 per cent of the total) were saving for somewhere to live (a condition of survival after brutal reduction in wages) – attacked the banks. They broke down the doors and won the support of the bank workers who were in fear of losing their jobs. *Cacerolazos* became *papelazos*: from the windows of factories which had closed workers hung 'archives' (records of their past work) which, like them, had been thrown into the street...

7.3 Example 3: France – the Strasbourg-Saint Denis McDonald's strike, 2002

Janos Borovi shows how young and inexperienced workers in 'service industries' are beginning to organise against their employers in new ways.

On 19 February [2002], the three-and-a-half months' strike at McDonald's in Strasbourg-St Denis ended. The strike was won, the sacked workers got their jobs back. Now management of the group is avenging itself on its employees at McDonald's St.Germain, 'guilty' of having launched the first strike some years ago and also of having actively supported Strasbourg-St Denis. The support committee born in the course of the conflict was enlarged as it supported other struggles: at FNAC (book chain-store), Go-Sport, Maxi-livre.

The balance-sheet published by the committee reveals the special features and innovation of this strike – the relation between the strikers, the support committee and the unions – and analyses the reasons for the strike's success. It analyses the strike, launched by a handful of young people, often originating from the urban neighbourhoods, most with no trade union experience and still less any political experience; how and why a strike led by a layer of youth until now virtually absent from this type of struggle, could succeed; how the initial handful of young people were able to unite a vast solidarity movement around them and force the giant slave-driver McDonald's to beat a retreat.

Those lucky enough to take part in the 'black Saturdays' (unpredictable pickets of different McDonald's branches in Paris) will not forget the joy of collective action (like the best moments of the struggle of the *sans-papiers* of Saint Bernard), nor the demonstration at the beginning of March by the strikers of FNAC, McDonald's and Go-Sport, together with the members of the support committee. The alleys of the Forum des Halles, packed with Saturday afternoon shoppers, filled with hundreds of young people chanting: 'Everything for us, nothing for them', moving with disconcerting ease beyond demands for wages and working conditions to questioning the whole profit system. For an all-too-brief moment, everything seemed possible.

Often political activists, seeing the break-up of the 'workers' movement', the lack of revolutionary perspective, the electoralist drift of the 'extreme left', ask how capitalism can be overthrown. How will a society which we still call communist, in the manner of the Paris Commune, succeed in sweeping away the barbarism in which we are living? References to the past are inappropriate, but if the revolution will not be a re-play of the storming of the Winter Palace in 1917, how will people arrive at 'mass communist consciousness'? Today the process of recomposition, of re-organisation of the consciousness of the exploited is different from the process of construction of the workers' movement in the past. The oppressed are forced to resist, while realising that the tools of the past, 'their' parties, 'their' unions, are ineffective, if not harmful, and even on the enemy side. It is highly significant that the young workers of McDonald's used trade union weapons, but did not receive actual support of any trade union, even those involved in the dispute, who might have been expected to understand the importance of the entry into struggle of insecure and casualised workers of the urban neighbourhoods. Self-organisation and the apparatus mentality decidedly do not go together.

At McDonald's the mixture of young people in struggle and experienced trade union and political militants gave rise to something new, a body where new experiences and whatever remains of value from the past could be welded together and produce a wealth of ideas, resolve in battle, resistance, inventiveness, rejection of melancholy. A sort of collective consciousness, although temporary, in part volatile, nonetheless a bit of the future, a bit of communism, has been brought from the future. All this is, to be sure, microscopic among the problems posed to the exploited of all France, of the world. But let us repeat: it has proved possible to add a little piece of this vast puzzle, the design of which we don't know, but which when it is finished, will perhaps show the new image of communism.

The 'Provisional Balance-sheet of the McDo movement' produced by the strikers contains the following:

The trade union empty space

The support committee easily gained legitimacy because of the completely stand-off attitude of the union structures connected to the strikers (Commerce CGT, UL, UD) in the day-to-day struggle, the weekend actions, or actions directed at mobilising beyond the usual support parties, meetings, demonstrations, etc. By occupying the space left vacant by the unions, the support committee was in a way the trade union of the strike with its own characteristics: leaving it to the strikers to take what they saw as the best measures, even encouraging them to express themselves directly (write their own leaflets, for example), not participating in negotiations, taking over a good part of the work of agitation and popularisation (150,000 leaflets distributed!), opening up the struggle to the outside (news spread and relayed outside Paris, and in the final month internationally), financial support....

The Paris strike is best seen against the background of the anti-union policies of this flagship of globalisation. In his revealing book *Fast Food Nation* (Penguin, 2002), Eric Schlosser writes:

> The McDonald's Corporation insists that its franchise operators follow directives on food preparation, purchasing, store design, and countless other minute details.... When it comes to wage rates, however, the company is remarkably silent and laissez-faire. This policy allows operators to set their wages according to local labour markets – and it absolves the McDonald's Corporation of any formal responsibility for roughly three-quarters of the company's workforce. McDonald's decentralised hiring practices have helped thwart efforts to organise the company's workers. But whenever a union gains support at a particular restaurant, the McDonald's Corporation suddenly shows tremendous interest in the emotional and financial well-being of the workers there.
>
> During the late 1960s and early 1970s, McDonald's workers across the country [US] attempted to join unions. In response the company developed sophisticated methods for keeping unions out of its restaurants. A 'flying squad' of experienced managers and corporate executives was sent to a restaurant the moment union activity was suspected. Seemingly informal 'rap sessions' were held with disgruntled employees. The workers were encouraged to share their feelings. They were flattered and stroked. And more importantly, they were encouraged to share information about the union's plans and the names of union sympathisers.

In 1973 the San Francisco labour commissioner ruled that McDonald's halt their practice of forcing employees to take lie detector tests. The company's job application forms specified that any employee refusing such a test would face dismissal. Schlosser recounts the story of two McDonald's restaurants which were closed in face of a union recruiting drive, the first when workers were successfully organising a McDonald's in Lansing, Michigan:

> All the crew members were fired, the restaurant was shut down, a new McDonald's was built down the block – and the workers who'd signed union cards were not rehired. Such tactics have proved remarkably successful. At the time of writing, none of the workers at the roughly 15,000 McDonald's in North America is represented by a union.

McDonald's is hardly an 'exception' when it comes to 'globalisation':

> The McDonald's Corporation has become a powerful symbol of America's service economy, which is responsible for 90 per cent of the country's new jobs. In 1968, McDonald's operated about 1,000 restaurants. Today it has about 30,000 worldwide and opens almost 2,000 each year. An estimated one out of every eight workers in the United States has at some point been employed by McDonald's. The company annually hires about one million people, more than any other American organisation, public or private.

7.4 Example 4: Africa – Algeria

7.4.1 Extracts from an editorial in *Carré Rouge* no.19 (autumn 2001)

It is very tempting to put the whole of this issue of *Carré Rouge* under the heading 'the emancipation of the workers is the task of the workers themselves'. Not only because the most substantial document in it, by Alain Bihr, is entitled '*Actualiser le communisme*', but because this idea – today more than ever before a 'new idea' in the working-class movement – is an important guiding thread in the political situation.

1. Algeria and France

Bringing the two together may seem incongruous, and of course has limits. But there is more than coincidence between the present movement of the Algerian masses against their corrupt regime and the demonstration on 9 June in Paris of 30,000 demonstrators mobilised nationally by rank-and-file sections of the trade unions from a number of enterprises hit by plans for sackings and job cuts. The two situations are different, but a deep underlying connection exists between them.

First Algeria. The movement started in Kabylie. It now covers the whole country. The Bouteflika government sought to limit its significance to that of simply an 'ethnic' revolt. It manipulated a number of youth in Algiers, signing them up to military security and the secret services in order to launch them against the Kabyles. The operation, bloody as it was, failed. The Kabyle demonstrators were recognised by all Algerians as their own. Countless testimonies show that the population identified with their rejection of oppression, extreme poverty, government corruption and trickery.

The origins of the great 14 June [2001] demonstration in Algiers are of considerable interest. It was built 'from below', by village committees, the archs, which are at the same time old traditional structures working on direct democracy at local community level, and a tightly closed local power insulated against outside manipulation. This channel of mobilisation had to be used for a fight which included both specific Berber demands and social and economic demands with which the whole Algerian people could identify, because experience of the 'traditional' parties had led the population to break with them.

'We expect nothing from them', said the demonstrators, and this rejection applied to both the RCD and the FFS, the traditional organisations for the Berbers' demands. These parties have more or less folded in the face of the existing power, in the case of the RCD to the point of participating in the power in the name of 'the fight against the fundamentalists'. (That term was designed to better control and terrorise the people, but has gone beyond the control of its creators.) 'We expect nothing from them,' they said, because poverty and injustice have reached intolerable proportions throughout the country, and because the political assault unleashed by the state in the name of 'we are the last barrier against fundamentalism' is no longer enough to contain the rage, the anger, the revolt against the nation's pillagers. This rejection is a radical and often rough one. Many would-be mediators have learned this to their cost.

Clashes initiated by the state provocateurs during the demonstration of 14 June must be understood as both a desperate attempt to terrorise the population (without being able, as in 1988, to turn machine-guns and cannon on the youth) and also as a political message: the archs, your traditional and democratic structures, are not for organising demonstrations. You must return to the 'traditional' parties. With variations, the message was designed to divert the river back into the old ruts of 'delegation': 'Vote for us, we'll do the rest!'

And so, the solution is not to put together some 'political' combination, or to build some new 'front', a sort of pluralist left [like the French '*gauche plurielle*' – CS]. All those who want to help the Algerian people sweep away the rot and take their destiny into their own hands must ask not how to take the road of the 'traditional' organisations again, but how to help the Algerian people build political representation for the existing movement, with all the specific social and economic demands of the demonstrations, demands which were directed against the state power, against the plunderers of the country's natural riches, and their allies. By this will those who work to help this movement be judged. In a word, how to assist the people and the youth to emancipate themselves, and not to substitute for them in the name of a supposed 'immaturity'.

7.4.2 'Light and Shadows in the Kabylie black spring'. There follow extracts from an article by Mohamed Arabi, member of the CPWB, in *Carré Rouge*, no. 19 (autumn 2001)

Some people have claimed that the origin of the events resides in the traditional demands of Kabylie, relating to language and Berber identity. Nothing of the kind. Old Berber fighters themselves recognised in their statements that the revolt had absolutely nothing to do with ethnic demands. What we saw in the black spring events was the birth of a democratic and fundamentally social movement, which inscribed on its banner, principally, the struggle against every form of hogra [Algerian expression signifying injustice and contempt].

After describing the plight of the Algerian people, the author continues as follows:

Such in outline is what 'filled the cup', and explains for the most part the despair and the rejection of the ruling power. These feelings were most strongly expressed and organised in Kabylie, but they were and are shared by virtually all Algerians, particularly the younger fringe among the workers and the unemployed. Those who went on to the streets to brave death, and those whose unreserved commitment led them to the supreme sacrifice, had the same cry of anger to show their rejection of social injustice.

The formation and nature of the committees and the differences between Tizi and Bejaia:

The question of organisation is another distinctive trait of the events. When the revolt began to spread (20 to 22 April 2001), we saw the birth of dozens of village and local committees. Declarations bearing the signature of these committees spread everywhere, calling the citizens to resistance against the forces of repression, and beginning to formulate the first demands of the population in revolt. It must be noted that these committees were created 'spontaneously', and had absolutely nothing to do with the directives of parties. Indeed the offices of the parties influential in Kabylie (FFS, RCD) were the first targets of the rioters, who lost no time in burning them down; a way of citizens showing that they had totally failed to represent them (as municipal and departmental councillors, MPs, senators) and at the end of ten years had brought about no meaningful change in the living conditions of the Algerians of Kabylie.

At the end of May, virtually all areas of Kabylie had committees. One of the most crucial tasks remained: to find a central hub, a catalyst which could federate all the committees and put in place a unified organisation capable of directing their actions and above all of formulating the political expression of the movement (i.e. its political-social-economic demands). On this question there is a clear difference between the structures established in Tizi Ouzou compared with Bejaia.

At Tizi Ouzou, after halting the young rioters and putting in place an inter-suburb coordination (in Tizi Ouzou town), it was decided at Beni Douala (a place in the mountains where the young high-school student Guermah Massinissa was assassinated) to adopt a principle of organisation on the basis of belonging to Aarouch. Aarch means literally 'confederation of tribes'. The mountains of Kabylie are dotted with villages; a village can consist of one or several families; several villages constitute a tribe (with kinship links); several tribes constitute what is called an Aarch. At Tizi Oouzou, organisation rested on a tribal base. But make no mistake, the concept of the Aarouch is very complex; it is a two-edged sword: on the one hand it can mobilise by the very fact of 'inborn' solidarity (familial and tribal links), on the other hand it is destructive, for it constitutes (in itself) the negation of the principle of citizenship. This will be verified in the course of development of the movement.

From the first meetings (mid-May) those coordinating the Tizi Aarouchs decided to exclude political parties, trade unions, women's associations and other organisations of civil society under the pretext of protecting the movement from all manipulation; the real reason was that the coordination at Tizi Ouzou was controlled from the start by petty-bourgeois layers of the population (shopkeepers, doctors, bankers, for the most part followers of the so-called Kabyle parties FFS and RCD), who wanted at all costs to reduce, even to conceal, the fundamentally social dimension of the black spring movement.

This explains why at Tizi Ouzoou the movement had a completely one-sided, even sterile platform, because it contented itself, under guise of political expression, with a few general, abstract, sometimes even contradictory formulae relating to the population's demands. Virtually all those in the committees of the villages, suburbs and communes belonged to underprivileged layers (young unemployed, workers, students and school pupils), but they were subjected to the dominant ideological influence of the petty-bourgeois elements.

7.4.3 Mohamed Arabi (cont.): 'The formation and political programme of the Bejaia popular committee'

Contrary to what happened at Tizi Ouzou, the town and department of Bejaia had a quite different dynamic. If the initiative for the creation of the first village and suburb committees came from the citizens (young unemployed, workers, students...), the catalyst was the presence of trade unionists. The first call for mobilisation and self-organisation (25 April 2001) was signed in the name of the university community of Bejaia, the leading group of which was constituted by the national Council of high-school teachers (CNES).

Some days later this leading group was joined by other trade unionists, in particular those of SETE (union of workers in primary, secondary and higher education). The attempt to organise brought the proclamation of the popular committee of the Wilaya of Bejaia (CPWB), consisting of delegates from the 52 existing communes and ten or so trade unions, as well as the presence of a Berber cultural association and a women's association. The popular character of the committee reflected the broad nature of the movement, involving not only underprivileged layers (young unemployed, workers) but also elements of the middle layers (small shopkeepers, teachers, public service doctors, etc.). It also signified above all a social and political definition of belonging, of citizenship. No committee, whether of village, suburb or commune, claimed for itself a Bejaia department tribal identity. Whereas at Tizi the platform of the coordinating organisation excluded the rights of women (contrary to the familial code), of journalists (contrary to the amendments to the penal code) and other political-social-economic demands, contenting itself with points related to the consequences of the movement (trial of the assassins, caring of victims' families) and demands (traditional to Kabylie) for the Berbers' linguistic and ethnic identity, the CPWB adopted a platform on 11 June with three main axes: immediate demands (caring for victims' families, trial of the assassins), political demands, and finally social-economic demands.

The CPWB platform emphasises the democratic and above all social aspects of the movement. The programme formulates in precise terms the necessity of rejecting the economic policies imposed by the international financial institutions, the necessity of starting public works, based on the State budget, to consolidate the working of the state sectors (hospitals, schools, etc.). Unfortunately, the CPWB platform, which ought to have constituted the basis for the programme of the movement as a whole (14 June 2001), was completely cut to pieces. The document finally adopted under the dominant political influence of the movement in Tizi Ouzou, the 'capital' of Kabylie, was inspired by the platform of El Kseur, of dwarf-like proportions compared with the real significance and strength of the movement.

7.5 Example 5: Africa – Subsistence Agriculture

'Subsistence agriculture, internationalism and nationalism in Africa' by Steve Drury. This was a contribution by Steve Drury to the preparation of a proposed African Workers' and Students' Conference, 27 November 2002.

Outside of South Africa, where nearly all land is still held by a minority descended from white colonists, the vast majority of Africans are subsistence farmers and pastoralists. The conditions under which they make a living vary greatly from area to area, depending both on climate and soils, and on the terms under which they can use the land. Although the climate seems to be changing, partly under the influence of capital's increasing release of the 'greenhouse' gas carbon dioxide by burning coal and petroleum, there is little to be done about that, while capital still dominates human affairs in general. The intricacies of Africa's climate and the generally poor nature of its soils makes peasant subsistence there the most difficult on any continent.

Until about 100 years ago, Africa's population was very small relative to its vast area. Huge tracts remained in their wild state because of the difficulties of extracting a living, partly because of poor soils and erratic low rainfall, and partly because of risks from disease (mainly carried by mosquitoes, tsetse flies and other insects) affecting both people and domesticated livestock. Populations have grown rapidly since the beginning of colonialism, with the introduction of modern medicine, non-indigenous food crops (such as mealies and cassava) that survive drought, more resistant strains of livestock and especially the growth of cash-cropping (dominated by cocoa, coffee, tea and cotton) that, together with mining, drew Africa into capital's world market economy. However, life for this growing population has not improved, and in many cases has become worse and more threatened by calamity. Traditionally populated areas now have to support more people, and increasingly poorer land has come into use as people have migrated.

The main outcome of the pressure of an increase in population, together with that of herds of livestock, has been deterioration of the already poor land. Tree cover has shrunk through demands for fuel and building materials, and because of commercial logging. Reduction in the period of traditional fallowing of farmland and grazing has increasingly exposed bare soil to the elements. Already poor in nutrients, many African soils have lost much of their natural fertility. In areas prone to heavy rains, bare soil has been pounded into mud which dries to give an unploughable, almost rock-like surface. Worse still, the loss of protection by vegetation makes soils prone to erosion, so the surface becomes a useless 'badland' broken by myriads of deep gullies. Highland areas are most at risk from soil erosion, and it is partly the loss of soil from the Ethiopian highlands and other rugged parts of Africa that lies behind the growing risk of catastrophic famine and the death and misery of millions. Another legacy of the colonial partition of Africa, the neo-tribalism that it fostered in order to rule more securely, and the nationalism that artificial borders created, is a continuing recent history of warfare that spans the entire continent. This drives people from the land on which their survival depends, to become refugees in such numbers that most cannot be fed by the meagre resources provided by imperialist-inspired agencies and a variety of liberal-minded charities. Even a short-term abandonment of the land sees it descend further into infertility.

Attempts to increase agriculture through large-scale irrigation schemes, based on large dams and river diversions, depend on loans from the international bankers (who demand interest and eventual repayment of capital) and so-called 'aid', which benefits transnational consulting and engineering companies not the local people. Dominated by state and agro-business interests, and therefore by cash cropping rather than growing staple foods, such schemes have a dreary history. Dams eventually silt up with sediment that otherwise would have replenished soils further downstream. Large bodies of water encourage diseases such as malaria and bilharzia, and displace many people from the more fertile lowlands that they fill. Irrigation itself deposits salt in the soil because of repeated evaporation in hot climates, to make the soil irrecoverably infertile. The large fields of single crops, unlike the traditional African 'garden' agriculture using many different crops, are stripped of soil by the wind, and the fertilizers washed from them pollute rivers and groundwater.

Ownership and access to fertile land pose the most burning question to the majority of Africans. In some areas, such as Sudan, a tiny minority of semi-feudalists own vast tracts, enriching themselves from tenants' rents and from produce that depends on rural labour. The last refuge of real feudalism was driven out by Ethiopian peasants in 1974, who brought the downfall of Haile Selassie and expropriated the land of the Amhara feudal lords, only to find themselves exploited in other ways by succeeding regimes. In areas in upheaval, such as parts of Somalia and southern Sudan, various 'war lords' with no specific rights to land exploit local people to support their forces. No African has agricultural land rights in South Africa; a legacy of its colonisation and apartheid, unchallenged by the ANC-SACP government. Consequently, there is no peasant class in South Africa, but many rural workers on white-owned, large farms. Before Africa fell under colonial rule, land was apportioned on a community basis, with some guarantee to a share of its quality by rotation of rights, although the forms taken by this distribution varied greatly across the continent. Likewise, grazing for nomadic pastoralists was organized by communal decision.

Islands of traditional land tenure remain, largely in West Africa. Land rights of this kind ensure both individual and communal interest in maintaining and improving land quality, together with sharing many of the most arduous tasks, such as ploughing, terracing and tree planting. Two factors result in its breakdown. One, as in the Niger Delta, is the overriding of traditional rights by more powerful interests of industrial capital and the monolithic state – in this case those of the Ogoni people, whose land has been ruined by uncontrolled drilling for oil and gas by Shell. The other is arbitrary 'nationalisation' of land, the most recent case being by the unelected EPLF/PFDJ regime in Eritrea. Never completely absorbed by the feudal Abyssinian empire, land tenure in Eritrea was on a communal basis with a five-to-seven-year cycle of rotation, administered by village elders, of good and poor plots among farmers living in densely packed villages. Although drought-prone and suffering from deforestation for building and fuel, and with part of the best land expropriated for commercial agriculture by Italian colonists, this communal ownership ensured continual maintenance and expansion of cropped land and common pastures. Sudden state ownership, even with guarantees for tenure of descendants who continue farming, removes incentive to maintain and improve land for future use. It also undermines the traditional rights of nomadic and semi-nomadic pastoralists to move wherever grazing is available on previously 'unowned' rangeland. In parallel with it are attempts to make such pastoralists live in fixed villages after centuries of migration, and the control of supplies of equipment and seeds by the state.

Dependence on others, whether 'state' or landlords, for access to land, to equipment and seeds, and therefore survival destroys any political freedom for peasants. In 'democratic elections' they vote as they are told by their landlord or by the self-appointed state authorities, in fear of sanctions. This is a major reason for the appearance of the oppressive Islamic fundamentalist regime in the Sudan, and why other monolithic governments, as in Kenya, retain power and privilege for long periods. In reality no peasant can be truly free through their efforts alone, simply because they are tied to the land in order to survive. The fragility of their lives means little time for reflection and education, even the youngest children being needed to till the land and look after herds. Consequently their horizons are narrowed to that of the village, and it is difficult for them to see other far-off people sharing common problems, interests and aspirations. This enslavement by the land and ignorance makes the mass of peasantry easily susceptible to the nationalism that plagues Africa, made more insidious by the legacy of neo-tribalism fostered by colonialism and the artificial national boundaries that it imposed. Nowhere is the latter more blatant than in South Africa, with its creation of artificial states such as Swaziland and Lesotho and so-called 'tribal homelands', and the former in the Belgian promotion of the Tutsi as administrators over the majority Hutu in Rwanda, Burundi and eastern Zaire, with the well-known disastrous consequences.

The most astonishing and absurd outcome of historical factors beyond the control of ordinary people is the nationalism astride the boundary between Eritrea and northern Ethiopia (Tigray). It is worth dwelling on the present situation there, because it presents some important lessons. The border is a creation of Italian and British imperialism at the start of the 20th century, submerged for 30 years by Haile Selassie's annexation of Eritrea in 1962, only to re-emerge from the defeat of the Bonapartist Derg regime that succeeded his unseating by the 1974 Ethiopian Revolution. After the Derg's physical liquidation of all democratic parties in the Ethiopian heartland and defeat of Somalis in the south-eastern province of Ogaden seeking to re-unite with Somalia in 1976-7, its only opposition consisted of forces fighting for regional self-determination in the north, mainly in Eritrea but later in Tigray. Conscription of peasants by both Derg and nationalist forces, together with the driving of peasants from their land by the Derg's terror tactics, made farming impossible. More so than climate shifts and land degradation, these were the underlying factors behind the catastrophic famine of 1984-5 that saw perhaps a million dying from starvation, particularly in Tigray. Despite the great ethnic diversity of both areas and a roughly 50:50 division between Christians and Muslims, intellectuals from the Tigrigna-speaking, Christian community of the highland areas became the leadership of both liberation fronts. The final act of the war against the Derg's repression, following stalemate in Eritrea, was the assault on Addis Ababa by the Tigray Peoples Liberation Front (loosely allied with less organized Oromo and Afar forces) armed, supplied and strengthened by the Eritrean Peoples Liberation Front.

The TPLF, assuming the name of the Ethiopian Peoples' Revolutionary Democratic Front, formed the new Ethiopian government. Subsequently it decreed a spurious form of self-determination to Ethiopia's major regions, but retained central power through elections thereafter. The EPLF suspended declaration of Eritrea's independence until a referendum (based on electoral registration carried out by the EPLF) gave that an overwhelming mandate in 1993. To the outside world this presented an air of peace and harmony in the area. Events in 1997-8, which culminated in open warfare over the common border and the Red Sea port of Assab, revealed a very different underpinning. It became clear that a Tigrigna axis had formed towards the end of the war against the Derg, seeking to parasitise the remainder of Ethiopia for the economic development of both Tigray and Eritrea and the enrichment of their respective bourgeoisies, described elsewhere (Alasdair Guest, 'Observations on the Eritrean-Ethiopian War', *International Socialist Forum*, No 3, 1998, pp. 73-7). It hinged on Eritrea's control of Ethiopia's access to the Red Sea via the ports of Massawa (also serving Tigray) and Assab and the flow of port dues which enabled, manipulation of the Ethiopian currency shared until 1997 by both countries, smuggling of cash crops to Eritrea from southern Ethiopia for re-export and hard-currency earnings, and diversion of capital to Tigray for its development by the TPLF/EPRDF government. A mixture of Tigrayan expansionism – its regional government claimed and began to occupy parts of Eritrea behind the original border of the former Italian colony – and the inability of the economic policies of the EPLF (now Popular Front for Democracy and Justice, albeit disinclined to institute any elections or constitution and ruling by decree) to improve conditions in war-ravaged Eritrea as the world economy began to descend into slump, broke apart this relationship. Eritrea invaded northern Tigray, while the TPLF/EPRDF attempted to regain the port of Assab. Hundreds of civilian lives were lost by bombing, with an unknown number of military casualties. At the time of writing, some one third of able Eritreans are said to have been conscripted, with a similar expansion of military forces by the TPLF/EPRDF.

Despite the fact that the opposing forces are mainly drawn from the same Tigrigna-speaking, highland Christian community, the hostilities are characterized by a wave of jingoistic nationalism voiced mainly by Eritrean petty-bourgeois elements as foul-mouthed diatribes against Tigrayans in general. The most common epithet is that Eritreans are 'proud and free', while Tigrayans are 'beggars'. The only differences between highland Eritreans and Tigrayans, is that the former were never subject to feudalism, lying at the fringes of the Ethiopian and Ottoman empires, whereas the latter had been serfs and suffered the full force of the 1984-5 famine. Tens of thousands of young people in Tigray are destitute orphans, many seeking a miserable survival by begging in the capital of Eritrea, Asmara, after the end of the war in 1991, only to be driven out by the EPLF in 1993. Thousands of bourgeois and petty bourgeois people of Eritrean origin, who had a prominent role in Addis Ababa, have been expelled to Asmara since the war started, their assets frozen by the TPLF/EPRDF. The full truth about this disastrous situation has yet to come out. However, what has emerged shows clearly that nationalism has nothing whatever to do with the interests and lives of the majority of people in the region. It is a creation that serves only the interests of the bourgeoisie that happen to live in this or that part of a continent artificially carved up by colonialism. Since the national bourgeoisie act as conduits for the exploitation of Africa's natural resources and its people by global capital, the regimes that represent them receive the support of imperialism and its agencies. Both the TPLF/EPRDF and EPLF/PFDJ were held up by the OAU, the UN and the US State Department as 'model' leaders of the 'new African order'. Now they are floundering in disarray.

Nationalism and the fact that a majority of peasants and millions of people are dispossessed of land and at the edge of survival are Africa's endemic problems. It would be disastrous for African workers seeking unity and a revolutionary solution to their own problems not to ally themselves with the rural masses. Indeed, the majority of African workers are not themselves immune from nationalist sentiments. The majority are but one or two generations removed from origins among the peasantry. Consequently, though having broken from life-or-death ties to the land, most workers have family in rural areas, remit part of their earnings to the countryside (sometimes hundreds of kilometres from where they work), and retain much of the culture from which they sprang. The last, having been bent in many ways to the interests of colonialism, poses great dangers, as anyone witnessing the role of the Zulu Inkatha in South Africa will know all too well. Yet workers soon learn that their problems are the same, no matter where they came from, and that they have a common source in capital. This pressure for unity comes from their working and living closely together, and from their increasing consciousness brought in part by the education that capital finds necessary in order to have a skilled workforce, and in part by their continual exchange of ideas. Though they must labour, generally under poor conditions, workers have a freedom of movement, expression and action that is impossible for those tied to the land. As well as being the creators of wealth, by being forced to combine and organize in trades unions and community associations ('Civics' in South Africa) to improve their conditions and defend those won in the past, workers have created organizations with great potential power for resolving Africa's problems. However, while these organizations have leaders whose interests lie mainly with governments who represent national and international capital this power remains sleeping or misused. At best it serves only sections of the working class, and at worst it is harnessed to support nationalist adventures, as in the propagandising for conscription of the state-created National Union of Eritrean Workers.

South African workers in particular, together with smaller groups of their comrades throughout Africa, have a great responsibility to show the African rural masses that their advancement is only possible through a continent-wide alliance with the working class, as part of a world unification of labour. Such a unity, standing above the mosaic of nation-states and over the many differences in ethnic origin, language and religion, cannot be one of words and ideas alone. At its outset it surely needs to focus on satisfying the burning needs of subsistence farmers and pastoralists through using the skills and abilities of workers. The rural masses could supply agricultural produce to working-class communities, in a co-operative economy that is independent of capital and its markets, which only serve to exploit worker and peasant alike. Equally, those students and intellectuals who see a common cause with the workers are in a position to take education and science to the countryside so that their knowledge can take on a concrete and useful form within this new economic relationship. What is needed seems to me to be nothing less than the opening of the socialist offensive on the principle of: 'From each according to their abilities, to each according to their needs'.

The huge size and diversity of Africa might seem to pose great difficulties in beginning such an epochal change. However, rural needs are neither complicated nor difficult to solve. From the standpoint of those people subsisting at the edge of survival, the following are their main requirements to ensure a future that can be sustained and built upon:

Home life

- Reliable and safe water for drinking and washing, that is close by
- Energy for cooking and heating that does not mean further deforestation or diversion of manure from agriculture
- Durable housing, free from pests
- Hygienic means of waste-disposal, involving recycling of wastes to fertilizers and energy
- Access to medical, recreational and educational facilities

Farming

- Reliable water sources for irrigating crops
- Improved soil stability and fertility, bringing new land under the plough and reclamation of lost land
- High-yielding, pest-resistant seeds
- Efficient means of tilling and harvesting
- Safe storage facilities
- Improved roads and transport
- Pastoralism
- Reliable and widely distributed water points
- Eradication of pests that carry disease, and improved stock

- Access to fodder and rangeland
- Means of keeping stock and wild animals from crop land and reserved grazing and fallows.

There are many other possibilities for improving rural life, such as planting trees, using small irrigation dams for fish-farming, and enabling coastal people to harvest marine life safely.

Socialism means the removal for all time of the market mechanism, the dependence on the commodity and on exchange value, which lie at the heart of capital and its exploitation. It demands the eradication of capital from the whole world, and that is not done without preparation. While capital remains there will be markets and exchange, either involving goods and services or money – peasants depend on them to get necessities they cannot produce themselves. However, co-operatives can turn the market to the advantage of worker and peasant alike, by cutting out the middlemen, guaranteeing fair exchange and preventing hoarding and speculation; by becoming centred on usefulness rather than exchange value. A major step forward would be cutting loose from the so-called 'food aid' supplied by imperialist agencies, which serves both to enrich the agro-business of America's great plains and the speculators on the Chicago grain market, and to depress prices on local markets and peasants' incentive to produce efficiently when famine recedes. 'Food-aid' administered by nationalist governments is one source of corruption and a means of controlling people's lives. Worker-peasant co-operatives could themselves seize the initiative and administer distribution, beginning at the docks, when famine does require the import of foodstuffs from other parts of the world. While they have their own problems, workers should surely support peasants' demands for land and the break-up and fair redistribution of the great estates of the colonists, and do all in their power to help them get it.

Africa's problems are not the responsibility of its people alone. In times of emergency, such as the great famine of 1984-5 in the Horn and the recurrent plight of refugees driven from their land by war, millions of people in the industrial centres of capital, especially youth, raise funds and materials to help. Up to now this genuine assistance has been channelled through liberal-minded charities. Many of these NGOs today are important means whereby UN, European Union and individual governments' 'relief and development' funds make their way to Africa. Because of this, these charities have become part of imperialism's manipulation of people's misery. Equally, they work through nationalist governments whose interests are those of the national bourgeoisie. NGOs are by no means independent, whatever the wishes of their organisers, field workers and their donors. There is no reason why worker-peasant co-operatives in Africa should not establish direct links with their comrades in Europe and North America in times of catastrophe, drawing into their ranks the best elements who work for existing charities. Workers Aid in Europe, set up by workers themselves to come to the assistance of their comrades in the former Yugoslavia, is a model for establishing this unity in the opposite direction. But there is also another side to this need for internationalism.

As capital's structural crisis worsens and spreads, it brings destruction to working-class communities in the major industrialized countries in Europe and east Asia, and soon to North America. Whole industries are wiped out with no alternative employment for workers who have lost their jobs. To the growing millions thrown out of work are added millions more school leavers who have no prospect of work while capital remains. Areas once renowned for their coalfields, steel works and engineering factories are virtual wastelands. Even high-tech industries, centred on the computer revolution and based on capital attracted by generous government loans and guarantees, suddenly close and ship their equipment to where labour is cheaper. Such devastated communities are inhabited by workers with the most sophisticated skills and high levels of education, yet who will never again put them to use while capital remains. They depend on the dole and social security, both threatened by cuts because government funds are dwindling and national economies sliding into slump. They too face a threat to survival, and of the total breakdown of all community life. The only sustainable solution is to put their skills to use in revitalising the abandoned factories to produce useful goods through development schemes organized by their communities, and in setting up co-operative movements to ensure affordable food. Again, these strategies are only possible if established independently of capital and with the workers themselves administering their own affairs. It is clearly essential that such co-operatives unite and work together with their counterparts in Africa and other areas abandoned by capital.

Africa's fate rests with neither nationalism nor the agencies of finance capital. The first sets people against one another, either by fomenting war or by parasitic economic relations with neighbouring nation-states. It is a legacy of colonialism and is administered by the agencies it left behind. It works only in the interests of the bourgeoisie in this or that country. Capital has abandoned the continent, except to exploit its natural resources and to safeguard its own interests. Lofty words of creating new 'tiger economies' along the lines of the collapsing economies of the Pacific rim are an illusion, despite the human and natural resources on the continent. Only African workers and their allies among rural people and sections of professional workers and students can halt the decline in the lives of the majority. United by independent organization of production and community relations, and linked with similar workers' movements internationally, they can build a truly human future that lasts and flourishes.

7.6 Example 6: Africa – Rwanda. Statement by the Workers International, 1994

As we write, the death rate amongst Rwandan refugees from cholera and other diseases is one person per minute. The sick are climbing under their mats to die so that others can wrap their bodies more easily, and the dead are lying so closely packed by the side of the roads that tyre marks are visible where vehicles have been forced to drive over them. The response of world leaders to the Rwandan crisis would be laughable if it did not signify the miserable death of thousands of human beings. American President Clinton has offered £200 million to alleviate the disaster, and the British Minister of Overseas Aid Linda Chalker proposes £6.5 million. To put these sums into perspective, Clinton's offer is worth .0004 per cent of the European fighter aircraft project, which costs £50 billion.

All the possible charity, voluntary aid, relief agencies' work in the world, even multiplied a thousand times, will not save the millions of men, women and children now facing extinction in Rwanda. In the open, under the equatorial sun on the Zairean border, they stand, hundreds of thousands of refugees – nowhere to go, nothing to eat, no water. The only people who possess the emergency supplies necessary to save these lives are the great multinational companies of Europe, North America and Japan and the governments which serve them. These companies publish profit figures of billions. These governments have budgets of billions – much of it for military expenditure. Unless some of this untold wealth is spent – now! – millions will die, today and tomorrow. In every one of the 'Great Powers' in Europe, North America and Japan, the trade unions and political parties of the working class must organise now to demand that their governments mount massive emergency operations, whatever the cost, to save the people of Rwanda. The working-class movement will win behind itself millions of working people, the majority of the population, for such an initiative. It means organising demonstrations and representations and preparing strike action if necessary to force this action by the governments.

It means industrial action, from non-cooperation to strikes and occupations to force the great multinationals, monopolies and banks, especially those which invest in Africa, to disgorge the money, supplies and transport necessary for this international operation. It means demanding the government commandeer the necessary fuel, aircraft, vehicles and food, medical and building supplies. Until now the governments of the 'Great Powers' have done this kind of thing only for war, for their own interests, to conquer more Rwandas.

In Britain, every trade unionist should fight for the Trades Union Congress and its international department to bring these demands immediately before the government – the same in every trade union. We organise for Bosnia the Workers Aid convoys to Tuzla. These take material aid, as part of the fight to sustain the workers of Bosnia while preparing with them to reconstruct the international solidarity of the working class which is the only basis for a solution in the former Yugoslavia. The scale of the problem in Rwanda, and the resources available to Workers Aid – given the extreme urgency of the situation – don't allow the same operation. What can we do, except to fight for the whole strength of the workers' movement internationally to begin to work on the problem?

It means organising and exerting their strength to force those who have the wealth – and they are the only ones – to give up some of it. We know very well that, even if they are forced to respond, they will give as little as they can, and they will want to make money out of it, and they will come back to the working people of their own countries and the world to make them pay in the end. We know this, and we say that a fight to save Rwanda will prepare us better to meet these problems when they come. As for the supplies to be sent, we should demand at every stage that the people of Rwanda themselves, helped physically by workers from Africa south, north, east and west and from the rest of the world, have control. We know also that the sectarians will tell us that it is 'not enough' to use 'pressure' to make the imperialists do this, you have to overthrow them. Yes, but the death of millions of our fellow workers in Rwanda is today, and what we can do to force our governments and exploiters to intervene with supplies will bring us a big step nearer to being able to overthrow them. It is just such international action and consciousness that are necessary to take us closer to that day. And so we say that this proposal is not utopian. Who has another proposal for what the workers' movement should do? Should we do nothing? Should we accept the message of the capitalist media and the system behind it: that it is all so awful that we are powerless to act? Let us call on the workers of every country to move their organisations to make these demands on their governments. In South Africa, for example, let the COSATU unions tell the 'Government of National Unity', Mandela and De Klerk, to commandeer whatever is necessary from Anglo-American, De Beers and the rest. The workers of South Africa will respond to such a call, as everybody knows. In Britain, France, Germany, the US, the ruling classes of these countries have built their vast wealth from the brutal exploitation of Africa, from the slave trade to the diamond and uranium mines. It is this exploitation and oppression of half a millennium, and not 'inter-tribal conflict', that has kept Africa economically backward and has starved to death or butchered millions in Somalia, Ethiopia, Algeria and Rwanda, just as it did in Vietnam, Malaysia, Cambodia and in every corner of the world.

7.7 Example 7: Africa – Social movements. All the following South African quotes were sent to me by Namibian comrades in 2002

7.7.1 Social Movements Indaba puts full support behind Anti-War marches to take place across South Africa on 15 February 2002. 'NOT IN OUR NAME! No to US Imperialism! No War Against Iraq! No Blood for Oil! Free Palestine!'

The member organisations of the Social Movements Indaba (SMI) from across the country, call on South Africans to raise their voices against the impending war on Iraq by joining anti-war marches and other actions taking place in various cities on 15th February under the banner of the Anti-War Coalition. It would be a crime against humanity if we remain silent while the US government and its madman President Bush, prepare to slaughter hundreds of thousands of Iraqis and plunge the world into a cesspool of capitalist violence, hatred and greed. In raising our voices, the SMI, alongside many other progressive forces around the world, is very clear what the coming war on Iraq is really all about. At its core, it is about making the world safe for US imperialism and the corporate capitalists whose interests it serves. It is about crushing the legitimate struggles for real political and socio-economic freedom waged by the poor and oppressed across the world, no more so than as applied to the struggles of the Palestinian people. It is about the global imposition of the barbaric capitalist principle of profits before people.

Unfortunately, the ANC government's public pronouncements of opposition to a war on Iraq are much murkier. Being against war means exactly that. It does not mean supporting a war simply because it is endorsed by a set of United Nations elites so comfortably ensconced, and so far removed, from those they claim to represent. Neither does it mean decrying the militarist unilateralism that the US government seeks to visit on Iraq while wallowing in the economic unilateralism that continues to be visited on the majority of South Africans. It does not mean pursuing the capitalist policies of GEAR (Growth, Employment and Redistribution) and NEPAD (New Partnership for African Development) that deprive millions of Africans of the most basic human services and needs and then hypocritically attacking a US imperialism that is the engine behind the implementation of the same on a global scale. And, it most certainly does not mean making grand claims to an anti-war moral high ground whilst simultaneously allowing South African arms companies to export weapons components that will be used to maim and kill more Iraqis and Palestinians or allowing US and British ships, laden with weapons of war, to dock at South Africa's ports. The SMI, marching under the banner of the Anti-War Coalition, will be raising its voice against all those capitalists, of whatever hue and/or nationality, who seek to collectively, if differentially, hide behind the veil of democracy, so-called human rights and false freedom in their deathly quest for money and power. With millions of others all over the world, we will be sending a message that is loud and clear: NOT IN OUR NAME!

7.7.2 Mandela Park AEC opens school for the poor, 3 January 2003. Released by: Western Cape Anti-Eviction Campaign

The Mandela Park Anti-Eviction Campaign, responding to issues raised in community meetings, has opened a school today at Andile Nose Community Centre, in Govan Mbeki Road, Khayelitsha. This school is a response to the exclusion of students from government schools because they cannot afford school fees, or because they are too old. Despite the promise of free education by the government, communities in Mandela Park, Tafelsig and elsewhere have found that school governing bodies are forcing parents to pay fees they cannot afford. Parents are forced to sign 'acknowledgement of debt' forms, and face having their furniture and clothes confiscated if they cannot pay these debts. The opening of a school at Andile Nose is part of the Mandela Park AEC's 'Right to Education' campaign, and is a sign that community meetings in the area are taking up all the issues of the poor. The media is invited to visit Andile Nose today, to see what can be achieved when a community stands together!

7.7.3 Social movements: 'Ultra-left' or 'global citizens?' by Drew Forrest, *Mail & Guardian*, 4 February 2003

Depending on one's viewpoint, they are the embryo of a 'global citizens' movement' in South Africa, or President Thabo Mbeki's ultra-left nightmare. They include the 'loony' organisations Minister of Water Affairs and Forestry Ronnie Kasrils has accused the labour movement of befriending. They are an extremely loose constellation of left-leaning, community-based social movements that vary enormously in focus, size and influence. Most are minuscule. What unites them is a shared desire to help the poor and downtrodden, and, in varying degrees, a common antagonism to hierarchies and bureaucracies, the profit motive, the unfettered market and corporate power.

They are, at the very least, independent of the government and the ruling African National Congress. Some, like the Treatment Action Campaign, are not necessarily anti-ANC, but have clashed with the government. A hard core see themselves as ideological opponents of the post-1994 South African state, which they regard as anti-poor and subservient to domestic and international business interests. Most would be opposed to corporate globalisation and emotionally partisan to the countries of the South. Some view themselves as part of what the ANC calls 'the Seattle Movement' and have links with grassroots activists in Third World countries like Brazil. Under the umbrella of the Social Movements Indaba, the latter made their presence felt during the World Summit on Sustainable Development. The movements focus on townships, squatter camps and rural settlements, generally organising around discrete issues of concern to the poor: HIV/AIDS, evictions, power and water cut-offs, land and jobs/ privatisation. This often brings them into conflict with the authorities, particularly local councils. Loose-knit and fluid, many have overlapping leadership structures, with the same names cropping up in different contexts. The leading lights include Marxist unionists or ex-unionists associated with the 'workerist' rather than 'nationalist' union factions in the 1980s, and radical anti-apartheid activists disenchanted with the ANC and its partner, the South African Communist Party.

An almost universal feature is a tactical attitude to the law : the movements will use it if it is to their advantage; flout it if they consider it unjust. Forms of defiance range from calls for the repudiation of apartheid debt and peaceful civil disobedience, through to violent protest and the invasion of land. In this respect, they can be seen as the offspring of the anti-apartheid resistance of the 1980s. The taste for 'direct action' further links them with the Seattle anti-globalisation campaigners. Given the small size of most social movements in South Africa, Mbeki's attempt to demonise them seems odd. In part, it may flow from resentment at the moral sanctimony of much left opposition, exacerbated by the fact that many of its shrillest ideologues are non-Africans. The ANC justly complains that the demand for instant economic justice, given the apartheid legacy, is droompolitiek (dreamy politics). It has a point when it says some of the activism is opportunistic and self-defeating. Blocking the relocation of chronic bond defaulters, for example, merely fuels 'redlining' by banks. But 'vanguardist' pretensions are also a factor: the ANC seems outraged by a competing claim to its poor black constituency. It has reacted in two ways: by calling for 'ultra-leftists' to be isolated and defeated; and by suggesting that the new movements should be brought under its 'leadership'. Hence the moves to breathe life into its moribund ally, the South African National Civic Organisation (SANCO). One can see the movements in another way: at worst they are a minor nuisance, at best an attempt to give ordinary people a voice and some control over their daily lives. With the ANC now the political establishment, SANCO an empty shell, and NGOs weakened by the state grip on funding, politics for most South Africans increasingly boils down to making their cross every five years.

7.7.4 Treatment Action Campaign, by Matthew Wilhelm-Solomon

Launched in December 1998, the Treatment Action Campaign (TAC) has been one of South Africa's most effective and active civil society groups. Founded by, among others, current chairperson Zackie Achmat and national secretary Mark Heywood, its aims include ensuring access to proper, affordable treatment for AIDS sufferers, preventing and eliminating new HIV infections and fostering HIV/AIDSs treatment literacy. The TAC has used a shrewd mix of civil disobedience, marches and court actions to force the hands of the government and international drug companies. Its branches nationwide use volunteers in campaigns. Members are from diverse political backgrounds – Achmat is a loyal ANC member – and the movement is not aligned to any political party, basing itself on a culture of universal human rights. It has close links with more than 170 local and international organisations, including the Congress of South African Trade Unions (COSATU). In its first major act of civil disobedience, in 2000, it imported a generic of Flucanazole in defiance of patent laws. It has agitated against patent laws and the high cost of medicines. In 2001 it ran a campaign for a countrywide programme to prevent mother-to-child transmission of HIV, winning a key high court challenge to the government. The ruling that the state ban on nevirapine outside pilot sites was 'unjustifiable' was upheld by the Constitutional Court. The TAC also stridently opposes attempts to deny the link between HIV and AIDS, accusing Mbeki of closet denialism.

The TAC is planning court action to force the government and business to sign the framework agreement for national AIDS treatment and prevention plan tabled in the National Economic and Development Labour Council last year, and will march on Parliament when it formally opens on February 14 to rally support for the accord. The march will end at the United States consulate, where a protest will be staged against 'inadequate' US funding for the United Nations Global Fund for AIDS. If the government fails to sign the national agreement by end-February, the TAC will engage in further civil disobedience.

7.7.5 Anti-Privatisation Forum

The Anti-Privatisation Forum (APF) was formed in early 2000 by radical left-wing trade unionists and former members of the SACP and ANC. Key figures are chairperson John Appolis, ex-ANC; secretary Trevor Ngwane, expelled from the ANC in 1999 for his radical anti-privatisation views; Rob Rees, an official of COSATU's most radical affiliate, the South African Municipal Workers Union (SAMWU); and treasurer Florencia Delvere, ex-SACP. Its launch was largely prompted by the Johannesburg Council's Igoli 2002 plan, seen as a move to privatise municipal services and the target of a (failed) SAMWU campaign, and Wits University's 2001 retrenchment plan,opposed by the National Education and Health Allied Workers Union. 'Basic rights cannot be commodified,' said APF spokesperson Dale McKinley, expelled from the SACP in 2000 for 'undermining the leadership'. 'Our agenda is to mobilise the majority of the working class against privatisation.' The APF acts as an umbrella for 16 smaller organisations, including the Soweto Electricity Crisis Committee, which Ngwane leads, the Katlehong Concerned Residents Forum and the Working Class Coordinating Committee. It has links with the Education Rights Project and the Centre for Applied Legal Studies at Wits University. Last year a group of APF activists was arrested after Johannesburg mayor Amos Masondo's Kensington house was stoned during a protest against his policy of electricity and water cut-offs. The 'Kensington 87', as the APF calls them, appeared in court last week for the fifth time on public violence and other charges. McKinley said the APF was a political rather than non-governmental organisation, serving as a socialist alternative to the ANC. 'Most ANC policies are no longer beneficial to the poor,' he said. The AFP engaged in 'mass struggle' like marches and protests to ensure 'the power of the people is heard by the government'.

7.7.6 The National Land Committee

The pioneer of South African social movements, the National Land Committee (NLC) was formed in 1987 from four land-rights organisations opposing apartheid's forced removals. It describes itself as an independent, non-aligned movement that helps communities gain access to land rights and development resources. 'Government's land programmes are severely limited and the promises made to the people have not been met,' said Zakes Hlatshwayo, a former Pan Africanist Congressman and now NLC director. It has affiliates in all provinces, including the Association for Rural Advancement in KwaZulu-Natal, the Rural Action Committees in Mpumulanga and the North West, and the Surplus People's Project in the Western Cape. Internationally, it is close to Brazil's Landless Workers' Movement. The NLC supports independent movements that 'share its values', according to Hlatshwayo, the most obvious being the Landless People's Movement, which the NLC assists through funding and political mobilisation. It acts as a network for land service organisations 'which cannot pressurise government on their own'. In

1999 the NLC launched the Rural Development Initiative, which laid the groundwork for the growth of rural organisations as social movements and saw the consolidation of NLC affiliates. The committee was active in the World Racism Conference in Durban in 2001 and a friend of the court in support of Minister of Agriculture and Land Affairs Thoko Didiza in the case brought by the Transvaal Agricultural Union to stop the expropriation of private farmland. It intends to oppose the Rights Bill, believing it fails to sufficiently curb the power of the chiefs. It espouses mass mobilisation rather than litigation, which Hlatshwayo says is ineffectual. 'Our pressure is from below. Unless the government faces the masses, there will be very little change.' However, Hlatshwayo himself now faces disciplinary action amid claims that ANC sympathisers on the NLC board are moving to disable the Landless People's Movement.

7.7.7 Education Rights Project

The Education Rights Project (ERP) started last February as a joint initiative of the Centre for Applied Legal Studies and the Education Policy Unit at Wits University. The project, which includes legal researchers, educationalists and civil society representatives, aims to enforce the right to basic education. Comprising a small core of employees and a large voluntary 'reference group', it works with community organisations and other social movements, including the APF and anti-eviction groups. Grassroots initiatives involve education rights awareness, legal community workshops and legal support. 'The ERP is not a social movement, but our work is linked to strengthening the social movements,' said Salim Vally, Education Policy Unit researcher and founding member of the project. Vally became well-known in the late 1980s as a member of the 'Trotskyist' faction in SACCAWU, COSATU's retail affiliate. The ERP's focal areas are free education; the lack of facilities at schools; sexual harassment of female pupils; lack of facilities for disabled learners; and adult education and training. Active in areas like Durban South, Orange Farm, Ikageng and Thembelihle, it has written legal letters to schools, brokered encounters between parents, schools and the government, and organised community meetings. It is considering court action to force the state to discharge its constitutional duties on education. The ERP has no party affiliations, but locates itself on the left. Though willing to work with the government in advancing education rights, it opposes the Growth, Employment And

Redistribution (GEAR) policy and its impact on education. Said Vally: 'The state is shirking its responsibility. The cost of education is passed on to parents and education is becoming marketised.' The ERP opposes globalisation, especially in relation to the privatisation of education. It was launched by the UN special rapporteur on education, Katerina Tomasevski.

7.7.8 Soweto Electricity Crisis Committee

The Soweto Electricity Crisis Committee (SECC) was formed in 2000 in response to Eskom cut-offs in the East Rand, Vaal and Soweto. Its campaign, Operation Khanyisa ('light'), involves the illegal reconnection of residents' electricity. 'It is criminal to rob people of the necessities of life,' said chairperson Trevor Ngwane. An avowed Trotskyist, Ngwane says SECC members believe the ANC serves the interests of big business. 'Mbeki uses revolutionary-sounding phrases and ANC struggle credentials to implement a capitalist agenda.' The SECC recently broadened its agenda to include a campaign against water cut-offs and privatisation (Vula Amanzi – 'turn on the water') and the eviction of township residents for defaulting on bond and rent payments. It was involved in the attempted reoccupation of Sebokeng's KwaMasiza hostel by 6,000 evicted people last September. Linked to the Anti-Eviction Campaign, the Concerned Citizens Forum and the Zimbabwe Anti-Privatisation Forum, it is part of the Social Movements Indaba, an umbrella formed during the World Summit that includes the Landless People's Movement, Jubilee South Africa and the APF. 'We dream of a society where no child will go to bed hungry,' Said Ngwane. He said the SECC believed in mass demonstrations and marches rather than litigation. 'We focus on direct action rather than discussion. We will cross the legal line when the law attacks the working class.' The SECC and the APF are planning a march next month against a war on Iraq, and campaigns on March 21 to mark Human Rights Day, and on June 16 to mobilise for basic education rights.

7.7.9 'The Landless People's Movement' by Vicki Robinson

The largest of the social movements, the Landless People's Movement (LPM) was formed in July 2001 by leaders of landless people's organisations against a backdrop of growing frustration with the slow pace of land reform. The NLC influenced its launch and funds it, and there is a large overlap between the leadership of the two organisations. However, the LPM describes itself as an independent NGO with no affiliates. The LPM believes the government's prioritisation of the global market is to blame for South Africa's land reform failures. 'Landlessness has been pushed under the carpet, largely because it is seen as a socialist concern. A people-centred rather then a market-orientated approach is needed,' said one LPM activist. Linked to local movements like the Concerned Citizens' Forum, it also has ties with the Brazilian peasant movement Movimento dos Trabalhadores Rurals Sem Terra. LPM members attended The Peasant World Assembly in Brazil last week. The LPM played a major role in the social movements' march at the World Summit, which embarrassingly overshadowed a parallel rally backed by the ANC and addressed by Mbeki. Declaring 2003 'the year of the landless', it plans a 'take back the land' campaign, which will involve land invasions if its land reform demands are not met. It also plans a 'free the farmdwellers' campaign to enforce farm workers' labour rights. It aims to have 100,000 paid-up members by July and to launch a campaign to boycott the 2004 elections if the government stonewalls its demands.

7.7.10 Jubilee South Africa

Jubilee South Africa is the local branch of the international Jubilee movement whose aim is the scrapping of the debt that burdens many poor countries. Launched in November 1998 at a conference of more than 60 civil society organisations, including COSATU, the South African NGO Coalition and churches, it focuses on global Third World debt; debt that financed the destabilisation of Southern Africa under apartheid; and debt inherited by the government from the apartheid regime, mainly to foreign banks. In 1998 Jubilee embarked on its Apartheid Debt and Reparations Campaign. It has agitated in Germany, Britain, Switzerland and the US for debt cancellation and reparation by banks that lent to the apartheid state and companies that invested in apartheid South Africa. 'Debt cancellation is not an act of charity, it's an act of justice,' said Neville Gabriel, Jubilee South Africa spokesperson.

Jubilee launched legal action in the US last year against eight banks and 12 oil, transport, IT and arms companies based in Europe and the US. The actions are based on the Alien Torts Claims Act, which allows foreigners to file claims against companies active in the US accused of human rights violations. The cases have been brought in collaboration with the Khulumani Support Group, which represents victims of apartheid state violence. Jubilee has close ties with the Alternative Information and Development Centre, undertakes research and has organised rallies against debt and such issues as the high prices charged by international drug companies. It avoids political alliances, preferring to empower individuals and communities to force issues on to the agendas of the powerful. However, it does believe in cooperating with the government without compromising its right to speak out.

7.7.11 Concerned Citizens Forum

One of the most effective and innovative of the social movements that have sprung up in post-apartheid South Africa, the Concerned Citizens' Forum (CCF), was formed in 1997, with Professor Fatima Meer and charismatic activist, writer and former University of Durban-Westville academic Ashwin Desai among its founders. It comprises a number of community movements in the Greater Durban area organising against electricity and water cut-offs, evictions and, more recently, racism. It has used the courts to halt evictions, has won cases where its members have occupied empty houses, and recently won a significant victory on council rentals and levies at the Housing Tribunal. However, it has also been involved in a number of violent skirmishes with police and council security officials. It openly supports the illegal re-connection of water and electricity for the poor and has trained 'struggle plumbers and electricians'. It has also marched on the houses of councillors who support disconnections. The CCF sponsored a march of about 5,000 people last year to support the payment of a basic monthly service fee of R10.

Currently locked in a battle with the council on plans to relocate rent defaulters, the CCF has clashed with all political parties. It says it is seeking to rebuild a sense of community in townships destroyed by apartheid and now by what it terms the ANC's 'brutal Reaganomics'. The CCF has no formal structure, preferring a loose association with leaders rooted in communities. Its community meetings are often boisterous affairs, with much music and dancing. It is criticised by some on the left for lacking ideological coherence – its T-shirts carry slogans like 'Smash GEAR' and 'Celebrate Life'. The CCF has spread into a number of Durban townships and has taken to sponsoring independent unions organising sweatshop workers. It has close links with the Landless People's Movement and the Anti-Eviction Campaign in the Western Cape.

7.7.12 South Durban Community Environmental Alliance

The South Durban Community Environmental Alliance (SDCEA) is an umbrella body formed in 1996 by five residents' and ratepayers' organisations in the South Durban industrial basin. Initially a pressure group on pollution issues affecting residents of the basin, it has begun to focus on broader community grievances. The alliance blames government economic policy for the loss of 10,000 jobs in the South Durban chemical industry alone. This, with the introduction of labour brokers, water and power cut-offs and evictions, has led to militant action against industry and the ANC council. During the Engen strike of 2001, for example, the Wentworth community tried to burn down the local police station. This year the alliance is planning an 'Anti-Forced Removal Campaign' with other militant communities under the banner of the CCF. It has made common cause with Chatsworth, Umlazi and other communities in opposing the Durban council's proposal to relocate poor Durban residents with rent arrears. There have been rumours of relocation in South Durban since consultants recommended an industrial future for the basin, saying residents were 'living in the wrong place' – a view echoed by new city manager Mike Sutcliffe. The alliance, in conjunction with militant factions of Friends of the Earth and Greenpeace, also has an 'anti-corporate criminal' focus, targeting South Durban's three biggest polluters, Engen, Sapref and Mondi. Its spokesperson, Anna Weekes, is a former SAMWU official. It also has links with two chemical unions opposed to outsourcing.

7.7.13 Anti-Eviction Campaign

The Western Cape-based Anti-Eviction Campaign (AEC) has been mobilising since November 2000 against evictions of low-cost housing bond defaulters and water cut-offs in council houses. It was officially formed in February 2001 as an umbrella body after community activists came on board after the establishment of the Tafelsig AEC. Anti-eviction groups have since been launched in areas like Khayelitsha, Blue Downs and Mandela Park. The AEC also acts as an umbrella for up to 20 residents' organisations. With no fixed membership, it operates only in the Western Cape, although it supports other anti-evictions organisations like the Anti-Privatisation Forum. Clashes with police in poverty-stricken areas across the Cape peninsula – most recently in Mandela Park – have led to a flurry of arrests and prosecutions on charges including trespass, intimidation and public violence. Last week AEC executive committee members Max Ntanyana and Fonkey Goboza were arrested.

The AEC's method is to move into an area to organise protests against pending evictions, stage sit-ins at homes whose owners are being evicted and, often, restore evicted owners to properties even if new occupants have moved in. 'The AEC has at times responded by making the contested property unliveable, saying if the people cannot have the land, then no one will,' says its website. Describing itself as 'a grassroots social movement' with no political affiliations, it is close to SAMWU and has established ties with left organisations abroad that took up the 'Free Max' campaign after the arrest of Khayelitsha AEC leader Max Ntanyana last year. The World Summit provided the opportunity to link up with other such groups under the Social Movements Indaba. Most AEC executive members are unemployed community members. Spokesman and executive member Ben van Heysteen is a former member of the International Socialists, a Trotskyist movement. This year the AEC also took up the issue of exclusion of school pupils who cannot afford fees. Next month it will launch its 'R10 Campaign', in terms of which township residents will gather at municipal offices to pay R10 for rates and water.

7.7.14 Palestine Solidarity Committee

The committee was formed in 1998 by former anti-apartheid community activists, Palestinian exiles, union members, youth activists and students, though many members had done solidarity work for years, even under apartheid. Aiming to educate South Africans about Palestine and to strengthen links between Palestinian and South African social movements, it is headed by Naeem Jeenah, a political science lecturer at Wits University, and Thembisa Fakude, a tour operator. It promotes the political, diplomatic, trade, academic and cultural isolation of Israel and campaigns 'against the torture of political prisoners in Israel and to counter the Zionist media spin that distorts the Palestinian struggle'. It also seeks the expulsion of the Israeli Labour Party from the Socialist International. The committee falls under the umbrella of the Social Movements Indaba. 'We don't limit our activities to support of the Palestinian struggle,' said Salim Vally, an executive member of the committee, 'There are struggles in South Africa against inequality and poverty.' The committee intends staging an international anti-Israel conference in Soweto this year. 'We decided to hold the conference in Soweto because of the parallels between the Soweto and Palestine uprising, and because of the symbolism Soweto has internationally,' he said. Vally said the ANC government should be 'in the forefront in supporting the Palestinian struggle' and more forceful in condemning US support for Israel. He accused it of 'hypocrisy' for supplying Israel with military equipment and maintaining trade links until 2000.

7.8 Example 8: Iran

From *Iran Bulletin and Middle East Forum* (summer 2003). Responding to the idea of a 'liberal democratic' solution imposed from the outside as thc alternative to the theocratic dictatorship in Iran, the editors write:

> The practical problems facing this analysis can be summarised thus:
>
> First: people may not be as amenable to the 'democratic revolution' as the White House wants. They may enter the arena independently and determined. They may reject privatisation and tax relief for multinationals, want socialisation of public resources and of mass consumption. Or even further, occupy factories, farms, pavements, take over empty property and land – as they did in the last revolution. Alliance with such people will be unacceptable to the White House. Will George Bush not do to them what he is doing to the people of Bolivia, Venezuelan poor, Colombian peasants, Argentinian unemployed? Or do they deserve any better than befalls Iraq and Afghanistan? Will George Bush not rather ally himself with the current rulers than these mutinous people?
>
> Second: People ignore the exhortations of Emperor Bush and his native mouthpieces and ignore the call to rise. The burden of the 'revolution' will then fall on ex-Savak agents, army officers, repentant ex-hezbollahis, and also the armed gangs of Rajavi and people of the same ilk – the scenario of the 1953 coup d'etat. What will such a 'revolution' bring other than another despotism of the Pahlavi or

Khomeini version?... In this world rights are being discussed at the grass roots level everywhere. Why impose a discourse on the Iranian people that is centuries behind what is taken as minimum rights and demands elsewhere? A break with the Islamic republic is genuine only when it can blossom into a break with the system of power hierarchy, and put an end to the concentration of power above and its rupture from the people. This means a power structure that is non-centralised, organised from below and based on the self-government and direct participation of all sections of society in running affairs to the extent that affects their lives. It is a system that in distributing natural and political resources dissolves all geographical, ethnic, religious and sexual inequities. Its institutional base is local and regional self-governing communities, equal in all aspects, and self-rule in production and consumption. It not only recognises political, social and cultural differences, but internalises their equality.

This shape of sovereignty is, however, not a vessel into which any policy can be poured, specifically not neo-liberal policies. Indeed this form of popular sovereignty and system of power finds its *raison d'etre* in a radical critique of the bourgeois state, and in particular its neo-liberal re-incarnation. Political and cultural freedoms (without restraints) are separated from economic processes and redefined as social rights. 'Human needs' replace the 'needs of the market'. Where a conflict arises between political intervention in things that affect their lives and their unequal access to the main resources of production and reproduction (that is, where private property becomes an obstacle) participatory democracy chooses the former against the latter. In this government no material resource, except the labour force (humans) has immunity against the need to be socialised.

Neo-liberal policies have brought to their knees most liberal democracies that implemented them. The 'vote' hardly seems to matter. Participatory democracy rejects neo-liberal policies, and especially by defying the capitalist globalisation on the one hand, and referring the power of decision-making to below on the other, slows down the direct access of the multinationals and impedes their indirect influence in the socio-political arena. In short, despite all the value parliamentarism, secularism and political and cultural pluralism have for societies such as Iran, without a restructuring of the power structure, and transforming the role of the state, they cannot protect the people from the brutal despotism of capital.

The other challenge that virtually all governments face is aggressive US imperialism. Here again 'people's representatives' in most countries have so often had to ignore the 'popular vote' as a price for supporting the Bush administration. The only realistic source of resistance to this bullying is the solidarity of people who stand on their own feet across our planet. The reality is that an imperial power with a military budget equal to that of ten big powers has been unleashed on the world, not by the back door but sitting on tanks, with a piece of paper justifying occupation in its pocket, and from the very first instant begins the 'privatisation' of all public wealth. In this new world order one either annuls oneself as a political unit or recreates political power in such a way as to be able to make a stand. This may take years, but in the political future facing our world it is difficult to find another way.

In Iran the only truly democratic alternative to the Islamic Republic is participatory democracy. This is no utopianism. There may be ideals involved but it is not fantasy. It is also not merely a theoretical expression of a necessity. In Iran today millions of nameless men and women try to reply to this necessity with their actions. Thousands of NGOs address such issues as poverty, addiction, prostitution, street children, runaway girls, homelessness, and ecology. Thousands of self-help groups provide interest-free loans and free services, distribute essential commodities, teach literacy, provide training and such like. The real content of workers' demands, mass popular action by the urban poor, the movement of the unemployed youth, teachers, women, nationalities, religious minorities, lawyers, journalists, artists, writers, intellectuals all speak volumes. They all seek their needs outside the market, side-stepping commodity relations, competition and profit.

They want to socialise consumption. They want to remove the sources and conditions of their reproduction from state control. They reflect a realisation that only through direct collective participation can they fill the gap between needs and what the system offers. These movements are nothing less than the existence of the embryonic infrastructures for a society based on self-government and a participatory democracy. Can people, and specifically those social forces whose demands are unanswered under capitalism and who cannot mediate to change their conditions within the existing political order, undertake this transition? The answer is a qualified one. Yes, if they can become organised as a wide-ranging movement against capitalism. No, if they remain fragmented or fall in behind one or other 'charismatic' leader. The key issue, therefore, is the organisation of such a movement....

Previous models cannot offer a solution. Success has been rare, and the majority of political movements of previous decades have either been suppressed, ultimately appeared as another authoritarian system, or been absorbed in the dominant power structures. Movements which were able to open up different vistas are rare and mainly confined to the 1990s. We need to start from somewhere else: a critique of the past with its elitist, leader-centred, paternalistic male-dominated traditions. Some of the main features of this movement can be summarised as follows:

First: power is conquered from below and reconstructed, moving upwards, on the foundation of self-government and self-management. This is a termite-like process that pulverises (i.e. eats away) political and economic authoritarianism from within. It spreads and expands the area of control, the 'liberated areas' of society, broadens direct participation, creates a new world in the depths. The empowerment of this movement is the other side of strengthening the mass of working people, the other side of their direct action.

Second: this movement is not merely a route but also the construction of the road; does not just train the player but sets the scenery too. It cannot ignore the political scene, which can speed up or impede, even block its movement. It therefore needs to intervene in creating the historic groupings that facilitate the goal. Its different views on power and its structure are no reason for it to stand aside from becoming active in the existing political scene. Like it or not, imperialism will be one of the major players in the Middle East and, of course, Iran for years to come, and the establishment of a government of participatory democracy in whatever form faces the twin obstacles of the religious despots and American imperialism. The movement for self-government cannot ignore these obstacles, nor the fact that other social groups and layers could be potential allies in this struggle. Others, with a different vision of democracy, including some liberal democrats, can unite with this movement under such a clear political framework as the slogan 'for secularism, pluralism, republicanism – against imperialism and neo-liberalism'. Such alliances can and must be sought by the movement for participatory democracy. A democratic forum can provide the appropriate space for different forces and tendencies to gather together.

Third: this movement is part of the global struggle against dictatorship and the domination of capital and for self-government. This movement will not breathe unless and until it ties in with the global anti-capitalist movement and with the global movement against the warmongering and domineering policies of US imperialism. Even more, it has a duty to be actively involved in the organisation of this movement.

Fourth: its organisation obeys a central rule: the source of solidarity is not uniformity but acknowledging differences. In its organisation social, cultural, ethnic, sexual differences are acknowledged and encouraged. Individual needs become collective needs and every part can see itself in the whole. Only then can all potentials be mobilised and the movement for self-government and participation be organised in the form of a movement of movements.

The structural equivalent is a voluntary network linking its different components, self-managed and horizontally organised. No social grouping, no specific movement, no particular institution, no person or personality can claim to be at the helm of this network, to represent it or give it identity. Leadership is not the expression of a centralised will, nor a hierarchy of leadership to be obeyed. Voting is not the fundamental mechanism for decision-making, which is mainly through a process of consensus.

The mechanism of choice is the social forum, that all-embracing umbrella that gathers under itself all the social movements, civil institutions, NGOs, trade unions, parties, the press, and political activists who believe in confronting capital and dictatorship, and have a share in the struggle for participatory government. This is the first and immediate step to plant the seed of that political presence that can take the role of architect for political transition towards the alternative order.

In Iran today, the only force capable of engineering this project is the left, a left that has said goodbye to its addiction to 'stages of revolution' and has abandoned puritanical isolationism, and is prepared to be involved in the day-to-day struggle to facilitate the road. The left, unless it can overcome its existing dispersion, cannot answer such a call. The project of Left Unity thus becomes doubly important. The radical socialist left is the only force that can see the dawn in the depth of darkness and turn it into an attainable reality. No time to lose.'

7.9 Example 9: The Zapatistas (Both parts of this section are taken from John Berger's book *The Shape of a Pocket*[2])

(a) From a letter of Subcomandante Insurgente Marcos to John Berger – Mexico, December 1995

Months later, the indigenous of south-eastern Mexico again reiterated their rebellion, their resistance to genocide, to death. The reason? The supreme government decided to carry out organised crime, the essence of neoliberalism, that money, the god of modernity, had planned. Dozens of thousands of soldiers, hundreds of tons of war materials, millions of lies. The objective? The destruction of libraries and hospitals, of homes and seeded fields of corn and beans, the annihilation of every sign of rebellion. The indigenous Zapatistas resisted, they retreated to the mountains and they began an exodus that today, even as I write these lines, has not ended. Neoliberalism disguises itself as the defence of a sovereignty which has been sold in dollars on the international market.

Neoliberalism, this doctrine that makes it possible for stupidity and cynicism to govern in diverse parts of the earth, does not allow for inclusion other than that of subjection to genocide. 'Die as a social group, as a culture, and above all as a resistance. Then you can be part of modernity,' say the capitalists, from the seats of government, to the indigenous *campesinos*. These indigenous people irritate the modernising logic of neomercantilism. Their rebellion, their defiance, their resistance, irritates them. The anachronism of their existence within a project of globalisation, an economic and political project that, soon, will decide that poor people, all the people in opposition, which is to say, the majority of the population, are obstacles. The armed character of 'We are here!' of the Zapatista indigenous people does not matter much to them nor does it keep them awake (a little fire and lead will be enough to end such 'imprudent' defiance). What matters to them, and bothers them, is that their very existence, in the moment that they (the indigenous Zapatistas) speak out and are heard, is converted into a reminder of an embarrassing omission of 'neoliberal modernity': 'These Indians should not exist today, we should have put an end to them BEFORE. Now annihilating them will be more difficult, which is to say, more expensive.' This is the burden that weighs upon neoliberalism made government in Mexico.

'Let's resolve the causes of the uprising,' say the negotiators of the government (leftists of yesterday, the shamed of today) as if they were saying: 'All of you should not exist, all this is an unfortunate error of modern history.' 'Let's resolve the causes' is the elegant synonym of 'We will eliminate them'. For this system which concentrates wealth and power and distributes death and poverty, the *campesinos*, the indigenous, do not fit in the plans and projects. They have to be got rid of, just like the herons ... and the eagles ... have to be got rid of.

(b) 'Against the Great Defeat of the World'. (John Berger here points to the anticipation of today's globalisation in Hieronymus Bosch's picture of hell in his Millennium Tryptich, painted at the beginning of the 16th century)

There is no horizon there. There is no continuity between actions, there are no pauses, no paths, no pattern, no past and no future. There is only the clamour of the disparate, fragmentary present. Everywhere there are surprises and sensations, yet nowhere is there any outcome. Nothing flows through: everything interrupts. There is a kind of spatial delirium. Compare this space to what one sees in the average publicity slot, or in a typical CNN news bulletin, or any mass media news commentary. There is a comparable incoherence, a comparable wilderness of separate excitements, a similar frenzy.

Bosch's prophecy was of the world-picture which is communicated to us today by the media under the impact of globalisation, with its delinquent need to sell incessantly. Both are like a puzzle whose wretched pieces do no fit together. And this was precisely the term that the Subcomandante Marcos used in a letter about the new world order last year.... He was writing from the Chiapas, south-east Mexico.[3] He sees the planet today as the battlefield of a Fourth World War. (The Third was the so-called Cold War.) The aim of the belligerents is the conquest of the entire world through the market. The arsenals are financial; there are nevertheless millions of people being maimed or killed every moment. The aim of those waging the war is to rule the world from new, abstract power centres – megapoles of the market, which will be subject to no control except that of the logic of investment. Meanwhile nine-tenths of the women and men living on the planet live with the jagged pieces that do not fit.

The jaggedness in Bosch's panel is so similar that I half expect to find the seven pieces that Marcos named. The first piece he named has a dollar sign on it and is green. The piece consists of the new concentration of global wealth in fewer and fewer hands and the unprecedented extension of hopeless poverties. The second piece is triangular and consists of a lie. The new order claims to rationalise and modernise production and human endeavour. In reality it is a return to the barbarism of the beginnings of the industrial revolution, with the important difference this time round that the barbarism is unchecked by any opposing ethical consideration or principle. The new order is fanatical and totalitarian. (Within its own system there are no appeals. Its totalitarianism does not concern politics – which, by its reckoning, have been superseded – but global monetary control.) Consider the children. One hundred million in the world live in the street. Two hundred million are engaged in the global labour force.

The third piece is round like a vicious circle. It consists of enforced emigration. The more enterprising of those who have nothing try to emigrate to survive. Yet the new order works night and day according to the principle that anybody who does not produce, who does not consume, and who has no money to put in a bank, is redundant. So the emigrants, the landless, the homeless are treated as the waste matter of the system, to be eliminated. The fourth piece is rectangular like a mirror. It consists of an ongoing exchange between the commercial banks and the world racketeers, for crime too has been globalised. The fifth piece is more or less a pentagon. It consists of physical repression. The Nation States under the new order have lost their economic independence, their political initiative and their sovereignty. (The new rhetoric of most politicians is an attempt to disguise their political, as distinct from civic or repressive, powerlessness.) The new task of the Nation States is to manage what is allotted to them, to protect the interests of the market's mega-enterprises and, above all, to control and police the redundant.

The sixth piece is the shape of a scribble and consists of breakages. On one hand, the new order does away with frontiers and distances by the instant communication of exchanges and deals, by obligatory free trade zones (NAFTA), and by the imposition everywhere of the single unquestionable law of the market; and on the other hand, it provokes fragmentation and the *proliferation* of frontiers by its undermining of the Nation State – for example, the former Soviet Union, Yugoslavia, etc. 'A world of broken mirrors,' wrote Marcos, 'reflecting the useless unity of the neoliberal puzzle.' The seventh piece of the puzzle has the shape of a pocket, and consists of all the various pockets of resistance against the new order which are developing across the globe. The Zapatistas in south-east Mexico are one such pocket. Others, in different circumstances, have not necessarily chosen armed resistance. The many pockets do not have a common political programme as such. How could they, existing as they do in the broken puzzle? Yet their heterogeneity may be a promise. What they have in common is their defence of the redundant, the next-to-be-eliminated, and their belief that the Fourth World War is a crime against humanity.

The seven pieces will never fit together to make any sense. This lack of sense, this absurdity is endemic to the new order. As Bosch foresaw in his vision of hell, there is no horizon. The world is burning. Every figure is trying to survive by concentrating on his own immediate need and survival. Claustrophobia, at its most extreme, is not caused by overcrowding, but by lack of any continuity existing between one action and the next that is close enough to be touching it. It is this that is hell. The culture in which we live is perhaps the most claustrophobic that has ever existed; in the culture of globalisation, as in Bosch's hell, there is no glimpse of an *elsewhere* or an *otherwise*. The given is a prison. And faced with such reductionism, human intelligence is reduced to greed. Marcos ended his letter by saying: 'It is necessary to build a new world, a world capable of containing many worlds, capable of containing all worlds.'

What the painting by Bosch does is to remind us – if prophecies can be called reminders – that the first step towards building an alternative world has to be a refusal of the world-picture implanted in our minds and all the false promises used everywhere to justify and idealise the delinquent and insatiable need to sell. Another space is vitally necessary. First an horizon has to be discovered. And for this we have to refind hope – against all the odds of what the new order pretends and perpetrates. Hope, however, is an act of faith and has to be sustained by other concrete actions. For example, the action of *approach*, of measuring distances and *walking towards*. This will lead to collaborations which deny discontinuity. The act of resistance means not only refusing to accept the absurdity of the world-picture offered us, but denouncing it. And when hell is denounced from within, it ceases to be hell. In pockets of resistance as they exist today, the other two panels of Bosch's tryptich, showing Adam and Eve and the Garden of Earthly Delights, can be studied by torchlight in the dark ... we need them.

7.10 In lieu of a conclusion

In lieu of a conclusion to these notes, I add here a section which is largely extracts, slightly modified, from a discussion article I contributed to the January 1998 edition of the London-based journal, *International Socialist Forum*. This is intended to underline my view of the important changes in outlook which have become necessary for Marxists who, through much of their political lives, had tried to work in the tradition of Lenin and Trotsky. What follows may benefit from being read in the context of my 'hypothesis' in Chapter 8.

There is of course no doubt that the power and pressure of the Stalinist bureaucracy, physical and ideological, on the working class and particularly on the Trotskyists, imposed grave and often impossible difficulties for the building of revolutionary parties. Today the physical pressure is no more and the ideological pressure residual. We are obliged not only to expose the manifest bankruptcy of Stalinism and social democracy as manifestations of capital's structural crisis, nor only to review the way in which these objective changes open up class struggle in new ways, but to review also our conceptions and methods of 'party-building', the 'subjective' side of things, as it were. Central to the thinking of all who have tried to continue the fight of Trotsky and the International Left Opposition has been the opening section of Trotsky's 1938 Transitional Programme: 'The world political situation as a whole is chiefly characterised by a historical crisis of the leadership of the proletariat'; and again, 'the historical crisis of mankind is reduced to the crisis of the revolutionary leadership.'

The 'crisis of revolutionary leadership' was understood in a dangerously wrong and narrow way. There was a tendency in our movement to assume that the crisis of leadership would be resolved by replacing one leadership by another (and that other was us). This took the most extreme forms in the proclamations by more than one group that they were indeed 'the (reconstructed) Fourth International'. Since the Fourth International was the name for a 'world party of social revolution', their claims were and are patently absurd. Much of what went under the name of 'party-building' was done with this conception that what was needed was to build an apparatus and train 'cadres' to replace the apparatuses of the existing parties. All those who have been working in the Trotskyist movement will recognise the outcome of this conception in the grotesque regimes which developed under the leadership of Healy in Britain and Lambert in France and no doubt in other countries.

History has shown that the results of the betrayals of social democracy and Stalinism, and their control over the working-class movement, involved not only the considerable fragmentation of the organisation and consciousness of the working class. It also helped give the space and time to capital for displacing its contradictions and achieving renewed expansion after the second world war, and prolonging its life. All this posed tasks which went far beyond merely replacing one leadership by another. Only in and through a wholesale, necessary reconstruction and regeneration of the class movement of the working class, achieved in the course of the growth of a mass socialist movement, could a new revolutionary leadership be forged in the vanguard of the class. I suggest that, particularly after 1945, there was another underlying and insufficiently questioned assumption. This was that, since the first act in the world socialist revolution (October 1917) the working class, except for short periods following defeats, was more or less in a state of latent readiness for revolution. It was implied that it required only our correct 'intervention' in the struggles inevitably forced upon it by capitalism in its 'last stage' – imperialism. Thus the working class, at boiling point as it were, because of 'the nature of the epoch' since 1917, needed only to be 'supplied' with a new party.

We must begin to learn how to develop the insight of István Mészáros in the closing chapters of his *Beyond Capital*, that the future mass socialist movement will be 'inherently pluralist', with its component parts developing through their growing and necessary ability to combine and coordinate their efforts (and thus to achieve class-consciousness), not to accept 'control' (and a supposed 'revolutionary consciousness' already formed by professed Marxists from above). Thus the revolutionary party which is necessary will play its part of striving to learn from and give direction to the mass movements of the working class through this self-combining and self-coordinating, from within the workers' movement and not from outside or above it, thinking to control it. This critique of the old 'party building' and of the errors deriving from the mechanical understanding of 'crisis of leadership' can have positive results if the following summary conclusions on strategy and on method are grasped: We actually had no real *perspective* for the revolution. Instead, we substituted for it the idea and practice of so-called party building, on the grounds that we were in the epoch of wars and revolutions, last stage of capitalism, etc. Lenin and Trotsky had their (at first different, then, in 1917, the same) perspectives for the Russian revolution, and even Mao had his for China. In Europe and America the Trotskyists had none. (I owe to Mike Banda the clear statement of this.) A perspective must after all be based on 'the concrete analysis of concrete conditions'. Instead, we persisted in the abstractions 'crisis of leadership', 'nature of the epoch' and so on. These abstractions lay behind our 'correct' denunciations of Stalinist betrayals, but we did nothing to analyse and understand the actual developments of capitalism resulting directly and indirectly from these betrayals, nor the specific consequences for the class struggle and revolution in each country.

That is why we now must face up to the fact that in the most important sense we were drifting without a compass. Opposition in the working-class movement to Stalinism and its 'socialism in one country' was essential, but the internationalism of the Fourth Internationalists remained an abstract internationalism. As István Mészáros so succinctly put it: 'One cannot grasp the "specific" ' (e.g. a concrete perspective for a given country or region – CS) without identifying its manifold interconnections with a given system of complex mediations.' We made no analysis of the 'given system of complex mediations' (i.e. the changing system of global capital, its 'economics' and politics) nor the 'manifold interconnections' of the class struggle in each particular country with that world system.

This critique of our past needs to be put in the context discussed briefly above (Chapter 4). The history and evolution of the capital system in the last century was dependent politically on the role of the Stalinist bureaucracy (and to a lesser but very important extent, social-democracy) in disarming and betraying the international working class as a revolutionary force. Mistakes and misconceptions are one thing, but the Trotskyists have the unique honour of having been alone in consistently exposing and combating Stalinism and its crimes and betrayals from the standpoint of the fight for a communist future. Far from putting that history aside in the new situation, we uphold that fight, in the tradition of the Communist Manifesto, against the ideological barrage of 'the end of communism'.

---

[1] Naomi Klein explained the meaning of *argentinazo* in the *Guardian,* January 25, 2003: '..."Argentinazo" [is] a word that is completely untranslatable into English or, for that matter, Spanish. The Argentinazo was not a riot exactly, although it sure looked like one on the television, with looters ransacking supermarkets and mounted police charging into crowds; 33 people were killed across the country. It wasn't an ordinary revolution, either, although it sort of looked like one on the face of it, with angry crowds storming the seat of government and forcing the president to resign in disgrace.

'But, unlike a classic revolution, the Argentinazo was not organised by an alternate political force that wanted to take power for itself. And, unlike a riot, it pulsed with a unified and unequivocal demand: the immediate removal of all the corrupt politicians who had grown rich while Argentina, once the envy of the developing world, spiralled into poverty.

'In reality, the Argentinazo was just what the word itself sounds like: a chaotic explosion of Argentinian-ness, during which hundreds of thousands of people suddenly and spontaneously left their homes, poured on to the streets of the capital, banged pots and pans, yelled at banks, fought police, revved motorcycles, sang football anthems and managed to send the president fleeing his palace in a helicopter.'

[2] Bloomsbury, London 2001; and Pantheon/Vintage International, New York 2002

[3] This letter was published in August 1997 throughout the world press, and notably in *Le Monde Diplomatique*, Paris.

8

THE TWENTIETH CENTURY: A HYPOTHESIS

Not Without a Storm has done no more than attempt to establish – on the basis of work that first became possible in the late twentieth century – the context within which working-class, socialist internationalism has to be developed, and urgently developed, in the 21st. Only now – as Mészáros above all has established – have we entered the period in which capitalism encounters its structural, its historical, crisis. Only now have the preconditions for socialist revolution, for socialism, matured. In these circumstances those of us, who once existed politically on the basis of exposing (and often correctly and importantly exposing) 'revisionism', must now recognise – as I noted in the Introduction – that we have to revise the things that *do* need to be revised. How do the ideas of those of us who have, over the last 50 years or so, been involved in the communist movement measure up to new realities?

We started from our conviction that Marx had demonstrated the necessity of socialist revolution. The October 1917 Russian revolution, and the ideas of the communists who led it, formed the basis of our view of the class struggle in the twentieth century. Those ideas can be summarised as follows. The question in early twentieth-century Russia concerned how it was possible to work as communists in a major, but backward, country. Trotsky wrote that the coming revolution would undoubtedly be *bourgeois* in character. But he went on to question which classes would solve the tasks of the democratic revolution and how those classes would relate to each other. He interrogated Lenin's formulation, the 'revolutionary-democratic dictatorship of the proletariat and the peasantry'. What, he asked, about the relationships between the proletariat and the peasantry? Which would be the *leading* class? The answer: only the proletariat was capable of such a leading role. The 'dictatorship of the proletariat and the peasantry' would

> have to carry through to the end the agrarian revolution and democratic reconstruction of the State. In other words the dictatorship of the proletariat and the peasantry would become the instrument for solving the tasks of the historically-belated bourgeois revolution. But having reached power the proletariat would be compelled to encroach even more deeply upon the relationships of private property in general, that is to take the road of socialist measures.[1]

Whether this would lead to socialism or not was dependent on 'the fate of European and world capitalism'. So far so good! Note well, however, that Trotsky assumes that the 'world economy as a whole, and European economy in the first place, is fully ripe for the socialist revolution.' With this perspective, Trotsky and Lenin (in his 'Testament') were able, quite correctly, to take a stand against Stalin's 'socialism in a single country'. But there is now more to be considered.

Trotsky and Lenin were right to see that the bourgeoisie could not carry through the bourgeois-democratic revolution. But for us there are new problems to take into account. Have there been *any* twentieth-century 'bourgeois-democratic revolutions'? In the main countries in which such 'bourgeois revolutions' were still to happen, they have been carried out by workers and peasants led by Communist (Stalinist) parties, or parties closely linked to the Stalinist international network. This is certainly true in the most important cases – in China; in south-east Asia; and, via the ANC and SWAPO route, in southern Africa. In these countries, and in all ex-colonial countries, there has been no 'solution of democratic tasks', that is to say, there has been no 'democratic revolution'. And this raises the big question: was Trotsky right when he wrote of the conditions being 'fully ripe for the socialist revolution'? Now that we know the fate of the Russian revolution and can make a confident prognosis concerning the likelihood of any genuine democracy in China, I think we must conclude that he was not. For Trotsky, 'the road to democracy [in backward countries was] through the dictatorship of the proletariat'. If he had simply said that it could not pass through the dictatorship of the bourgeoisie, he would have been right. But this 'dictatorship of the proletariat' – it very soon took the form of what he (and we) called 'degenerated and deformed workers' states' – was not at all a 'road to democracy'. It was a road to a capitalism that has proved itself, to put it mildly, far from democratic.

In summary, I would say this. We came to understand the last century as the era of working-class socialist revolution, opened up, in 1917, by the Russian October. We learned to understand its failure to spread and its degeneration in Russia as the result of betrayals of leadership, consequent on the utopian doctrine of 'socialism in a single country', and the bureaucratisation of the Bolshevik Party and the Soviet state apparatus. We saw the collapse of the Soviet Union and Stalinism in 1989-91 as confirmation of Trotsky's prognosis: without a political revolution to remove the Stalinist bureaucracy, the Soviet Union would see a restoration of capitalism. We either persisted in the notion that 'resolving the crisis of working-class revolutionary leadership' was the essential problem, the objective conditions for socialist revolution having matured; or at best, if we now expressed doubts about that theory, we failed to replace it with any explicit alternative.

I have criticised these notions of crisis of leadership and the associated ideas of 'party-building', 'intervention' in the class struggle, and so on, elsewhere, notably in my *A New Party for Socialism?*[2] in the mid-1990s. This acknowledged the collapse of Stalinism as essentially positive, opening up opportunities for building the 'alternative leadership'. At the same time, I, and those I was working with most closely, began to understand that all ideas of 'imminent revolution', of a working class somehow needing only new leadership before assuming its true, revolutionary role, were misplaced. We saw – very late – that the period following the October revolution, with a series of revolutionary situations (Germany, China, Spain) was over, and that the new period needed new thinking, new practices. Mészáros's work laid the basis for such thought and action, showing as it did that only now does the capital system enter its structural crisis (that is, its crisis *as a system*, its *historical* crisis), as against its cyclical, boom-slump crises of the past. At the same time, this maturing of the conditions for socialist revolution – structural crisis, 'globalisation', the end of the possibility of spatially displacing contradictions, 'universal intercourse' and advanced productive forces – is fatally infected with the fact that the self-reproduction of capital is now predominantly *destructive.* It cannot be viewed just as 'preparation of the objective conditions for a socialist order'. This surely must change our ideas of how the workers' movement orientates itself, its strategy, and tactics, its alliances.

But there is more to be said. *Was the twentieth century, as we believed and as we took as the basis of our work and lives, 'the century of working-class socialist revolution'?* There was no such revolution in a major, developed capitalist country except the failed one in Germany – though of course there were many struggles of a revolutionary nature. The Russian October took place in a country where capitalism had only recently begun to develop – and had begun to develop under conditions where capitalism had already become 'imperialism'. Tsarist autocracy stood in the way of Russia's development. Trotsky tried to comprehend this 'uneven and combined development' in countries like Russia with his theory of permanent revolution. In October he came to agreement with Lenin to the – to be sure, very important – extent that they saw the proletariat as the only class able to make the 'democratic' revolution, leading to a workers' state that would then be joined by the proletarian revolution in the advanced countries.

Looking back over the twentieth century, however, we have to acknowledge that there has been no 'bourgeois-democratic' revolution. This suggests that a democratic regime for transition of late-developing nations to capitalism is, in the conditions of the twentieth and 21st centuries, impossible. In all ex-colonial countries, the emerging regimes, taking their place (such as it is) in globalised capitalism, have not been in any sense 'democratic'. They have not successfully tackled the 'democratic tasks' of establishing a democratic state, solving the agrarian problem, and so on. They have resulted in bourgeois, non-democratic dictatorships. Where revolutions have overthrown the old regimes – as in China, Russia, south-east Asia – led by Communist (Stalinist) parties, with the workers and peasants as the revolutionary force, the resultant regimes have after some decades become capitalist. And the form of capitalism adopted has, inevitably, corresponded to the requirements of the stage that *now* exists in the 'globalised', world arena.

Recognising this, is it too sweeping to say something like the following? It was correct, with Lenin and Trotsky, to see that it would need the proletariat to take the leading role in overthrowing feudalism, serfdom, or whatever *ancien regime* existed. But we have now to go further in analysing the history of the period since Lenin's and even Trotsky's death. It was *only* via this path – and not via the bourgeoisie – that national capitalist states could be achieved; and *that is the historical role* the various Stalinist regimes, 'workers' states' played. They prepared, and effected, the transition of the nation to capitalism. They did it in an unprecedented way, but that is what they did. Not only did they build up the economic infrastructure at least to the point where the new national bourgeoisie could exist and compete in the globalised capital system. They also created a larger and *disciplined* working class – and surely the creation of such a dispossessed working class is the main condition necessary for capitalism to begin – with a massive movement from country to town adequate to the next step of the transition. That stage began with the collapse of Stalinism in 1989-91. As this chapter was being written – in July 2005 – large-scale pitched battles were being waged in villages in many parts of China as peasants resisted the seizure of their land for capital investment by members and friends of the 'Communist' state bureaucracy. These people have become the modern perpetrators of the expropriation that took place centuries ago in the land enclosures in England and lowland Scotland, and in the Highland Clearances, and which destroyed the peasantry and created the proletariat necessary for Britain's own transition to capitalism.

Furthermore, the proletariat prepared and disciplined by the Stalinist regimes is employed to produce for the 'globalised' market at rates of pay and under conditions which were long ago left behind by the workers of the advanced capitalist countries, giving China, Russian and other ex-Stalinist countries an enormous competitive advantage, a new edition of the 'privilege of backwardness', and with immeasurable consequences for every aspect of the global economy.

Contrary to what we believed and based our political lives on, then, *the twentieth century was not the 'epoch of working-class socialist revolution'*. Rather, it was *the epoch of the maturing of the conditions for socialist revolution*, by way of great increases in the productivity of labour and 'globalisation', bringing the capital system to the onset of its structural crisis; and within this process, *the transition of historically backward countries to capitalism.* In those backward countries, beginning with the October revolution in Russia, the attempt was made to institute planned economies regulated by a centralised state, in conditions where capitalist market relations were only partly, even hardly at all developed. In the light of what happened, Marx's words in his *Grundrisse* now seem highly prophetic: in capitalism, 'Each individual possesses social power in the form of a thing (money). Rob the thing of this social power and you must give it to persons to exercise over persons.'![3]

The capitalist classes now in power in these countries are of course not (as in the familiar 'classical' transition from feudalism to capitalism) a bourgeoisie that has built up its economy and social relations within a feudal society and then been strong enough to effect a bourgeois revolution. On the contrary, they are capitalist classes formed by Stalinism and the system of state-bureaucratic – 'extra-economic' – extraction of surplus product. They consist of ex-members of the state bureaucracy and of new 'entrepreneurs' promoted by them. These origins of the new capitalists and their connections with, and their insertion into, the system of globalised capital give us a class very different from the bourgeoisies that emerged from the old bourgeois revolutions in Europe and – with its own particular characteristics – in America. The only alternative to this mode of transition, it should be said in parenthesis, was in

Japan. There an autocratic regime could in the late nineteenth and early twentieth century 'incorporate' the development of capitalism and transform itself into a capitalist state, retaining the traditional ideological controls and the existent repressive state apparatus. This, it would seem, was the only other way to discipline a working class for the 'modern' transition to capitalism. And even this 'other' way had striking similarities to the first. It is surely not surprising that it was soon necessary to turn to a form of fascist dictatorship in Japan to continue preparation of the essential prerequisite of 'modern' capitalism, a *disciplined* proletariat.

This book has been a report on 'work in progress'. It is work that must continue and be carried forward in a collective way. Its precise direction cannot be laid out in advance. It is not for those who cling to old shibboleths, who will not abandon the hope that the real world will eventually correspond to their long-held certainties. But the new thinking needed cannot productively be an unguided adventure either. It must be rooted in an ever more critical analysis of how we have arrived at where we are now. This is the spirit in which *Not Without a Storm* has been written. And the very preliminary thoughts in this brief final chapter are no more than a hypothesis for discussion, as part of the necessary re-evaluations for which I have been arguing. They are by no means intended as a complete re-evaluation of the twentieth century. But I think they may point the way to an understanding of one important aspect of something that needs to be understood. In the twentieth century the objective conditions for the social revolution had in fact *not* matured; and this is contrary to what many of us – not without cause – believed. They were coming to maturity only over (say) the last quarter of the century – in today's conditions of the onset of capitalism's structural crisis and globalisation.

For many of us, and for many of those I have had in mind in writing this book, developing these ideas can, I believe, assist in necessary new thinking, new practices, new ways of engaging with the unfamiliar forms that anti-capitalist protest has taken in the last decade. The refoundation of working-class, socialist internationalism – without which there can be no socialism, no human future – will not come from continuing with business as usual. The world of business (the world of capital) has changed, and the business of changing the world has to be re-evaluated. Marx and Engels' *The Communist Manifesto* of 1848 established the basis for understanding the modern world and the necessary forces of progressive change. But it has never been more true that a new communist manifesto is needed, and that it must come from the collective of socialists grappling with the new age of globalisation.

The chains from which the world's workers must free themselves are not only material. They are intellectual too. There is a – very dangerous – world to win.

---

[1] All quotations are from Trotsky's *Permanent Revolution*, published in many editions.

[2] Cliff Slaughter, *A New Party for Socialism?: what? when? by whom?* (London, 1996).

[3] Marx, *Grundrisse*, pp. 157-8

AFTERWORD

A last word … from Walt Whitman, first published in 1860.

I hear it was charged against me that I sought to destroy institutions,
But really I am neither for nor against institutions,
(What indeed do I have in common with them? Or what with the destruction of them?)
Only I will establish in the Mannahatta and in every city of these States inland and seaboard,
And in the fields and woods, and above every keel little or large that dents the water,
Without edifices or rules or trustees or any argument,
The institution of the dear love of comrades.

APPENDICES

Discussing Marxism at the Millennium

by Terry Brotherstone

Appendix I: Marxism, history and the future

This appendix is an abridged version of 'Thinking about the Future of Marxism', the report of a discussion in July 1999, first published in *Work in Progress,* no. 1 (1999). István Mészáros (IM) and the American historian, Theodore Koditschek (TK), were in conversation with Terry Brotherstone (TB) and Cliff Slaughter (CS). The discussion began from the volume, *History, Economic History and the Future of Marxism: essays in memory of Tom Kemp*, edited by Terry Brotherstone and Geoff Pilling, published three years previously – to which Brotherstone, Koditschek and Mészáros had all contributed substantial essays.

TB: ... [O]ne of the key things about *History, Economic History and the Future of Marxism* was the juxtaposition within the same covers of Ted [Koditschek]'s essay [on Marxism and British social historiography] and István [Mészáros]'s [on historical temporality] ... [But the book has not been widely reviewed.]

TK: A number of articles in it are dealing with really important questions in a substantial way.

IM: It is a shame that historical scholarship can get away with ignoring these questions.

TK: Tom [Kemp] knew so many kinds of people, [making it possible to] put together a book ... that does not have a central theme, but in which there is a consistency in the pieces ... [It] centres on some kind of engagement with a Marxist agenda, and on aspects of the historical and philosophical questions which arise in actually existing capitalist society. There are not too many books coming out today which do that.

TB: [One important] point that ... concern[ed] me [as co-editor was] to understand better why it is that Marxism is pre-eminently an historical theory, and yet the Marxist history that has dominated over the past generation or two [was] successful without really engaging with Marxist philosophy.

TK: There has been a really dramatic delegitimation of Marxist historical analysis within the historical profession. It has been very rapid and astonishingly complete. There were, and remain, some big names ... who had ... [an] impact [in the 1960s and 1970s]. But they didn't create an ongoing presence, which could resist the revival of conservative history. Much of what is published now as history is narrowly political, rooted in the contingent. The impact of postmodernism and of poststructuralism has resulted in a very fierce assault. It is very hard to be practising in the historical profession with anything like the Marxist paradigm.

IM: I find the same thing in philosophy and social theory. I remember I participated in 1981 or 1982 in a journal called *Problemi de Sozialismo*, a really left-wing journal in Italy, which initiated a discussion with a theme something like 'The Crisis and Future of Marxism'. At the beginning of the 1980s it was still quite alive. But since then the political parties, which considered themselves Marxist have simply disintegrated. In Italy not only the CP but also the Nenni Socialist Party.... When you think of the political contrast between Nenni and Craxi it sums up the situation that created such a devastation.... [Intellectuals too] have turned away from [Marxism], or even against it. This is all to do with what [Ted is] talking about. But it is also to do with how the parties themselves have abandoned transforming society. Look at what a disaster the former CP has become. When you think about Jean-Paul Sartre and his role in the CPs and the left parties – from a very critical position. That has evaporated. Sartre would now also be ridiculed. It is a colossal transformation in attitude....

But my own attitude to the so-called crisis of Marxism is that Marxism is not a disembodied set of ideas. If you want to talk about a crisis of Marxism you have to relate it to some material and organisational structural crisis which then can appear as though it is a crisis of ideas. Some of the mainstream of the left considered itself to be openly Marxist or at least Marxist-oriented. When they started unravelling then of course they talk about the crisis of Marxism. But it is not the ideas themselves but rather the ideas as they relate to actual historical events and to social bodies. And after the mid-1980s, let's say, this change took place in a big way. After that only very small groups, really tiny, tiny groups retained some allegiance to Marxism as political movements; and it has been so ever since. We are still in that predicament. Those who consider themselves Marxist, who remain Marxist, are rather isolated.

TK: That's the critical thing, the isolation. Not to be part of anything that is any kind of a collective movement. It's difficult both for emotional reasons and as a political activity.

IM: Yes, and when you think even of people like Eric Hobsbawm who was both considered, and considered himself, a Marxist ... if you look at the last five or six years of his activity, it is standing on his head. It has turned, in so many ways, quite reactionary. I remember that on his 80th birthday, ... [he was asked] how it was possible that Hitler, with his authoritarian system, didn't have to have labour camps, while they did have labour camps in Russia. The response of our great historian and theoretician was [that] Hitler had charisma, Stalin had none. That ... as an historical explanation! That in a way sums up how puzzling and sad these events are. Also, in relation to his own past....

TK: That's what really strikes me. These people are going back on their entire history.

IM: Yes. How is that possible?... [S]o much has to be repudiated....

TB: [When] Hobsbawm [spoke on] *The Communist Manifesto* ... [in 1998, he argued that, because] 1989-91 had not proved to open up Utopia for capitalism, 'this guy Marx' ... could be seen to be relevant again. But he said that Marx made one really big mistake. You can see how relevant the *Manifesto* is only if you get this big mistake out of the way – and the mistake was about the working class. That's Marx's mistake! ...

CS: ... I was struck reading Will Hutton's book, *The State We Are In*.... It is a very interesting book because he is a liberal Keynesian who thinks that all that can be revived. But the theoretical position, if there is one, is the same as Hobsbawm's. Namely that the problem with capitalism today is that it has lost touch with the institutional bits and pieces it inherited from previous societies. It is too economic, too 'rationalised'. And Hobsbawm says the same thing. There's no Marxism in it whatsoever. [He comes] to the same conclusion as Will Hutton....

IM: Also in the introduction to the edition of *The Communist Manifesto* Terry referred to, there are two points at which he brings theory into the picture. At the first hand he relies on Lichtheim – a writer with a fairly right-wing position – and at the other on Leszlek Kolakowski, with an equally or more right-wing position. He totally subscribes to this. It is all a jumble of... not even ideas really. It is all thrown together and shaken in a hat.

CS: And he says that nothing should be done about Pinochet or it will disturb democracy in Chile....

TK: Exactly what the US State Department has been saying....

IM: I remember also the time when David Owen was still a figure in British politics [in the 1980s]. It was before an election. Hobsbawm gave a press conference saying to vote for David Owen. From the left of Robert Owen to the right of David Owen: quite a trajectory! ...

TB: The one consistency in Hobsbawm's political life has been his genuine support for the Popular Front. And this is where he's ended up. Is what he is saying now therefore so surprising? Right from the 1930s, he's had the position that the only thing the working class can do is to prevent fascism – the Popular Front is therefore alive and well. And, secondly, the whole education in the British Stalinist party was (wasn't it?) to secure the high ground in the profession you were in – and, in that sense, you can say that Hobsbawm has been marvellously successful. His ideas do inform a new generation. But he doesn't ask what sort of ideas he is informing a new generation with. In this sense his CH (Companion of Honour) was [perhaps] ... the apotheosis of the Popular Front – a Popular Front with the Queen.

TK: But he did make many people think. He certainly helped create my vision of Marxist history. For all his problems – and Terry is right that they go way back and that there's maybe more consistency if you look below the surface – [but] for all that Hobsbawm made some effort to fuse theory with history, however ultimately unsuccessful.... In that respect he is a contrast to someone like Thompson, who was probably more influential.

IM: And remains so.

TK: Yes, remains so. And yet Thompson's relationship to Marxism is extremely problematic. The relationship between the kind of history that the *Making of the English Working Class* – far less *Customs in Common* – represent ... in what way is it Marxist? His efforts to deal with that problem in *Poverty of Theory* only compound the problem, it seems to me. For me anyway, I was very influenced as a historian by Thompson, but I very much felt the need to engage with theory at a different level because it just wasn't there in Thompson. For me Hobsbawm was more ... there was at least a sense that he was operating from a theoretical basis in writing his history ...

IM: Undoubtedly he had merits in the past. That's why his past five or six years of development – no, it's more than that: it started when [Neil] Kinnock became Labour leader [in 1983].

TB: Or in 1978 with *The Forward March of Labour Halted.*

IM: Kinnock called him a great inspiration. You jettison more and more until the working class – as Terry mentioned with regard to the edition of *The Communist Manifesto* – is jettisoned altogether. What remains? A kind of wishy-washy talk of progress-ism. But a progress-ism which cannot refer to any agency. What is the meaning of progress if there are no historical agencies in sight. A historical transformation without a tangible human agency makes one laugh ... or cry. That is unfortunately what has happened. And I can't see much prospect for improvement as far as the historical profession is concerned. The historians are part of an intellectual landscape I characterise as full of tumbleweed. Without any obvious basis for their ideas in the social reality of the world they are blown to and fro in the changing winds. And I fear that, unless there is some improvement in the social base ...

TK: I teach] undergraduates in the middle of Missouri, where it is very conservative. They read *The Communist Manifesto* and it seems relevant to them. Their attitude is like Hobsbawm's. They are interested in the critique of capitalism but the working class doesn't resonate for them. But they read it with great interest, much more so than the professional historians. I wish there could be a way to channel that ... [This] question of agency ... is central. ... What is the agency that we can attach to progressive causes today – and what is its relationship to the working class? And how is its relationship to the working class going necessarily to be different than the working class that existed (say) from the late nineteenth century to the mid-twentieth century? This is really what is being wrestled with in the US, including by many people whose relationship to Marx is quite tangential – I think in part at least because they don't see, within Marxism, any resolution to this issue. They see that what you might call the classical working class doesn't exist any more, and it is not clear what kind of working class is emerging and how it can mobilise politically ...

IM: [A piece of mine, in interview form, in] *Science & Society* deals with this kind of issue.... One of the questions I was asked was on the working class, the role of labour and the proletariat. One of the things I was saying is that Marx never considered simply the manual working class when he talked about social transformation. He was talking about the *process of proletarianisation* which is something qualitatively different as a concept. Proletarianisation as a process applies to most categories today. To manual, blue-collar, etc.; increasingly to office labour.... When you think of how office labour is absolutely decimated, including in the most advanced capitalist countries where hundreds of thousands of people are simply rejected. Where can they go? They can't become chef's assistants in the Ritz Hotel. They have to manage somehow. That is the crucial question.... But for me the really central question is the onset of the structural crisis of the capital system as a whole. Roughly from the early 1970s – that's where we can locate the structural crisis, which includes the end of Keynesianism, of left Social Democracy and of the Communist parties. If you look at the mass CPs, in France and Italy primarily, their disintegration started in that period. There was the notion of a new Popular Front – the so-called 'historic compromise' which the Italians very much propagandised. All they managed to get out of that was that they totally compromised themselves. There were no other parties to the compromise. That had to be explained in terms of the structural crisis itself. Then they started to write about the long cycle. The little cycles didn't explain anything, so you had the theory of the long cycle appearing every 25 years. But now we've passed the 25 years and there is absolutely no perspective of the capital system getting out of this crisis. This has to be related to the question of agency.

Another equally important concept ... what I call the downward equalisation of the differential rate of exploitation. The differential rate concerns how the working classes in the capitalistically advanced countries have much better conditions and benefits – a much lower differential rate of exploitation than others.... The first time I wrote about this was in my Isaac Deutscher Memorial Lecture, written in 1970 and delivered at the London School of Economics in January 1971. If you think of the 30 years that have passed, it is absolutely pronounced how the equalisation of the conditions of the working class have deteriorated and continue to deteriorate. This idea has either to be refuted – and I would like to see a convincing refutation – or taken on board. To assume that all these things will make no difference is very rash.

From the point of view of intellectuals, the question often is not about how they relate themselves to the working class.... Most of them don't directly. Some individuals, as a result of the circumstances of their own life, their own personal history, might have some direct relationship. But, as a rule, it is through some organisation – a party, a trade union perhaps. And that is what has badly deteriorated through this same period of time. The structural crisis and its deterioration mean that the mass organisations of the working class tend to follow the line of least resistance. Instead of embarking on a different and more radical strategy they follow on whatever seem to be the dominant trends – the social-democratisation of the Communist parties, the liberal-bourgeoisification of the social-democratic parties. It all plays into the hands of established power relations. It is crucial to grasp this. But it must reach a point at which this will change. I am convinced that we must see a revival of labour activity ... not in this category or that category, but in the labour movement as a whole. I think this is the answer to the question of agency. It is the only agency that I can see. Of course this doesn't mean that women, and other movements, cannot be part of it. Indeed they *must* be part of it. That is vitally important. But such movements on their own have no totalising strategy. It is labour *as such* – as the structural antagonist of capital – which has this, or rather it *potentially* has it. It has such a strategy *given favourable historical circumstances*. And I am convinced that the circumstances must develop in the direction of providing them, that we are heading toward an ever-deepening crisis with some quite horrendous developments on the horizon, the revival of imperialism in its most aggressive form. And what can then oppose that? Certainly not some marginal force. It has to be the system's most elementary antagonist ... elementary in the sense that it can have an alternative mode of social-metabolic reproduction to capital. The alternative to capital has to be *at the level of control* – the overall control of society.

CS: Going back to the *Science & Society* interview where István talks about proletarianisation ... I was struck by what might appear a very simple point, but which I think is the basis for our discussion about agency. We've said some of this already. The proletariat doesn't simply coincide with what we have been used to thinking of as the working class. The essential question in a discussion of proletarianisation is that we're talking about all those millions of people who are subject to the control of capital. They have to work – or can't get work – in all kinds of impossible conditions. This widens the concept of what proletarianisation is; and what kind of movements will feed into it politically. This is a very important point.

IM: Also, when you think of the different categories of working people in whatever walk of life. In the past some of them had at least a minimum autonomy.... Of course the overwhelming mass had none. Cliff's grandfather, and mine, were both miners. They couldn't even dream about autonomy. But when you think about the foreman in a relatively advanced factory, they had traditions.... Marx wrote in these terms. You had the sergeant, and the officers, and so on ... of course with the relative autonomy always granted on the authority of capital. But what has in the past been *some* autonomy – in banking, insurance, middle management, and so on – is now being thrown out of the window, decimated. Tens of thousands of such people are losing their jobs. The computer takes over whatever areas they can where once there was devolved autonomy.

CS: Certainly people working in banks are now only adjuncts to the computer.

IM: Yes. The old local branch manager has become a laugh. There is no call for a local bank manager in the old sense. What is there for such a person to manage?

TK: The most dramatic example of this in the US in the last five years has been doctors. Once Clinton's national health plan failed and it became clear that everything in the future would be going through private insurance, the HMOs [Health Maintenance Organisations] basically took over private practice. Private practice has virtually disappeared because everyone gets their health care through insurance which is regulated by the HMOs. Doctors, in a very short period, have been turned into proletarians managed by these health insurance bureaucrats with regard to what tests they can perform, what procedures they can perform....

IM: It is now all actuarial ...

TK: They may not have been autonomous before but at least they thought they were. Now they *know* they are not. They are quite upset about it but their reaction doesn't seem particularly political.

IM: Not yet. I have also heard that there are quite a lot of office workers associated with these doctors.... The doctors dictate their memos and so on; and then they have to be transcribed. And how is that done? They are beamed to India. Indian computer wage-slaves transcribe them and send them back to California, or wherever. All these levelling processes tend towards the total disappearance of autonomy. Who is now autonomous? At what level in the decision-making process can you identify autonomy?

TB: If you look at what is happening in academic life ...

TK: I was restraining myself from pointing out the obvious about that as it is too close to home for me. But the other point – the point about equalisation – is very important and connects in my mind to these other movements. They seem to be taking the focus away from class but in practice may be making possible a more extended future definition of class. For example, gender.... Part of what is going on, particularly in the US, is the feminisation of labour at the same time as it is proletarianised – and this is connected with this downward equalisation. A particular occupation becomes feminised and then is paid at a lower level for everyone....

Also in the States, there is an obsession on the left with race, and it usually takes the form of multiculturalism, which may be very justifiable on its own terms. But what's going on with this downward equalisation is that you now have different groups that are culturally very separate, very disparate in cultural and political terms ... and the language of multiculturalism doesn't in itself reflect any clear totalising consciousness. It is, I think, a necessary prelude. When you have these people who are accustomed to certain earnings, to a degree of autonomy, to holding certain positions, and they are faced with downward equalisation, will this generate all kinds of reactionary feelings against those they are being equalised, with ... right-wing responses, fascistic even? Or will they be able to move in a more positive direction? I think multiculturalism is a way of engaging with those issues: it may not appear to be related to class, but it actually perhaps paves the way.... The same can be true of gender analysis. It is a way of forcing men to see that their relative autonomy in the past has been based on gender privilege which in itself is a form of, or is certainly tied up with, class oppression.... It seems to me that race and gender have to be factored into our understanding of the practices in the past which sustained hierarchy and privileges. And this was perhaps not recognised at the time ... and only now that these things have come under challenge can they be recognised. The critique of those privileges can, I think, sometimes be most effectively pursued through analysis of gender. That is not to say that it is something which exists outside class, and class analysis. But the class questions are easier for people to recognise first in these other spheres such as gender and race.

IM: Yes indeed. In some ways when we say 'class' we have to understand that there are different ways of identifying it.... And I think too that we need to recognise that sociological definitions of class often miss the most essential thing. In a fundamental sense there are only two classes in society: those who control and those who are controlled. The controlled – the working class or whatever other name you want to give it – have quite a number of sociological stratifications. That is a big problem for organisational and political work. But what is coming to the fore – and this is where the proletarianisation concept is so important for Marx, because what he had in mind was the two classes and their antagonism which defines their mode of life – is the tendency for the division into the small number of controllers and the mass of the controlled to become more a matter of real experience. These are the alternatives when we begin to think in these terms.

When you think of the working-class movement in the nineteenth century – Chartism or whatever else – it was always primarily orientated towards some political objectives. And if those political objectives were achieved, very often they added up to very little ... or, because usually they were not achieved, to nothing. Just think of the demand for the vote for workers – most of the Chartists didn't even call for the vote for women, only for male workers. And since the vote was conceded to the generality of workers, including females, its importance had been very seriously weakened. Parallel to the process of enfranchisement there was a process of disenfranchisement. It takes the form – you have had it in the States for much longer but now we have it in Britain too – of there being two parties you can't separate in any significant way. What is the difference between the Tory party and so-called New Labour? So you'll end up with a vote where 23% bother to turn out, and Labour get 8% and the Tories get 6% and that is be called democracy! I think the big challenge in the future in terms of the social agency is that it cannot be simply political in orientation. Much more fundamental is its social orientation. That is to say, the alternative which is offered in how to control the vital, reproductive process as a whole. Rather than seeing everything in terms of these ridiculous parliaments that we now have in our societies.... People think about elections with cynicism ... and then they are all over. What percentage usually turns out in the States?

TK: A good turnout for routine elections is 25%.

IM: Well, in Britain, in the European elections we had 23%. In Hungary where there was great happiness after the big change, there was a fairly big turnout. But in three years people had become so cynical that there were some by-elections where they had 2% voting and had to cancel the result.

TB: The one place where there is still interest is South Africa ...

IM: But there there was the question of trying to revise the constitution, so there are still illusions ... once we revise the constitution everything will be all right....

TK: In the US the tabloidisation of politics has made dramatic strides in the last decade. In a way it is positive because it makes much clearer what was always true but is now totally on the surface. Most people have no interest in electoral politics – or if they do, it is only at the level of a scandal. So there is really quite a realistic attitude – though it is called cynicism in the American press. But that cynicism, that realism, needs to be mobilised for something else ... and it's that mobilisation that is missing.

IM: Yes, and when you think that various left groups in the last two or three years in Britain have been expending energy fighting each other about which candidate to put forward, or about how to coalesce in some sort of electoral unity ... for maybe 1% of the vote. That's if they are lucky ... it may only be half a percent. It is all terribly trapped, the whole process.... [But] the crisis of party politics is only a manifestation of the underlying general crisis and the complete lack of any perspective to overcome it.... [I saw Barbara Castle] on TV [saying] that the great danger was that the politics of New Labour would make people bored and that they wouldn't turn out to vote. So long as people vote – whatever it achieves – she thinks that's great. But not to vote ... my God, what a calamity! In fact it would be a true achievement if people didn't vote! And it wouldn't make much difference! We need a true alternative to which we can give a name, and, for the last twenty years, I've been calling it extra-parliamentary action. Not some way of reviving this rotten thing that has allowed people the vote while disenfranchising them.

TK: What sort of extra-parliamentary action?

IM: Well, you cannot say, 'Do this' or 'Do that'. But you can identify the direction. Namely, that it is action independent of the existing system. It takes an initiative on its own behalf. It is addressing issues of critical social control, of the control of enterprises; and it sets its own objectives. The trouble with the kind of framework the left groups operate in is that they are forced into a situation in which they are only reflecting at a distance on what the big parties have – and they are aspiring to have the same things, to proceed in the same ways, even if they convince themselves they will be different. It is a complete illusion. It ignores the essential irrelevance of parliament....

I was at a conference last year on the 35-hour week and there were representatives of left parties there from all over Europe, some of whom had been quite successful in their own way. I had dinner one evening with a group of these people and a woman from the Swedish party was saying: 'We are going to make big advances at the next election.' I said: 'Yes, and when you become members of the government, you'll become purring pussycats!' She misunderstood and protested that they were not pussycats. I said, 'No, not yet!' It invariably happens. The Greens, on entering the government, totally changed their policies. For me it says something about the nature of government, and ultimately about the narrowing margins of capital. Capital has to define narrower and narrower limits for what political activity is, and can accomplish. Let me correct something I said earlier – that New Labour is the same as the Tories. For me, the characteristic of New Labour is that they are *worse* than the Tories because they are doing things the Tories didn't dare to do....

TK: And that is exactly Clinton's role. When he was first elected, I thought he would move everything slightly to the left, and that the left could then be a real opposition. Instead it has been the exact opposite. Clinton has legitimised the worst of the Republican agenda; and was responsible for the Republicans winning Congress – which is much more important than the White House. There has been a fundamental change in American society and politics. It is much worse than Reagan.

IM: And in Britain, the Tories didn't dare to impose student fees. Labour did. The Health Service has become worse. Social Services have greatly deteriorated.... There is *nothing* these people are shying away from. They do it because the narrowing margins of capital compel it. It is happening everywhere. The same thing in Germany. Just before the election people were talking about what would happen ... would [Oskar] Lafontaine prevail and move everything to the left? Instead he was kicked out in no time and things have moved to the right. And in Italy ... the role the former CP has played is quite unbelievable....

Ted raised the possibility of the social movement becoming something very authoritarian, that resentments may be exploited by very authoritarian tendencies. That danger is certainly there and, unless there is a very solid socialist movement to take its place, it can become a deadly danger, leading to all kinds of adventurism. On the other hand I am convinced that this wouldn't resolve any of the problems. In the 1930s fascism was not only a possibility; it was also a probability for both social and political reasons. It corresponded to a certain stage of capitalist development. Today is a period of an absolutely horrendous crisis of accumulation.... When you look at the economic roots of what is going on, there is a terrible crisis of accumulation which manifests itself in all kinds of adventurism in international finance. There is an inability to invest capital in a profitable way in reliable industrial enterprises.

What we have is the production of fictitious figures. The last issue of *The Economist* shows that they are moved by what may happen to the American economy, to American financial institutions – the stock market is over-extended, etc., and they are very scared about it. But underneath that is this terrible crisis of accumulation and, in my view, authoritarian measures, authoritarian tendencies of development, would not address this crucial dimension of the crisis. They can take the wind out of the opposition and direct popular forces of dissent in a very negative direction, but only by leading them into a dead end, not into something that would last even as long as Hitler lasted – and even that, after all, was only twelve years. We have to be thinking in terms of a much longer period. This is what underlies the need for a really vital organisational and political movement – and, as I've said, not even just *political* because I don't believe in the future viability of political movements as such. On their own, and in the way they've played their hand in the twentieth century particularly, such movements have fulfilled their historical role, their historical moment is past.

It is necessary to have a new form of movement, one that is not just parliamentary. It has to be a movement which involves direct action.... All this will include taking over productive enterprises and running them – though this will require favourable circumstances which are not easy to envisage today. The appearance today, as we have said, is of fragmentation. They produce statistics to say unemployment is going down, but that is only because most of the new jobs are tiny jobs for casual, part-time workers. They get two or three jobs for the statistics out of one serious one. Feminisation was mentioned in this respect, and it goes along with fragmentation and fractionalisation. In that respect the situation gets worse and worse – and in *every* country not just in Third-World or 'backward' countries, but also in the capitalistically most advanced countries....

TB: [When there are big factory closures, the government scarcely intervenes. The politicians say that they have] 'policies in place' to alleviate the unemployment figures – [New Labour's] so-called 'New Deal' and so on.... [They accept] that the role of government is reduced to picking up – or appearing to pick up – the human pieces left behind by capital's rapid changes of orientation, the lack of its ability to make stable investment István was talking about.

IM: And they only *appear* to do even that, because they are falsifying statistics, notably unemployment statistics, all the time. Look at Health Service statistics too. They don't put you on the official waiting list now until you meet the consultant, so you don't count statistically – but you're still waiting.

TK: ... [T]his relates to another big problem in the US. The right controls huge think-tanks through which they issue all sorts of figures, which then get on radio and TV, and that's how 'realities' which actually contradict the truth are defined.

IM: Because they are not solving anything, they have to lie about it all the time and they now do that very systematically. The statistics are often cynical lies. But often, even on TV and radio, you hear people saying this. There is so much untapped resentment that has to be channelled into something real. But it has to be something real which brings us back to the political problems we've been discussing, and the need for thinking which breaks out of the traditional assumptions of the labour movement. Take [Arthur] Scargill – a decent man, the best of militant fighters especially in the 1984-5 [miners'] strike – but he launches his Socialist Labour Party, a totally delusory movement.

TB: Are there any practical ways out of this discussion, that might lead us to talk about how we might ourselves work more collectively – of course also involving others – in the kind of developments we are saying are needed? Some of us are in involved with what we call the Movement For Socialism, and – without it being very clearly theorised – I think it has begun to bring together various activities which do relate, in different ways, to the emergence of the opposition to capital, which, of course, has to be international. We have linked up with an interesting group in Perm in the former Soviet Union; participated in a miners' conference in Tuzla, Bosnia-Herzegovina, against privatisation; been involved in solidarity work with the Liverpool dockers; and with the teachers and miners of Kosova in Prishtina and Mitrovice....

TK: I think the use of the internet is something we have to consider more. I'm involved in an internet group in the States which is in its early stages but which I hope will contribute to breaking down the sense of isolation I certainly feel.

CS: This is something the Liverpool dockers, assisted by Dave Hookes, are looking at in their Initiative Factory which they are developing out of, and on the basis of, the lessons in international solidarity drawn from their over-two-year-long dispute. I do think it is an immediate thing to try to establish a central website.

IM: I have been gratified to hear about reading circles in the US around my book *Beyond Capital.* And as many as 2,000 attend the annual Socialist Scholars' Conference. An organic link with the working class is what is needed and the work of some people in the MFS with the Liverpool dockers, the discussions on the situation in north-east England and so on are moving in that direction. The left-wing papers simply don't do this. They simply make propaganda to try to make members. How can they waste their life in that way?

CS: That *is* their life!

TB: Friends active in the trade unions on the question of the Balkan war ... [say] that the kind of protest politics the left groups insisted on at that time, and their inability even to discuss the need for prioritising the question of practical solidarity over largely futile protest made [them] think: 'This is the death of the "left"'. [Or]at least of what has previously been understood as being the 'left': 'The groups are showing their complete irrelevance.'... An advantage of the sort of contacts I was talking about is that we begin to see real struggles emerging in situations much wider than the intellectually comfortable, but pretty bankrupt, world of the British left groups....

TK: Tom Kemp used to say ... that in the 1930s politics was very different from today. It seemed relevant to get on the soapbox and give the party line. But that's not meaningful any more. Politics is more difficult. It is more difficult to mobilise, to pinpoint the real political issues. But the other side of that is that it is clear that that old propagandist politics has run its course.

IM: In the conditions of the 1930s it was relatively easy to organise; but it has become increasingly hard to answer the question: 'Organise for what?' There used to a story about two old Hebrew friends in Israel. One asks about the other's three sons. One is in Prague 'building socialism'; another is in London 'building socialism'. And the third? 'He is here in Israel.' 'And is he building socialism?' 'Are you completely insane? *In his own country*!'

The way in which socialism was articulated was in a very narrowly political sphere and with a narrow political orientation. It was essentially defensive – on the margins of expanding capital. If capital can expand relatively undisturbed, there is a margin from which more and more can be conceded to the working class. But this has gone. It disappeared nearly 30, or at least 25 years ago. There has been no significant advancement for the working class. The Welfare State has essentially finished, the question is only how long its agonies will continue. There is no way capital can keep it going. This is why I think the crisis of politics we've been talking about is so absolutely profound; and it is why the political crisis has to be radically redefined in such a way as to get out of the political vicious circle.

Some of the initiatives we've mentioned – in Liverpool and so on – could be the basis in different parts of the country (and in other countries) for develoing new organic links between socialist ideas and the working class. If we look at turn-of-the-last-century socialist activities, a lot of it centred on workers involved with Rosa Luxemburg and others in very serious, demanding discussions on Marxist economics, Marx's *Capital*, etc. Things are very different now, and we've been talking about how new ideas are needed. But it may not be beyond the bounds of possibility to revive some of that spirit, to try to counter the kind of intellectual devastation that has taken place within what used to be regarded as the socialist movement.

APPENDIX II: Problems of Globalisation – and of its apologists and critics

This is a report by Terry Brotherstone (who is responsible for its contents) of the meeting organised by **Movement for Socialism** in alliance with WLU – **Workers Left Unity (Iran)** – at Birkbeck College, University of London, on 3 February 2001. The meeting's significance lay in bringing the two main speakers – István Mészáros and François Chesnais, editor-in-chief of *Carré Rouge* – uniquely on to the same public platform. It was chaired by **Yassamine Mather** (WLU).

Mészáros began with recent discussions about what should always be called *capitalist* 'globalisation' or '*mondialisation*', between the ideologists of capital and their opponents; and with a *Financial Times* editorial stating that 'if poor countries are to benefit they must recognise that their problem is too little globalisation, not too much.' He compared this with the impact of 'globalisation' on a rich country, the UK. In the previous two days, the headlines had all been about the privatised steel corporation, CORUS, which had sacked 6,000 steelworkers, mainly in Wales. The 'Labour' government had accepted this on the ground that 'globalisation' made such events inevitable. And another recent *Financial Times* editorial had called the opponents of globalisation – who had met in Brazil – 'assorted idealists and romantic revolutionaries'. This exemplified 'the idiotic paternalism and arrogance' with which decision-makers respond to the vital concerns expressed by critics of capitalist globalisation.

Mészáros examined further what the 'realism' the ideologists of capital contrasted to romantic idealism meant. The President of Mexico, Fox, proposed to bridge the divide between the rich and poor nations by rejecting 'crass materialism' and harnessing the 'intense undirected desire for spiritual rebirth.' The solution was to find a new engine for growth involving advanced expansion of economic citizenship that would bring millions of the excluded into the world of computers and the internet. Mészáros ridiculed the idea that, under the rule of capital, the excluded millions, including all the peasants of Mexico, would soon have free access to the internet – but that was the level of the realism being promoted. The actual reality to be confronted was that of globalisation as a destructive force. The CORUS sackings had been only the latest in a long line of such affairs in rich Britain, never mind the real prospects for poor countries.

What of the trade-union movement? Its leaders only criticised the government on the ground that it had failed to sign the Brussels directive that said that the workers must be consulted before being sacked. They would not face the reality that the same devastation found in Britain was happening elsewhere. The German steel industry had been decimated, despite 'consultation'. In the US in the last few weeks eleven major steel companies had had to declare bankruptcy. The challenge of 'globalisation' could not be met by playing 'some stupid game ... with a Brussels directive.' The same day as CORUS announced redundancies, the stock value of the company leapt up 13%.

What was to be done? The economics editor of the *Guardian*, Larry Elliot, had recently criticised an article in *The Economist* by Claus Schwab, the man behind the world forum for economics, entitled 'Opening Gambit Without Strategy'. This formulated the seven challenges that globalisation had to confront. They were the need for environmental and social sustainability; international peacekeeping; the narrowing of the technological and social gulf between rich and poor; the need for higher standards of health and nutrition; a common understanding of human rights; and the safeguarding of cultural identity in an increasingly homogenised world. Elliot rightly pointed out that this echoed the 1942 Beveridge Report. Then and now, this was all 'motherhood and apple pie'. But Elliot's own solution?: 'What they need is debt cancellation, access to the rich markets of the north and an increase in aid.' Under conditions of capitalist globalisation, said Mészáros, that was just more 'motherhood and apple pie'.

Faced with the movement that began with the Seattle demonstrations, Mészáros argued, the decision-makers saw that they had real problems, had to play a better public-relations game. They would now try to ensure that their summit meetings were 'pre-cooked', with carefully managed expectations; and that carefully selected opponents were apparently involved in debate. Better have them in the tent pissing out than outside pissing in, as President Johnson had said. And a former prime minister of France had claimed that, after all, the decision-makers had been elected by millions of people. That was presented as a conclusive argument: you could not question the legitimacy of this type of representation. But in practice people *were* questioning. There would be no end to the debates and to the challenges because the ravages of globalisation could not be fictionalised as the success of globalisation. Everything had become extremely problematic, contradictory and antagonistic, and the antagonisms could only multiply.

What should be the approach to all this in socialist discourse? The ideologists of capital had presented globalisation as a great new discovery. But the idea of the inseparability of globalisation and capitalism – pushing towards some kind of global integration – was a commonplace to Marx. Globalisation was part of the logic of capital and that was the tremendous challenge. The ravages and destructive contradictions of globalisation would not be resolved into a happy ending without confronting capital itself, for quite fundamental reasons, four of which Mészáros dealt with.

First was the globalisation of ever-growing unemployment, which could not be concealed by the falsification of data, and by the device of casualisation, producing the appearance of five jobs instead of one. An improvement in the statistics was producing no improvement in standards of living. Mészáros referred to his work on this in *Iran Bulletin*. Second was the destruction of the environment – an integral part of the economic and social processes underlying globalisation. The Kyoto agreement, like similar previous ones, would go into the waste-paper basket, because the ferocious drive of capital towards devastation could not be halted by dealing with the environment as a discrete issue. Nobody was even talking about the underlying causes. At best the establishment journals, and the single issue campaigners, could point to the effects.

The third problem was more serious still – the fact that no capital-system *state* existed, only national states. The consequence was that the globalising drive of capital for integration in economics and finance had to operate on shaky ground, full of contradictions, some already evident, others bound to erupt sooner or later. Despite tendencies to nullify this, the ultimate implication was war. In the past imperialist powers had expressed their interests and fought for them through devastating world wars. Now we had many localised wars only. But imperialism, and the threat of world war, had not gone away. The very real and fundamental contradiction was that there was no state corresponding with the capital system as a whole. The logic of capital, therefore – this globalisation of capital at the level of economy and finance – cannot find an equivalent at the political level. This brought many adventurist possibilities into the picture. The power currently able to explore them, the United States, was already doing so in different ways. At present, there was only one hegemonic global power, but that would not be a permanent condition. It was also possible that smaller regional groupings and contradictions could intervene. The name European Union, for example, looked like a bad joke, considering the internal squabbling.

Then there was the question of the 'countries of the south' – the miscalled 'Third World countries' (actually subordinated parts of one world). 'Underdevelopment' was referred to as though the underdeveloped countries should blame themselves. In reality, conditions of underdevelopment were forced on the poor countries. The triumphalist propaganda of the past held that, after this phase of underdevelopment, there would come a great modernisation and everywhere would conform to the American model and be happy in the capitalist paradise. But now nobody in development studies was talking about modernisation in that sense. Permanent underdevelopment is required if only because of the need to buy 'pollution rights', allowing the US to suffocate us all.

The final point dealt with was that any solution to the challenges of globalisation in the foreseeable future would have to find some way of solving these underlying contradictions and tremendous antagonisms. No solution was conceivable within the horizons of capital. One crucial concept had therefore to be borne in mind if there was to be a world in which economic processes would be integrated in a positive way so as to enhance the potentialities of the people and serve their needs. The need was for the concept of planning – a word that the anarchy of the existing system could not embrace. In due course an order of planning would have to be established, in which the participants – the people of all countries operating on the basis of equality – could manage their own lives. This was inconceivable within the framework of capital.

Chesnais introduced himself as a member of the editorial board of the journal *Carré Rouge*, a journal trying to overcome the problem that there had been no proper discussion for decades within the framework of revolutionary Marxist thinking. Those, like him, who had fought against capitalism and Stalinism, in various Trotskyist organisations, went along with a very stultified form of Marxism. The explanation for this, however, was not what he would deal with in this presentation. But it had to be recognised as a major problem. A starting point was to think afresh about what Engels said at Marx's graveside – that Marx was first and foremost a revolutionary, and that this imbued everything he did. The primacy of action imbued everything he wrote. And Engels himself, who lived a long time and faced huge changes in the capitalist system, exemplified what we needed to reflect on today. He, with Marx when he was alive, always tried to deal with the implications of those changes and with developments in the class struggle, and new political situations. We had to recognise that there was no *Marxist system*. There were Marxist *approaches*; but no ready-made system. The great Marxists lived the whole time in struggle – Luxemburg, Lenin, Trotsky – dealing with a changing reality from a practical point of view. To judge their work from the point of view of *system* would be to find many contradictions in it. But those of us who had been educated in a sort of Talmudic approach to their work had now to reject that absolutely.

On the 'problems of globalisation', Chesnais drew attention to the need to look again at Marx's famous text about the contradiction between productive forces and social relations, and about the fact that productive forces become too big to be contained in given social relations of production and property. It had been written in the mid-nineteenth century: what did it mean today? The system of class domination had shown incredible flexibility and the ability to ride out a great number of crises. The enemy could not be taken lightly. The more he re-read *Capital*, said Chesnais, the more he had come to understand that, to use this central work, it was necessary to throw out everything in it that might *seem* to make a bridge between Marx's conceptions and classical and neo-classical economics – and thereby to Keynesian and contemporary economics. It was necessary to rid ourselves of everything encouraging the idea that the working of the capitalist economy is something autonomous, mechanical, obeying purely economic laws.

One of the major problems in understanding globalisation was the strength of *fetishism* – the fetishism of commodities, the fetishism of finance, the autonomisation of the power of capital as if it were simply the power of 'the economy' seen as the natural order of things. In fighting against this, *Capital* was vital, particularly because of everything in it relating to the reality that what we should be talking about was a social form of class domination, not simply an 'economy'. When Marx said that capital was a relationship of production and that the expansion of capital was the expansion of that relationship, he was inviting us to look at things from this angle.

The history of the late-nineteenth and the twentieth centuries was a history of a growing movement in the direction of the organisation of conscious forms of class domination – a domination organised both through state power, and through the use of the 'industrial reserve army' of the unemployed. Mészáros had talked about globalisation and unemployment. This had to be understood primarily from the angle of the unemployed as the 'industrial reserve army'. There had been a recent debate between a *Financial Times* team and one from *Le Monde Diplomatique*. One of the arguments the *FT* people had made was: how could workers whose factories were being closed in advanced countries complain, since this was allowing factories to be opened in east Asia? We needed also to think about the way the fetishism of commodities and of finance had been able to bring the media into the picture to play a major role in the organisation of capitalist class domination and the reproduction of system. We should remember Lenin who said that there was no 'final' crisis for capitalism – unless workers' power was created on a broad enough basis to survive and expand.

It was important to look at capitalism as a system of class domination which, because it is based on the market and because the realisation of surplus value on the market is central to it, brings different centres of capital and of its accumulation constantly into competition with one another. This would allow us to tune into the numerous contradictions of capitalist production. The system was ridden with contradictions, as the approach of *Capital* showed. In many key chapters, Marx stressed that every time capitalism found temporary solutions to one of its contradictions, this only reproduced the contradiction in a new form and on a higher level. Understanding the 'problems of globalisation' meant detailed work on the realities of today's contradictions. We had to reveal the internal dynamics of the economic and social processes, which, far from representing an inevitable and natural order, were creating the conditions for the overthrow of capitalism.

Mészáros's second concluding point had highlighted the central question of globalisation and environmental destruction. We had entered the phase where the rate and scale of environmental destruction was increasingly affecting the basic reproduction of human existence. Capitalist reproduction in the 21st century, by its nature, was tending to destroy the very reproduction of social existence on this planet. Mészáros's point about how the US had imposed a scheme whereby it bought pollution rights had made the point exactly. Such issues, and the others Mészáros had dealt with, would become more acute over time.

What would be likely to develop faster, however, were all the contradictions related to finance, and it was on this area that Chesnais had decided to concentrate in conclusion. In the twentieth century, the type of regular periodic crisis that Marx studied in the nineteenth century had not occurred. In the 1880s Engels hypothesised that there were now new structural changes in capitalist economy which would lead to other types of crisis. And, indeed, the twentieth century really did become an era of 'wars and revolutions'. The century's wars, and the Cold War, had been intimately related to the process of capitalist accumulation, and to the way the capitalist class responded to its changing contradictions. These 'political' developments could not be walled of from our understanding of the workings of the economy of capital.

There had also been one major directly and obviously economic and financial crisis – the crisis of 1929, with its impact on the whole of the 1930s, ending only with the war economy of the second world war. Chesnais suggested that the context in which we were now living now was similar ... or – to be more careful and precise – had similarities to ... the late 1920s. The central feature was the growth of fictitious capital. To make use of Marx on this question we had to turn to the very incomplete chapters on finance in Volume III of *Capital* – the chapters dealing with interest-bearing capital, fictitious capital, on the relations between industrial and money-bearing capital. Incomplete though these were, they were important for thinking through many of the characteristics of the situation today. The most important representative of the capitalist class was the chairman of the Federal Reserve Bank. *The Economist* some years ago had had an article on 'The Central Banker as God', and that more or less was what Alan Greenspan, as FRB chair, had been for the system as a whole. Wall Street and the other stock exchanges represented the incredible phenomenon that Marx called the shadow or ghost of capital, the form in which it comes to life again, leading a second life, acquiring huge values on these markets, and convincing people that they have real wealth.

The greater part of US consumers had become used to projecting their whole consumer expenditures on the basis of the wealth they were supposed to have, which was supported by a second form of fictitious capital – the huge development of the credit system. So fictitious capital, either in the form of investment capacity – more stock and more bonds – or in the form of the capacity to consume was how the new economy had basically become organised. It operated around the interconnections between different forms of fictitious capital. But it could not be overlooked that, under the governance of corporate capital, there had been a real increase in the rate of exploitation. The pick-up in productivity that there had been was essentially an increase in the rate of exploitation, the rate of surplus value. This had been obtained through a new form of relations between industrial and finance capital with the fund managers looking at every dimension of corporate capital.

The US stock market was totally dependent on the position of the US in the world economy. This mass of fictitious capital had been there for seven years, since the early 1990s, and the actual activity of the US financial markets had made every kind of legal or illegal earnings available in the form of money to be invested. This nearly permanent flow of capital to the US now constituted 5% of the US GDP, a huge amount to be represented by this financial bubble, this growth of fictitious capital.

Chesnais said that, at that point, nobody could know when and how this was going to end. The final point he stressed was that the amount of finance flowing constantly to the US has been so strong, the pumping of new fictitious capital so important, that this process which had started in 1982 weathered the 1987 Wall Street market crash and the US savings and loan crisis. It had only been somewhat battered by the financial recession in the building crisis of 1990. It had taken off again and had hardly been dented by the Mexican crisis. It had weathered the Asian and Russian crises, and the loss last year of half of the supposed NASDAQ value. Not even that last crisis had bought the whole edifice down.

In conclusion, Chesnais said that the way finance had developed, the way in which rental types of capital had been fostered by the policies of globalisation, meant that those who govern the system, and those they governed, were confronted with a 1929-type of crisis. No timescale was possible, nor were precise predictions about immediate causes and consequences. But these points were very relevant to determining what we had to do – for example in the anti-globalisation movement Mészáros had mentioned. At least a part of the young generation – the students and young teachers were the people he knew best in France – were coming to politics in a quite different way from their predecessors. It was important to do everything possible, in the context of this movement, to provide a Marxist interpretation – explaining what unemployment actually is and why it is an unsatisfactory term; the real nature of the environmental crisis; and the threat of the financial crisis.

Chesnais had concentrated on the financial crisis because this was how there would be a plunge into social and political chaos sooner or later. The important and practical conclusion from all this – the thing that made this discussion so important and the political preparations we might be able to make so germane – was that it was necessary to understand that there was real chaos at the centre of the system. This would actualise itself in the lives of millions sooner or later.

The meeting then took the form of questions and answers and discussion.

INDEX

Titles published by Index Books and a range of former New Park Publications titles are available from Index Books, including:

Peter Fryer

Hungarian Tragedy and other writings on the 1956 Hungarian revolution, 1-871518-14-8 192pp. £11.99

Aspects of British Black History, 1-871518-04-0 56pp. £4.95

Politics of Windrush, 1-871518-24-5 56pp. £6.99

Cliff Slaughter
A New Party for Socialism: why? how? when? 1-871518-15-6 100pp. £2.00

Norman Harding
Staying Red: why I remain a socialist, 1-871518-25-3 300 pp. £12.99

Bob Myers, ed.:

Revolutionary Times, Revolutionary Lives
South Africa Series No. 1, 1-871518-19-9
117pp. £4.99

Is This Really What We Fought For?
South Africa Series No. 2,
1-871518-20-2 104pp. £4.99

www.indexbooks.co.uk sales@indexbooks.co.uk